Holiness for Every Day

Devotional Meditations for Each Day of the Year

by
G. B. Williamson

Beacon Hill Press of Kansas City
Kansas City, Missouri

Copyright 1980
Beacon Hill Press of Kansas City

ISBN: 0-8341-0636-1

Printed in the
United States of America

2

Dedication

To the hundreds of students
who have received instruction in my classrooms,
and to the nearly 1,000
men and women of many lands and languages
on whom my hands have been laid
in holy ordination to the Christian ministry,

THESE MEDITATIONS ARE DEDICATED

with the prayer
that they will be faithful.

Foreword

Here is a devotional book written by our own beloved general superintendent emeritus, Dr. Gideon B. Williamson. It is penned in the epoch of his maturity. The years have taught him, and he shares his strength in these day-by-day devotions. He does not write essentially as a technical scholar or even as a skilled church statesman, but as a seasoned, lifetime student of the Bible and a pastor-at-large to all who would follow the One called a Nazarene (Matt. 2:23).

Variety and balance are implicit in the wide range of Scripture studied and employed. This book's marked charm and strength lie in the writer's expositional insights found on every page. They read deceivingly simply but afford both remarkable clarity and perspective. They challenge us to read and then contemplate.

This book also affords food for the soul to the beginning Christian as well as for the ripest saint. The tone throughout is healthy and invigorating. Its message is redemptive. There is a light that shines in every page; it is the light of holiness. Always there is the practical application to our daily lives, but its author counts on the Holy Spirit (who is the Spirit of Truth) to aid us. The author believes and teaches the ethical approach to truth. (We learn as we obey.) The Holy Spirit makes it personal to us, one *by* one and One *to* one. This book is more than a road map; it introduces to us the Holy Spirit himself as our personal daily Guide.

This book is not sectarian in the narrow sense; it is broadly evangelical in its appeal to the needs of men and women everywhere. There is a light here that will shine on you if you will give it some 15 minutes a day. May your soul be refreshed as you meditate on these pages.

—Samuel Young
General Superintendent Emeritus

Preface

"Holiness adorns your house for endless days" (Ps. 93:5, NIV).

The word *house* is used as a figure of speech to represent the household. It is not the building but the occupants. It is the church composed of people. The building may be dedicated to sacred purposes in appropriate ceremonies; those who by choice are members of the church are moral beings who must dedicate themselves to God to be cleansed and made holy.

The metaphor of the text implies that holiness is a tailored garment which becomes all who wear it. Holiness is a spiritual experience which harmonizes the nature of man with the nature of God. It is obedience to God's command, "Be ye holy; for I am holy" (1 Pet. 1:16).

It is like a garment suitable for all occasions. It is comely for the person who worships God in the beauty of holiness on the Sabbath Day. It does not become spotted or soiled when worn in the office, the shop, the factory, or the field. It never becomes threadbare or worn-out. It is appropriate if worn at a wedding feast. It is a comfortable shroud in death, and for the one who is clad in it there need be shed no tears of sorrow. It will be wonderful to be clothed in robes of white when the dead in Christ shall arise and those who are alive and remain are caught up to meet the Lord in the air (see 1 Thess. 4:16-17). Those who are adorned in robes pure and spotless will be qualified to sing, "Holy, holy, holy is the Lord God Almighty" (see Rev. 4:8), in the great celestial choir. Holiness will be the bridal gown worn by the Church when she is joined forever to Christ the Bridegroom.

That holiness which harmonizes the nature of man with the divine nature is for every day and all occasions.

January 1

The New Start

Phil. 3:13-14

The good life is progress toward a compelling goal. To live in the past is to forfeit the prize. Thank God, the sins of yesterday, both voluntary and inadvertent, can be forgiven. There is no need to live defeated by a guilt complex. The mistakes and failures of the past are to be forgotten. To be haunted by their memory is to be hindered in the race. To dwell on the successes of the bygone years would breed conceit and discount confidence in God and ourselves for further achievement.

Reflection on the past is profitable only as a means to needful correction. That is important. A few degrees of error on the compass now may mean a wide miss of the mark. Striving for the goal is good only if the aim is accurate.

New Year's resolutions are made only to be broken unless reinforced by persistence and determination. Pressing toward the mark is rewarded in progress. That is the incentive to reach for the ultimate goal, which is Christlikeness. Each day will bring a nearer approximation. This is the high calling of God. It is not only onward, it is also upward. The prize most to be coveted, and that will be the most satisfying reward, is to see Him and be like Him. The anticipation of that high moment is the inspiration for the day-by-day concentration on the pursuit. The Psalmist said, "I shall be satisfied, when I awake, with thy likeness" (17:15). Paul said, "I press toward the mark for the prize."

January 2

Man Was Created by God

Gen. 1:26

Of all the theories that have been advanced concerning the origin of man, none is so satisfying to a devout and humble person as the story of creation found in Genesis, chapter 1. Here God is postulated as the great and adequate First Cause. The eternal God had no beginning. At an undated moment in eternity, "In the beginning God created the heaven and the earth" (v. 1).

The climax of God's creation came when He said, "Let us make man in our image, after our likeness" (v. 26). "So God created man in his own image, in the image of God created he him" (v. 27).

God's image or likeness in man is seen in the fact that he is a spiritual being capable of immortality. All other creatures live and die, and that is all of it. When human life begins, it never ends. Every human being will spend eternity somewhere in conscious existence.

God made man in His own likeness, a moral being completely holy in his original state. But to make man like himself it was necessary that he should have the right of self-determination.

God also created man an intellectual being with capacity for reason and rulership. The ability to reason lifts man above the beast. For the right exercise of his reason, man is accountable to God.

"What is man, that thou art mindful of him? and the son of man, that thou visitest him? For thou hast made him a little lower than the angels, and hast crowned him with glory and honour. Thou madest him to have dominion over the works of thy hands" (Ps. 8:4-6).

January 3

A Holy Day for Holy Men

Gen. 2:2

"God blessed the seventh day, and sanctified it" (v. 3). The observance of one day for rest has its origin in the example God set for man. He rested on the seventh day from all His work. The fourth commandment came much later. With benevolent concern for the well-being of man, God gave the law of the Sabbath. Upon the obedient He promised a blessing. Upon the transgressor He pronounced judgment. Proper rest and relaxation for the body and renewal for the mind and spirit can only be found in a day set aside for meditation and worship. It is written into the very constitution of the universe that there should be one day in seven for rest.

Free men may violate this principle, but they are sure to pay the penalty. Some must do their work on the Sabbath Day. In such cases another day ought to be set apart for rest and renewing of body and soul. It is the principle that must be kept, not the same day on the calendar necessarily.

Some things should be done on the Sabbath, such as works of mercy and unquestioned duty. All should remember the words of Jesus who said, "The sabbath was made for man, and not man for the sabbath" (Mark 2:27).

A corollary of the command to keep the Sabbath holy is the requirement to work or be profitably engaged six out of seven. For him who would be holy time is sacred and must not be squandered.

Keeping the day for rest and worship is a criterion for obedience to all God's will.

January 4
Eden

Gen. 2:8

Many things have been said about the garden of Eden. The important fact is that when God had made man with the built-in power to choose good or evil, He placed him in circumstances that were maximumly favorable to a right choice, a worthy life, and the highest possible destiny.

There was the one tree which bore the forbidden fruit. Why was it there? Had there been no possibility of man turning from the good way, then he would have been in a fixed state of being. A person, either divine or human, craves a voluntary devotion. There was everything for the man of Eden to have and to do that he might have pleasure, inspiration, challenge, and fellowship with God. There were positive commandments, such as "Be fruitful, and multiply, and [fill] the earth, and subdue it" (1:28). There was only one prohibition—"of the tree of the knowledge of good and evil, thou shalt not eat" (2:17).

There has not been found another Eden for man, who forfeited his home in that ideal environment. Nevertheless, Christ the Redeemer has conquered the foe. He has made of sinful man a new creature. He has won for himself a total victory over the tempter. And, potentially, He has made it possible for man to live in the world and not be of it. The Christian can be elevated above the evil environment. He can change his immediate surroundings by receiving the Holy Spirit and bearing His fruit.

January 5

God Initiates the Family

Gen. 2:18

God sought to provide for man everything that would add to his happiness. God said it was not good that man should be alone.

To have a family there must be a wife and mother, as well as a father. In fact, without a mother there could be no father, and without children there would be neither father nor mother. God envisioned earth populated by thousands, millions, now billions of inhabitants. He provided for man the greatest pleasure, comfort, and well-being. God started with one man and one woman. With them the race began. To elevate man above all other creatures, God laid the foundation for marriage, family, home. Today nothing can replace the home for the dignity, security, and enjoyment of life as God planned it.

There are powerful forces in operation today to destroy the redeeming influences of the home and the family. Infidelity of partners in marriage, which leads to divorce and dissolution of the family, is a vicious attack upon that which God intended to be a strong bulwark for righteousness and happiness of man.

Augustine is reported to have stated, "Woman was created from the rib of man, not from his head to be above him, nor from his feet to be walked upon, but from his side to be his equal; near his arm to be protected; close to his heart to be loved."

"Therefore shall a man leave his father and his mother, and shall cleave unto his wife: and they shall be one flesh" (v. 24).

God wanted man to be holy and happy.

January 6

Holy Men Are Tempted

Gen. 3:6

Before man was created, evil existed. "Lucifer, son of the morning," had sought to exalt himself above God. He was cast out of heaven and became the personification of evil. (See Isa. 14:12-15.) After the creation of man, Satan renewed his attack upon God at the most vulnerable exposure. It was against the man God had made in His own image with the ability to choose good or evil.

The appeal of Satan was first to Eve at the point of physical desire. The fruit of the tree was good for food. All people experience desire. When the will unites with the desire for something forbidden, sin is conceived.

Satan also appealed to Eve's intellectual curiosity. The fruit of the tree, if eaten, would "make one wise." The inclination to experiment, to discover for oneself is an innate disposition of the human mind. Sanctification does not remove it.

Third, Satan appealed to that in man which causes him to desire to exercise his right of self-determination.

None of these human traits is wrong in itself. But when to give expression to them leads to disobedience to God's command, they are evil. "The way of transgressors is hard" (Prov. 13:15). It brings one under the dominion of sin and the reign of death.

In this life there is no escape from temptation. Even Christ was tempted to the end of His life on earth. We must all fortify ourselves against our mortal enemy. Victory over temptation is possible by faith in Christ. He won the victory for himself and for us.

10

A Redeemer Is Promised

Gen. 3:15

In God's foreknowledge He anticipated the Fall and had a plan of recovery to put into effect. He said to the serpent, "I will put enmity between you and the woman, and between your seed and her seed; he shall bruise you on the head, and you shall bruise him on the heel" (NASB). Christ is the Lamb slain from the foundation of the world. "He was bruised for our iniquities: the chastisement of our peace was upon him; and with his stripes we are healed" (Isa. 53:5).

That first promise of a Redeemer grew upon the consciousness of men groping for light, until through added revelations of God's eternal purpose it crystallized into the great Messianic hope of Israel. This hope came to fulfillment that night at Bethlehem when the angel announced, "Unto you is born this day in the city of David a Saviour, which is Christ the Lord" (Luke 2:11). The Lamb of God had come to take away the sin of the world. Finally, on the Cross, the bruising for the Redeemer was completed. He cried, "It is finished." The price for "so great salvation" was paid.

In that Calvary deed Satan's head was bruised. Jesus the Savior had conquered. He rose from the grave in victory. His triumph over the dread enemy of God and man was potential victory for all who will trust and obey His word. "He is able also to save them to the uttermost that come unto God by him, seeing he ever liveth to make intercession for them" (Heb. 7: 25).

January 8

The Blood of Sprinkling

Gen. 4:4

No two persons are alike. Cain and Abel, although they were brothers, were different in their basic nature and characteristics. Adam was a gardener. Cain became a tiller of the ground, and Abel was a keeper of sheep. The contrast between the brothers is much more evident when their traits of character are considered. Cain was arrogant, self-sufficient, easily provoked, bent toward envy. He was quick to coddle his evil thoughts. Abel, on the other hand, was humble, trusting, gentle, simple in his faith and dependence on God.

Somehow in their minds had been implanted the idea that it was right to offer sacrifice to God. This practice of an offering as a part of worship had doubtless been maintained by the family. Cain brought of the fruit of the ground. Abel brought a firstling of the flock. The Lord accepted Abel's sacrifice, but He rejected Cain's.

What was the difference? The attitude in which the offerers came could have entered into the distinction in their acceptability. But there was more. Cain came with only the product of his labor. There was no confession of sin and no acknowledgment of the need of atonement and forgiveness. In his way he sought salvation by works rather than by faith. Abel's sacrifice pointed to Calvary and the five bleeding wounds of Jesus. His was "a more excellent sacrifice than [that of] Cain, . . . and by it he being dead yet speaketh" (Heb. 11:4).

"Ye are come . . . to Jesus the mediator of the new covenant, and to the blood of sprinkling, that speaketh better things than that of Abel" (Heb. 12:22, 24).

January 9

Enoch Walked with God

Gen. 5:24

In an age of almost universal unbelief and darkness Enoch walked with God. We have only a brief biography, but what we know of him is a great encouragement to a life of faith and holiness. Twice in the short story of his life it is recorded that he walked with God.

Evidently some good influence led him early to dedicate his life to the Lord. He must have lived much alone as far as human companionship was concerned. Therefore, God received him into a very exclusive fellowship.

12

There was close agreement between God and Enoch. In his day he was partaker of the divine nature. Can two walk together except they are agreed? If with his limited knowledge Enoch had clear testimony that he pleased God, is it not possible that men today can walk with God? We have the Word of God to be a Lamp to our feet and a Light to our pathway. We have the abundant grace bestowed on us through faith in Christ. We have His blessed example to inspire and guide us. We have the Holy Spirit to be our strength as well as our Teacher.

God rewarded the faith of Enoch by translating him that he should not see death. But all who walk with God in the way of righteousness and faith here can meet death without fear. "Thanks be to God, which giveth us the victory through our Lord Jesus Christ" (1 Cor. 15:57).

January 10

Noah Was a Just Man

Gen. 6:8

The life story of Noah is interlaced with the history of the Flood. There are some obvious lessons to be learned from what happened in those days of destruction. First, we should note that judgment for sin is inescapable. God never condones or excuses sin. The mercy of God is extended to nations because there is a righteous remnant. They are the salt of the earth, a saving influence restraining the wrath of God.

The second observation to be drawn from this ancient story is that righteousness is indestructible. Never in all the history of the race has God been left without a witness. God said, "I will destroy man whom I have created from the face of the earth" (v. 7). But Noah found favor in the eyes of the Lord. One righteous man became the salvation of the race.

Noah was just. He was upright. He was perfect in his generation. God spared him and his family and in their descendants preserved His own creation.

Noah built the ark exactly as God instructed him. He took

into the ark all God told him. When the waters receded, Noah and his family and all in the ark came out to replenish the earth. Noah built an altar and offered sacrifices of thanksgiving to God. God established a covenant with Noah. The rainbow is the sign of that covenant. God keeps His promise. God is faithful to all who trust and obey Him.

January 11

God Will Humble the Proud

Gen. 11:9

Pride is at the bottom of all sin. It was pride that caused Lucifer to seek to exalt himself above God.

It was similar motivation that led the descendants of Noah to settle in Shinar instead of scattering over the earth to replenish it as God had commanded them. In pandering their pride they proceeded to build a city and be self-contained. They would live there together in the most fertile valley known to them. They built a tower to achieve the ultimate good in their own wisdom and skill. It might be implied that atop the tower there would be a temple dedicated to some god to compete with the Creator and Preserver of the race of man.

When God saw what they were doing and knew their intent, He confounded their language and scattered them upon the face of all the earth. The breakdown in understanding those of different speech has caused or aggravated the hatred of men for one another. It has resulted in bloodshed and war, times without number. God has always and will always judge the sinful pride of man.

At Pentecost we have Babel in reverse. Men of many languages understood the wonderful words of life. By God's Spirit they heard that whosoever shall call on the name of the Lord shall be saved. Instead of pride God teaches men humility. In place of hatred, which is the companion of pride, God sheds love abroad in our hearts by the Holy Spirit. Instead of strife there is peace. "Where the Spirit of the Lord is, there is peace." There is unity because there is humility.

14

A Man Responds to God

Gen. 12:1

God is omnipresent. Those who have recognized and responded to the calling voice of God are the ones who have been lifted to a higher plane of life than their fellows. Something like 4,000 years ago God called Abraham.

How God gained the attention of Abram none can know. Possibly as he grew into manhood, he asked himself, "Is physical existence all there is to mortal man?" He then reached out to find spiritual realities and a Voice began to speak to him. Perhaps as he gazed into the starry heavens when the shades of night were drawn about him, he heard a clear, strong Voice say to him, "Get thee out of thy country, and from thy kindred, and from thy father's house, unto a land that I will shew thee."

It was no passing emotional impulse that moved him to go. It was a firm conviction in his soul that he had heard God's voice. By faith he obeyed.

It was a costly course of action for Abram. He became a migrant. He and his were sojourners in a strange land. They declared plainly that they sought a better country, that is an heavenly.

But Abram received his reward. He became the father of the faithful. He earned the coveted title "the Friend of God." In him the chosen family had its beginning. Through him and his seed came Jesus, the Savior of all mankind. In him all families of the earth are blessed. The willing and obedient are never disappointed. God is faithful.

The Man of God Builds Altars

Gen. 12:7

Abram moved from place to place. He had no title deed to the land, yet God had promised him that it should belong to him and his seed forever. Every place at which Abram lingered he built an altar and worshipped God. Obedience to God was the hallmark of his character.

Abram's altars were visible reminders of the promises of God. Devout men live by faith in God's promises. Abram did not in all his life possess the land of Canaan. Because of his faith in God, possession was a reality. He enjoyed it as though he held the deeds. In like manner holy men of all ages have lived in the reality of things as yet only possessed by faith in the promises of God.

Abram's altars were a testimony to his obedience. He believed God and he obeyed God. Such faith is accredited to the believer as righteousness.

Abram's altars served as a call to worship. An altar built to God is as meaningless as a heathen shrine unless the builder meets God there in attitudes and acts of sincere devotion. He must worship God in spirit and truth. It is more than lip service. It is keeping God always before us. It is the practice of the presence of God. It is keeping the will of God as our constant frame of reference. Jesus said, "Not everyone that saith unto me, Lord, Lord, shall enter into the kingdom of heaven; but he that doeth the will of my Father which is in heaven" (Matt. 7:21).

January 14

A Holy Man in a Wicked World

Gen. 13:12

Holiness and worldliness never blend. The story of Lot is an illustration of that indisputable fact. Lot's choice of the well-watered plain of the Jordan revealed his character as a worldly-minded man. He pitched his tent toward Sodom.

Once the direction of his life was determined, he was soon drawn into the wickedness of Sodom. Doubtless he prospered; his fellow citizens recognized his ability. He sat in the gate— the place of honor.

Evidently Lot did not take on the manners of the environment in which he lived. Peter, centuries later, characterized him as "just Lot." Abram's good life was a saving influence

16

upon him in spite of the materialistic, sensuous world around him.

Lot was saved as one escaping out of the fire. But how great was his loss! The material values were all swept away. Some of his family perished in the holocaust of fire and brimstone. His wife fled, but her heart was with her treasures; therefore she turned to look back, and in righteous judgment she became a pillar of salt. The two daughters who escaped with their father had taken on the sins of Sodom. They made their father drunken, led him into incest, and produced offspring to plague future generations of Abram's seed.

It does not pay to court friendship with the world. Better choose the high country as Abram did. Enjoy life's best here and the values eternal hereafter.

January 15

The Record and the Reward of Faithfulness

Gen. 15:1

"After these things" recalls those meaningful events that had already transpired in the story of Abram. Included, certainly, would be his call and his response to it. The record is one of unhesitating obedience.

There is also the wholesome paternal attitude toward Lot. When both of them prospered and their herds increased, although Abram was the senior and the benefactor, he gave Lot first choice of the land before them. In unselfish love Abram took what Lot's choice of the fertile valley left to him.

Then came an invasion by an overpowering enemy. Lot was among the captives carried away. Abram could have said to himself, "It serves him right." Instead, he organized his household into an army. He pursued the invading host, fell upon them by night, routed the captors, recovered the prisoners, including Lot, and brought back the spoils. Thus Abram proved himself a magnanimous benefactor to one who was undeserving.

Abram gave further demonstration of his noble character when the king of Sodom offered him the spoils if only he would

17

return the captives. Whereupon Abram said, "I will not take any thing that is thine" (14:23). He had done nothing for gain.

There is another important part of the story. Abram did pay a tithe of all the spoil to Melchizedek, king of Salem and priest of the most high God. It was after these things God said, "Fear not, Abram: I am thy shield, and thy exceeding great reward."

Faithful men always have God for their protection and their reward. What more can one expect or need?

January 16

Total Consecration
Is Required for Holiness

Gen. 15:17

As God renewed and amplified His covenant with Abram, Abram asked, "Lord God, whereby shall I know that I shall inherit [the land]?" Then God said, "Take me an heifer of three years old, and a she goat of three years old, and a ram of three years old, and a turtle dove, and a young pigeon" (vv. 8-9). The animals were to be three years old because they would by that time be in their prime. The birds' age was not a factor. This was to be an acceptable sacrifice. It tells us that God always wants the best men can give.

There is no designation here of the significance of each offering. The sum of these sacrifices seems to indicate that God does ask for all, not a part.

It is noteworthy that when Abram had prepared the sacrifice and placed all in order—the animals cut in pieces, the birds dressed but whole—he stood guard over his offering lest birds of prey devour that which he had prepared for God to receive. The answer from God is not always immediate. There are times when God tests man's faith by delayed action. But if man will keep the offering complete and drive off the vultures of doubt and impatience, God will surely come as He did to Abram. A smoking furnace and a burning lamp spoke of the

18

presence and acceptance of God. And again Abram heard God saying, "Unto thy seed have I given this land" (v. 18). This was God's answer to Abram's consecration and faith. He does answer the faith of men with sanctifying grace.

January 17

God's Ideal Is Perfection

Gen. 17:1

The fact that God looks for perfection in His creation follows from the fact that God himself is perfect. In the world of nature we say a rose, an apple, or a tree is perfect. When a son who had an older sister was born, the obstetrician said to the mother as she returned to consciousness, "You have done it again, another perfect baby."

Strange but true, in the realm of Christian character we are invariably afraid to speak in terms of perfection. We mean by the use of the term that the subject of our comment is capable of complete fulfillment of the purpose for which it has being. We are inspired by the word of our Lord: "Be ye therefore perfect, even as your Father which is in heaven is perfect" (Matt. 5:48). Christians can, by the grace of God, be so fully committed to the way of obedience that they can be what God intends them to be and do what He bids them to do.

This is what God said to Abram in his time: "Walk before me, and be thou perfect" or blameless. The perfection of God is absolute; that of men is relative.

It is clear that God said Abram's performance was to be in His sight, not before men. God is the All-wise. He knows the measure of light one has received. He judges accordingly. Abram did not have the light that shines to believing men today.

God prefaced His call to Abram to be perfect with the identification of himself as the All-sufficient One. In Him is our salvation and our adequacy. By Him we may be overcomers— more than conquerors. Our sufficiency is in our God through faith.

January 18

Abraham's Faith Tested

Gen. 22:1, 14

God promised Abraham and Sarah a son. It was not easy to believe. Sarah was past age for child bearing and her husband was 10 years older, being 100 years of age. But God asked Abraham, "Is any thing too hard for the Lord?" (18:14). At the proper time Isaac was born. God assured Abraham that He would keep His covenant with him.

When Isaac had grown to manhood, God did test Abraham. He said, "Take . . . Isaac, whom thou lovest, and get thee into the land of Moriah; and offer him there for a [sacrifice]" (22:2). His obedience was prompt and without protest.

When the site for the sacrifice was in view, Abraham said to the young men that accompanied them, "Abide . . . here with the ass; and I and the lad will go yonder and worship, and come again to you" (v. 5). Already his faith was shining through.

As they walked in silence, Isaac said, "Behold the fire and the wood: but where is the lamb for a burnt offering?" Again Abraham's faith was strong, for he said, "My son, God will provide himself a lamb for a burnt offering." Abraham, having made all necessary preparations, lifted the knife to plunge it into the heart of his son. The angel of the Lord spoke, saying, "Lay not thine hand upon the lad . . . for now I know that thou fearest God, seeing thou hast not withheld thy son, thine only son from me" (vv. 7-12).

God provided the ram for the sacrifice.

Abraham passed the supreme test of faith. His beloved was not too much to give to God.

January 19

God Guides in Difficult Assignments

Gen. 24:27

Sarah was dead. Abraham was advancing in years. It is understandable that he would be concerned about a wife for his beloved son, Isaac. He was certain that he should not marry a Canaanite woman. That would compromise him with the ungodly—too great a risk. He was also just as clear that Isaac should not return to the country of his kindred. He would then, no doubt, become enmeshed in the materialism by which they were in bondage. He desired for Isaac a wife who, for the love she had for her husband, would leave father, mother, brother, sister, all her kindred, and her homeland.

Abraham commissioned his servant to go to his native country to find a wife for Isaac. Upon arrival at his destination the servant, being a man of prayer and faith, put out his fleece. He came to a well that supplied water for the people, their flocks, and their herds. He prayed to God to prosper his journey. His proposition was that the girl who came to draw water would at his request for a drink give to him and offer to draw enough for his camels too. Rebekah—beautiful, virtuous, and industrious—was first to come. She would be an ideal wife in any day. Her response was according to the specifications the servant had laid down. From there until the marriage contract was complete, everything worked perfectly. The family approval of the marriage of Rebekah was soon given. When the decision was referred to Rebekah, she said, "I will go."

Isaac received Rebekah and she became his wife and he loved her.

"Being in the way," God leads all who put their trust in Him.

January 20

Family Faults and Failures

Gen. 25:28

Esau and Jacob were twin brothers. Certainly they were not identical twins. They were different in complexion, in disposition, and in character. Their differences did not justify the strife that developed between them. Esau was a man of the field, a hunter. His genteel father admired his rugged way of life and loved the venison he brought to him. Esau became his favorite. Jacob, more fair, more domestically inclined, was the favorite of Rebekah. The parents who might have bridged the gap between their sons only made it wider. Their poor judgment brought greater pain to themselves and estrangement between their sons.

Nevertheless the brothers bore responsibility for themselves. The mistakes of parents do not justify deception and resentment in their offspring. Each must bear his own burden. The grace of God is available to fathers and mothers as it is also to the siblings.

Esau was a man given to appetite. He must satisfy his hunger *now*. He sold permanent values for present gratification.

But Jacob was the heel grasper, the supplanter, the deceiver. His hand was on Esau's heel when they were born. He wanted to be first. He bargained when he knew he had the advantage of his hungry brother. Rebekah knew God had said the elder should serve the younger, but she would not trust God to work out His plan and purpose. God is wise and good. He can bring about His will if humans can be patient and trustful. God will forgive sin and overrule the mistakes of men. Simple faith in God and sincere obedience might have preserved a family in peace and love.

January 21

Jacob at Bethel

Gen. 28:22

Esau, having sold his birthright and having been tricked out of his father's blessing, was angry at his brother, Jacob. Isaac and Rebekah sent Jacob away to Padan-aram, ostensibly to seek a wife, but also to save him from Esau's wrath.

At the end of his first day's journey he made ready to spend a lonely first night away from home. He used stones for his pillow. Doubtless he had troubled reflections more than happy anticipations of finding a wife. Adventure and romance were submerged in feelings of loneliness, guilt, fear, and uncertainty.

When sleep came to the fugitive, his troubled thoughts seemed to leave him. Possibly he sought and found God's par-

22

don. Then in his dreams there came a first great confrontation with the God of Abraham and Isaac. He saw a ladder which reached from earth to heaven, and angels of God were ascending and descending upon it. It was prophetic of the time to come when the Son of God would become the Son of Man to bring the message of God's love to men and open the gate of heaven to whosoever believes.

God renewed to Jacob the promises He had made to Abraham and Isaac. And in a very personal promise to Jacob, God said, "I am with thee, and will keep thee in all places whither thou goest" (v. 15).

Jacob awoke and said, "Surely the Lord is in this place . . . this is none other but the house of God, and this is the gate of heaven" (vv. 16-17). Jacob called the place Bethel—the House of God.

January 22

Jacob at Peniel

Gen. 32:28

Twenty years had passed since Jacob spent the night at Bethel. Much had happened meantime. God had prospered him. He was returning to the land of his fathers.

A meeting with Esau was inevitable. Fear caused Jacob to prepare for the worst. The memories of more than a score of years flooded his mind.

Jacob expected to spend the night alone. It was, however, the opportune moment for a second meeting with God. God, in likeness of a man, wrestled with Jacob. The struggle was actually with Jacob's reluctance to face up to his own double mindedness. It was an inner conflict. It was typical of the battle all men have who seek to live for God in spiritual victory over sin and self. The victory is won in the moment of confession and surrender.

The God-man said, "Let me go, for the day breaketh." In desperation Jacob said, "I will not let thee go, except thou bless me." Then came the moment of truth. "What is thy name?"

23

was the question Jacob hated most. But he had now the honesty to confess: "Jacob"—heel grasper, supplanter, trickster, deceiver (vv. 26-27). Then the mighty conqueror said, "Thy name shall be called no more Jacob, but Israel: for as a prince hast thou power with God and with men, and hast prevailed."

Jacob was an outward label on an inward nature. Now the nature was changed by the cleansing power of God's all-prevailing Spirit, and the name became Israel, having power with God.

January 23
Joseph the Dreamer

Gen. 37:3-4

Jacob loved Joseph because he was Rachel's child. But Joseph was not in favor with his brothers for other reasons. He was a tattletale. He told evil stories about his brothers. Their dislike turned to hatred.

Jacob could be excused for entertaining especially tender feelings for Joseph. But for making a show of it he is to be blamed. The coat of many colors was too much for the brothers to accept without deep resentment.

Besides the father's indulgence Joseph dreamed dreams in which he saw himself exalted above his brothers and even his parents doing obeisance to him.

The brothers waited their opportunity to show their bitter feelings for Joseph. They were away feeding their father's flock. He sent Joseph to see how they were. This gave the brothers the chance to take revenge. Their first thought was to kill the lad. They said, "We shall see what will become of his dreams" (v. 20).

But Reuben made another proposal. He said, "Let us put him into a pit," intending to return and deliver him and send him back to his father. They agreed and stripped him of his coat of many colors.

While Reuben was absent, Judah proposed to sell Joseph to

merchantmen who carried him into Egypt and sold him as a slave. They drenched the coat in blood and sent it to the grief-stricken father. The brothers were guilty. But the father provoked their jealousy and hatred. And Joseph contributed to his own fate. Let all fathers and sons take the lesson.

January 24

Joseph the Slave

Gen. 39:2

Joseph could have lived in resentful protest against his brothers and their spiteful treatment. Instead, he made the best of the bad lot which was his. His personal charm and his efficiency soon caught the attention of Potiphar, his master. He was promoted to the highest position a servant could occupy. It was more than attractive personality and unusual ability that elevated Joseph. It was the favor of God. Joseph kept his faith in the God of his fathers. The hand of God was upon him for good. He was being prepared to fulfill the purpose of God for his life. The tests of life do not defeat strong men. They are opportunities to prove themselves.

Potiphar was a high-ranking officer in the Egyptian guard. His wife was pampered and self-indulgent. Joseph, strong and virile, became the object of her undisciplined desire. Repeatedly she sought to entice him. He refused, saying, "My master has trusted me with all that is in this house. How then can I do this great wickedness, and sin against God?" (see vv. 8-9). When no others were present, the temptress made her final appeal. Being rebuffed again, her unrequited love turned to uncontrolled rage. She told the men of the house that Joseph had sought to rape her. Then she retold the story to her husband and convinced him that her story was true; so Joseph was thrown into prison.

He might have fled from the house at the first temptation. But he was a slave, not a free man. He went to prison, but he went with untarnished integrity.

January 25

Joseph the Prisoner

Gen. 39:21

Prisons are for criminals. Joseph was without guilt and blameless. But he was in reproach with the outcasts of society. He could have mourned over the injustice done him. Instead he went about to prove himself. Soon he flowered like a snow-white lily in a mud pond. He was not afraid to be different. The contrast between him and his fellow prisoners brought him to the attention of the keeper. He became much more than a trusty. The Lord was with him and made all he did to prosper. That which breaks most men, makes strong men even stronger. But promotion did not come soon. There were years of delay.

Pharaoh's wrath was kindled against his butler and his baker. They were both thrown into prison. One night each had a dream. They were puzzled by them. They related their dreams to Joseph and he interpreted them. It was good for the butler, for he was soon to be restored. Joseph asked to be remembered to the king. Nevertheless the butler, when liberated, forgot his benefactor. For two more years Joseph was put to the stringent tests of prison life. In all that time his faith did not falter, nor did he fail in his duty.

Pharaoh had dreams which his magicians could not interpret. The butler then remembered Joseph, and the king brought him out of prison to interpret his dreams. Steadfastness in righteousness was now rewarded. The path to promotion and power led through slavery and imprisonment.

January 26

Joseph as Ruler of Egypt

Gen. 41:41-43

To be vested with power spoils most men. The mettle of Joseph's character had been so tested and proved in 13 years of slavery and imprisonment that sudden elevation to be the most powerful man in Egypt did not corrupt his morals or inflate his ego. Righteousness is an essential factor in administering the affairs of men with wisdom and fairness.

When Joseph was summoned from prison to interpret the dreams of Pharaoh, he demonstrated such understanding and foresight that the king recognized him immediately as a man of unusual value. Pharaoh made him prime minister in a time of national crisis.

It is noteworthy that the preparation for his great responsibility came to Joseph in slavery and imprisonment, not in a university. Begotten in him was faith in God. The great trials through which he passed had purged his spirit of selfish ambitions until he could be trusted to guide a nation in years of great prosperity that it might survive the seven long years of famine. And because of that wise leadership Egypt had food to share with other nations round about her.

Faith in God was firm when he wore the king's ring and gold chain about his neck. Let all who would prepare themselves for performance of great duties in wisdom and righteousness, accept the tests of adversity with faith in God.

January 27

Joseph and His Brothers

Gen. 45:4-5

There is no more convincing proof of the greatness of the mind and spirit of Joseph than in his treatment of his brothers. Instead of smoldering hatred, he showed them love and forgiveness. He did watch them climb over some rather high hurdles. But when the showdown came, he showed kindness, mercy, and compassion.

He gave them corn and restored their money. When finally he made himself known to them, he not only showed forgiveness; he also sought to relieve their guilt feelings by saying it was in the wise providence of God, for he was sent before them to preserve their lives and their posterity. He urged them to bring their father down to Egypt. He settled them on the most fertile land in the nation.

27

When Jacob died, the brothers were fearful lest Joseph would take revenge on them for their evil deeds. They sought his forgiveness and promised to be his servants. He said to them, "Fear not: for am I in the place of God? . . . ye thought evil against me; but God meant it unto good, to bring to pass, as it is this day, to save much people alive. . . . fear ye not: I will nourish you. . . . And he comforted them, and spake kindly unto them" (50:19-21).

Joseph lived to the age of 110 years. Before he died, he instructed his brethren to carry his bones with them when their exodus came. He did not want identification with Egypt but with those to whom the promises of God were given.

January 28

Moses, Man of Destiny

Exod. 3:14-15

Moses should have been thrown into the river when he was born, according to the Pharaoh's decree. By the daring and faith of his mother he was spared to be the son of Pharaoh's daughter. As he grew to manhood, he had opportunity to become learned in all the wisdom of the Egyptians. At the age of 40 years he made his choice to identify with the Hebrew slaves rather than the court of Pharaoh. He assumed the role of judge and defender of the Hebrews. His action in rash judgment forced him to flee to Midian to become a shepherd for 40 years.

For four decades he was learning the important lessons of obedience to God, discipline of himself, and patience in dealing with people. Moses accepted the discipline of delay. When he was ready, the time to lead his people out of bondage would be right. God does match His man with His hour.

Another discipline hard to accept was isolation. Moses used the unbroken silence to train his ear to listen when God spoke to him.

Moses also accepted a distasteful task. Here was a prince

from the king's court and a university graduate herding sheep. Moses did his work to the best of his ability.

There under the desert sun a bush burned and was not consumed; and as Moses looked, he heard God say, "Moses . . . put off thy shoes . . . for the place whereon thou standest is holy ground" (vv. 4-5). Holy because God was there, holy because it was the place of splendid vision.

January 29

Moses and His Rod

Exod. 4:2

The self-confident young prince of 40 years ago is now humbled. God cannot use the man who acts independently of Him. On the other hand, God does need men who have sufficient self-esteem to believe that when they are fully possessed of God, He can use them to bring to pass all that is included in His will. That Moses should shrink from the great work God assigned to him is understandable. God-called men have a feeling of inadequacy.

God told Moses, "Say unto the children of Israel, I AM hath sent me" (3:14). The Eternal, the Almighty, the omnipresent God is the All-sufficient One. With Him a man of finite, limited powers becomes the *adequate man*. Moses replied, "They will say, The Lord hath not appeared unto thee" (4:1).

It was then God said, "What is that in thine hand?" Moses answered, "A rod." It was no doubt a shepherd's crook. Then God gave Moses full proof that to him would be given the miracle-working power needed to convince Israel and Pharaoh, too, that he was sent of God to lead Israel out of their slavery in Egypt. It is not how much one has to offer to God, but how completely he is in God's hands. "Little is much if God is in it."

The rod of Moses became the rod of God. A man who is wholly and forever the Lord's is sufficient for the fulfillment of God's eternal purpose. Let God possess what is in thine hand.

29

January 30
"When I See the Blood"

Exod. 12:13

Nine plagues had been visited upon Pharaoh and the Egyptians, but the heart of the stubborn ruler was yet hard. The 10th calamity which was to come was the most terrible of all. The next stroke of God's righteous judgment was to be the death of the firstborn in every Egyptian family from the maid behind the mill to the Pharaoh on his throne and all the firstborn of beasts. What judgment!

After the third plague God had made a difference. The people of Israel in the land of Goshen were spared. Now, however, if they were not to know the visitation of God's wrath on Pharaoh and the Egyptians, they must follow explicitly the instructions God gave them by Moses.

Every household as led by the father was to take a lamb without blemish, a male of the first year. The blood of the lamb was to be placed on the two side posts of the door and on the upper post of the houses wherein it was eaten. God said, "I will pass through the land of Egypt . . . and will smite all the firstborn in the land of Egypt, both man and beast; . . . and when I see the blood, I will pass over you."

This Passover feast was to be kept perpetually. It was being observed on that Good Friday when Jesus, the Lamb of God, died on the Cross. Voluntarily He bore our sins in His own body on the Cross.

Whosoever will may come and in obedience and faith find pardon and cleansing.

January 31
With God All Things Are Possible

Exod. 14:13-14

God allows impossible situations to develop and then shows His power in a miraculous deliverance. In the Exodus, God led Israel by the way of the wilderness of the Red Sea. When

30

Pharaoh knew them to be in an impasse between the mountainous wilderness and the sea, he ordered all the chariots of Egypt with their captains, and he pursued after them.

They reproached Moses, saying, "Were there no graves in Egypt, that you have brought us into this wilderness to die?" In calm courage he said, "Fear ye not, stand still, and see the salvation of the Lord . . . The Lord shall fight for you, and ye shall hold your peace."

Moses was crying to God. The answer came clear and strong, "Wherefore criest thou unto me? speak unto the children of Israel, that they go forward." The impassable sea lay in their path. God told him, "Lift thou up thy rod, and stretch out thine hand over the sea, and divide it" (vv. 15-16). God would magnify His obedient servant in the sight of those fear-stricken people. The God of miracles uses human instruments.

The angel of the Lord in the cloud changed from going before to going behind them. That cloud was glowing with light for Israel all night, but it was darkness to the Egyptians. A pathway through the sea was opened. Israel went over dryshod. The chariots of Pharaoh followed in pursuit. When Israel was safe over, God said to Moses, "Stretch out your rod again," and the sea closed in on the chariots. The waters returned in their strength. "God specializes in things thought impossible."

February 1

Bread from Heaven

Exod. 16:15

Murmuring is the common indulgence of those who live in their doubts and fears. Those who have faith in God never murmur; neither do those who murmur believe God. "Without faith it is impossible to please him" (Heb. 11:6).

The children of Israel were chronic in their complaints against Moses. He reminded them that in fact their malcontent was with God. This habitually negative state of mind which

31

was so frequently the mood of the people whom Moses led out of Egypt is more excusable than among the enlightened people of our day. They for long had been slaves, and their minds had degenerated until they did not know how to live in thanksgiving and praise to God even though they had seen His miracles. Christians today have no such excuse. They have a Greater than Moses as their Leader and the abiding presence of the Comforter. We pray, "Give us this day our daily bread," and our prayer is answered.

It is understandable that this mass of people should hunger for food. The supply they brought with them was exhausted. God promised and supplied their daily need. He wanted them to be constantly reminded of His miracle-working power.

The manna gathered each day was to keep them aware of their dependence on God. That it came on only six days was to renew in their minds the fact that God did rest the seventh day. Sabbath keeping is still a criterion of obedience to the known will of God.

The pot of manna which was kept as a memorial of God's providence was prophetic of the coming of Him who said, "I am the bread of life" (John 6:35).

February 2

The Smitten Rock

Exod. 17:6

Another crisis had arisen. Now it was lack of water. There were over 600,000 men able to bear arms besides women and children. There were unnumbered animals. All required water to live. The situation was desperate. The people were so angry at Moses that he said they were ready to stone him. He reminded them that it was God with whom they were impatient and angry.

Moses knew to whom he should go. With confidence that God was almighty and equal to the emergency, Moses called on Him.

God directed Moses, "Take the rod with which you smote the river, and go stand on the rock; and you shall smite the rock, and there shall come water out of it." Moses did so in the sight of the elders of Israel. The people and the beasts drank until their thirst was quenched. Travelers to that part of the world are today shown a fountain of water flowing out of a rock. It never runs dry.

Paul wrote in 1 Cor. 10:4, "They [all] drank of that spiritual Rock that followed them: and that Rock was Christ." Jesus told the woman at Sychar's well, "Whosoever drinketh of the water that I shall give him shall never thirst; but the water that I shall give him shall be in him a well of water springing up into everlasting life" (John 4:14). Isaiah cried, "Ho, every one that thirsteth, come ye to the waters" (55:1).

February 3
Prayer Does Prevail

Exod. 17:11

A new and different crisis had arisen. A ferocious enemy was harassing the camp of Israel. It was not open combat until now, but Amalek was attacking the unarmed people and inflicting damage and loss to those incapable of helping themselves. The time had come to face the enemy. Moses here introduced Joshua to be a military leader.

The untrained men under Joshua's command were not equal to the toughened fighters of Amalek. But Moses with his rod was yonder on the hill. When his hand was uplifted, God was with Joshua in the battle. When his hand in weariness fell to his side, Amalek prevailed. When doubt and independence of God take over, failure is sure to come.

Moses' arm grew weary; he needed prayer partners. Aaron and Hur were there to support his hands. With their help he was strengthened, and God's power brought victory to Joshua over Amalek.

The constancy of our prayer to God and our faith in Him is

the secret of victory over every foe. Satan, our truculent, persistent, frightening foe, flees when he sees the believing saint on his knees.

One alone may win the victory but all need help. A praying mother needs the support of a devout husband. A godly pastor can win by his own prayers and faith in God, but he needs a church board and a group of prayer partners to win total victory. Prayer does prevail.

February 4

Share Your Burden

Exod. 18:21-22

Moses was being crushed under a burden too heavy for any mortal to bear. Someone must share the load of possibly 3 million people, and to whom else could they go?

Jethro, Moses' father-in-law, came to pay him a visit. He was a man who had knowledge of God and insight in dealing with people. He saw that being judge of all the Israelites would shatter even a man as strong as Moses. Jethro advised that the load should be distributed among the most reliable men in the camp. He said, "You hear the great causes, and let the small matters rest with your appointed helpers."

It was good advice. Evidently God approved, for later He gave the same guidance to Moses, and He let Moses know that other men could be endowed with the same Spirit that had been given to him. Few if any have exclusive access to His wisdom. It was good for Moses and good for all who had responsibility thrust upon them.

The sharing of burdens and problems is sound psychologically. There is relief in the very act of sharing. It is good for those who accept their responsibility. People are happier if they are useful. They catch the spirit of cooperation; furthermore, the cause is promoted by the work of many. Most of the work of God will not be done unless the help of many is enlisted.

Share your burden of responsibility.

The Law Leads to Christ

Exod. 19:4-6

Israel had come to Sinai. Their sojourn at this encampment was a landmark in all their history. Here God would begin to mold a nation.

God proposed to take this people into a covenant relationship with himself. They would be a possession of His own. In them the promises made to Abraham would be fulfilled. In the midst of most awesome circumstances God spoke the terms of the covenant. Those terms are spelled out in the Ten Commandments. God's law has never been abrogated, abridged, or amended. Christ said, "I am not come to destroy, but to fulfil" (Matt. 5:17).

These commandments are transcendent. They came down from the high and holy God to Moses at Mount Sinai. They also transcend history. They are timeless. They speak to the conscience of God-fearing men today.

The Ten Commandments are permanent. God wrote them on tablets of stone, not on perishable papyrus. This signifies that they were to be the lasting foundation for civilization for as long as men live with other men on the earth. God gave orders to Moses to place those tables in the ark of the testimony for safekeeping as a sacred trust.

This law is beneficent. In the keeping of it there is great reward. John Wesley said, "Every one of God's commands is a covered promise." Keep those precepts with a clear conscience and receive unnumbered and unmeasured blessing.

For all its worth the law is inadequate. Its primary value is in the fact that it points to Christ the Redeemer.

February 6

The Holy Anointing Oil

Exod. 30:25

In the Old Testament the Holy Spirit is often represented by meaningful symbols. One of them was oil. This holy

35

anointing oil which Moses was commanded to make, with the several ingredients, is especially symbolic of the Holy Spirit and His blessed work in the souls of men.

The mixture was to contain 500 shekels of pure myrrh. This spoke of the purifying work of the Holy Spirit. Purity is the necessary preparation for maximum growth toward maturity.

Two hundred and fifty shekels of sweet cinnamon were to be added for fragrance. The presence of the Holy Spirit makes lives fragrant, attractive, charming. He makes life beautiful.

There were also included 250 shekels of sweet calamus, a hot spice. Those who know the fullness of the Spirit are never lukewarm. Calamus also has a healing quality. The Holy Spirit is an antidote for supersensitive persons who enjoy hurt feelings.

In the composition of the holy anointing oil there were to be 500 shekels of cassia. This was a sweet spice. It was to add a preserving effect. This the Holy Spirit does for those who receive Him.

The base for the holy anointing oil was one and one-half gallons of olive oil. Olive oil does not harden or grow stale. The Holy Spirit keeps the Christian's life fresh and up to date. Olive oil is a lubricant. It eliminates friction. Olive oil is an illuminant. It makes whatever it touches to shine. The Holy Spirit dwelling within produces a holy radiance which does not grow dim.

February 7

Would You Believe It?

Exod. 32:1

It is incredible but true. After years of bondage and cruel treatment by their taskmasters; after witnessing the miracles God performed to bring release to them; after the mighty deliverance at the sea; after the supply of food from heaven; after they drank water from the rock; yes, and after they had heard the Ten Commandments spoken audibly to them amidst the display of God's power at Sinai; after they had said, "All that the Lord hath spoken we will do" (19:8); when Moses was gone from them for 40 days, they said to Aaron, "Up, make us gods, which shall go before us." This was a flagrant transgression of the first and most important command which they had heard and agreed to obey.

God warned Moses of what was happening and sent him down from the mount in haste. When he saw them in the midst of their idolatrous orgy, Moses cast down the tablets of stone, and they were broken in pieces beyond repair. Was it a fit of carnal anger? No, it was the kind of indignation that is holy. All holy people must retain the capacity for righteous wrath. They must abhor evil. But more, if Moses had not broken the inscribed conditions of the covenant, it would have been in effect, and for violation of that covenant those idol worshippers would have been guilty beyond pardon. Now God could give them another chance.

In answer to the intercessory prayer of Moses, God spared the people. They returned unto God and He returned to them. How merciful is God!

February 8

The Shining Face

Exod. 34:29-30

It is no wonder that Moses' face shone, for he had been in intimate communion with the God of glory for 40 days and 40 nights. Such continued practice of the presence of God may still produce a spiritual glow that can be seen in the countenances of devout men.

The late Dr. H. E. Jessop, teacher, preacher, and author, has left his testimony in a little book entitled *I Met a Man with a Shining Face.* Dr. Jessop tells of going to a conference, where he heard a man speak whose face was illuminated with heavenly radiance. He went home to seek until he found that fullness of the Spirit. To him was given the inner light that shone in his face.

Of Stephen, sitting before the council while false charges

were lodged against him, it is written, "His face [shone] as it had been the face of an angel" (Acts 6:15).

It is notable that Moses did not know that his face shone. The spiritual glow is evident to those who see. Paul concludes his commentary on the shining face of Moses with these words of encouragement to believers: "We all, with open face beholding as in a glass the glory of the Lord, are changed into the same image from glory to glory, even as by the Spirit of the Lord" (2 Cor. 3:18).

This is not a radiance for preachers and leaders only. It is a glory all God's people may share. But wouldn't it be wonderful if more preachers had their credentials written on their faces, not just on parchments?

February 9
God Has Something for All to Do

Exod. 35:29-31

While Moses was in the mountain, God gave him detailed plans and specifications for building the Tabernacle. He was to make the plan known to the people to the last item. But Moses needed help. He called upon the whole congregation of Israel to bring a willing offering. Everyone could bring something useful.

God gave to the people a willing heart. And wonder of wonders, the people brought and kept on bringing until Moses had to ask them not to bring more!

Then Moses named the men to lead in the construction of the Tabernacle. There were those who had the skills to put together the materials according to the blueprint God had given to Moses. Bezaleel and Aholiab possessed the special talents for all manner of workmanship and the ability to teach their helpers. There is in God's plan a work for all to do.

Soon the Tabernacle was built as the Lord commanded Moses. How beautiful the product! How perfect the workmanship! How happy the people who heard and obeyed the command of God! From the nameless persons to Bezaleel and to

Moses, all had done as God commanded. Then a cloud covered the tent of the congregation, and the glory of the Lord filled the Tabernacle. The glory was so great Moses was not able to enter the tent.

What would happen in the Church today if all would bring their offering and be careful to hear and obey the still, small voice of God? Could there not be a glory of God's presence that would be overpowering?

February 10

Bring an Offering

1 Chron. 16:29

The Book of Leviticus is a manual for worship. It assumes that man coming to God to worship will not come empty-handed. He will bring an offering. There was to be a sin offering. Sinful man must have an atonement made that he may have access to God. The offering was to atone for sins of ignorance. For voluntary transgressions of the covenant there was no sacrifice. This ritual was prophetic of the redeeming work of Christ who was delivered unto death for our offences, and was raised again for our justification. Thank God that this atonement was made that our willful sins might be forgiven as well as sins committed in ignorance.

There was also a burnt offering. The entire offering was to be burned with fire as a sacrifice to God. This signified that Christ would offer himself in total surrender to the Father's will. The New Testament calls for believers in Christ to present their bodies (i.e., the whole personality) a living sacrifice, holy, acceptable unto God, their reasonable service.

There was also the meat or meal offering which suggests the consecration of our work to God. "Whether therefore ye eat, or drink, or whatsoever ye do, do all to the glory of God" (1 Cor. 10:31).

A fourth sacrifice was the peace offering. This implied that the offerer was in fellowship with God.

These offerings all have their fulfillment in Christian experience. There is symbolized pardon, sanctification, service, and fellowship. All are provided in Christ, the antitype of those sacrificial rituals.

February 11

Holiness the Central Theme of the Bible

Lev. 19:1-2

The fundamental reason for consistent emphasis on holiness is that God said, "I am holy." Being holy includes God's transcendence, His separateness, and His absolute purity. For a holy God to have full fellowship with man, he too must be holy. The fulfilling of this requirement brought the Son of God down to earth in an infinite condescension. It sent Him to the Cross to die. It was all because God had said, "Ye shall be holy: for I the Lord your God am holy."

The Book of Leviticus has been called "the fountain of holiness." Chapter 19 is the heart of the holiness code. It is a restatement of the Ten Commandments, which are a transcript of God's holy being. It also anticipates the ethical principles of the New Testament. It is a preview of the Sermon on the Mount. It includes the first and greatest commandment and the second which is like unto it.

The verse which we are considering for this day tells us that the source of all holiness is in God himself. And only in a relationship of active faith, love, and obedience can man be holy. It also makes it clear that the standard for holiness in man is seen in the holy character of God. "Be ye holy; for I am holy" (1 Pet. 1:16). That holiness involved separation from all the evil of the world. It was separation unto God. In this text and the chapter which it introduces we learn that God desires to bring life in its totality to complete commitment to Him. It calls for holiness of heart and righteous conduct in every phase of life. Leviticus points up the necessity for a better way. It implies clearly that what it offers is not the ultimate. It prophesies the coming of an adequate Savior.

February 12

The Lord Give Thee Peace

Num. 6:24-27

These verses are known as the Priestly Benediction. "The Lord spake unto Moses, saying, Speak unto Aaron and unto his sons, saying, On this wise ye shall bless the children of Israel" (vv. 22-23).

There is implied in this benediction the great mystery of the Trinity by the repetition of the name Lord or Jehovah. There is one Lord. There is perfect unity in the Trinity. Father, Son, and Holy Spirit are One.

"The Lord bless thee, and keep thee." Here is the assurance of God's protection and safekeeping. "As the mountains are round about Jerusalem, so the Lord is round about his people from henceforth even for ever" (Ps. 125:2). John Calvin said, "The blessing of God is the goodness of God in action."

"The Lord make his face shine upon thee, and be gracious unto thee." It is Jesus the Son who bestows grace. We are saved by grace through faith; it is the gift of God.

"The Lord lift up his countenance upon thee, and give thee peace." It is the Holy Spirit who gives peace to those who love God and keep His commandments. The fruit of the Spirit is peace. This includes prosperity and total well-being. It means harmonious fellowship with the Father and with His Son, Jesus Christ, and fellowship one with another among all God's consecrated people.

There is a New Testament benediction that reflects this one. "The grace of the Lord Jesus Christ, and the love of God, and the communion of the Holy [Spirit], be with you all. Amen" (2 Cor. 13:14).

February 13

God Leads His People

Num. 9:17

Very soon after the Israelites left Egypt, God gave them guidance by a pillar of cloud by day and of fire by night. When the cloud lifted and moved, the camp of Israel journeyed. When the cloud stood, they pitched their tents and abode there.

The cloud was the assurance of the presence of God. How completely confounded and helpless would this moving mass of humanity have been without the knowledge that God was with them. He was with them in all their journeys for the 40 years of their wilderness experience. Even in the years of their unbelief and rebellion, while they lived out their sentence to wilderness wandering, God did not reject His people. In lovingkindness and patience God continued His presence and His protection. This is eloquent testimony to the disposition toward mercy in the heart of God.

To be sure, there was human leadership; Moses was God's chosen servant to bring His people from Egypt to the Promised Land. But it was God who showed the way. Moses heard God speak to him. Nevertheless the people needed to be persuaded that God was with them. This visible evidence of His presence reinforced the leadership of Moses.

Human leaders of the nation and the Church always need the help and guidance of God. Today God gives to human leaders and to all His willing and obedient people, His Word as a lamp to their feet and a light to their pathway. Furthermore His Spirit speaks to the inner consciousness in unmistakable words of guidance and assurance.

February 14

Crisis at Kadesh

Num. 14:34

Nearly a year had passed at the mount of God's revelation. The time to move toward Canaan had come. The Passover was celebrated at God's command. The cloud was taken up and the tribes went forward.

They had not journeyed far until they came to Kadeshbarnea. There according to Moses' record in Deuteronomy, the people proposed to send spies to search out the land. Moses accepted the plan and God permitted it.

Twelve spies were chosen, one from each tribe. They were gone 40 days. Their report was unanimous at one point. It was a good land flowing with milk and honey. But alas, 10 gave a majority report that was negative. They said there were walled cities and giants so great that the spies were like grasshoppers in their own sight and the giants'. They were defeatists. They recommended that the undertaking be abandoned now.

But Caleb and Joshua were men of faith. They brought a minority report. They said, "If the Lord delight in us, then he will bring us into this land, and give it us . . . [God will make those giants] bread for us: their defence is departed from them, and the Lord is with us: fear them not" (vv. 8-9). These two men believed that with God all things are possible.

But the congregation accepted the majority report regardless of consequences.

That generation of rebellious people would wander in the wilderness a year for every day they searched out the land. All above 20 years of age died in the wilderness.

February 15

Timing Is Important

Num. 14:42-43

The die had been cast. The Israelites had made the fatal choice. They would believe the 10 spies who slandered the land which they had explored. They were condemned to wilderness wandering.

They slept over their decision and then reversed themselves. They said, "We . . . *will* go up" to possess the land. But alas, they had missed their day of opportunity, and crushing defeat befell their vain attempt.

Any effort to do the task without God's help is futile. The secret of success is God in the midst. There are times today

43

when men rush ahead of God only to suffer defeat or at best delay. At other times the hour for faith expressed in active obedience is past. The tide that was running favorably has turned.

This happens in the lives of individual Christians. It may be in making the commitment to follow Christ which some suppose can be made at a time of their own choosing. All such settle for second best. In most cases those who do not seize their opportunity go beyond the point of no return. Let all consider this inspired word: "Behold, now is the accepted time; behold, now is the day of salvation" (2 Cor. 6:2).

This can happen in the Church and its related institutions. The ones involved can grasp their opportunities and go on to great achievement and glory. But they can also miss their day to arise and follow the Master.

Shakespeare's famous lines are a warning: "There is a tide in the affairs of men . . . and we must take the current when it serves, or lose our ventures."

February 16

The Choice Is God's

Num. 17:5

For great spiritual adventures God has chosen His man. That God prepared and called Moses to lead Israel from Egypt to the Promised Land there is no reasonable doubt.

It is also clear that God chose Aaron and his sons to perform the sacred duties of the priesthood. God said to Moses, "Take thou unto thee Aaron thy brother, and his sons with him, from among the children of Israel, that he may minister unto me in the priest's office" (Exod. 28:1). The Lord proceeded to order specified garments to be made to distinguish the priests from the other Levites and all Israel; then He declared, "Thou shalt make a plate of pure gold, and grave upon it . . . HOLINESS TO THE LORD" (v. 36).

All this bore testimony to the choice God had made for

44

the priesthood. With the choice came great responsibility. Upon the breastplate of judgment worn upon the heart of Aaron were graven the names of the children of Israel. He represented the people before God, and he represented God to the people.

There still arose a rebellion against God's chosen leaders. Korah challenged the priesthood under Aaron. Dathan and Abiram, among others, told Moses that he took too much on himself. Moses declared it had never entered his mind to do all these things; it was God who had put upon him his responsibility.

When the rebels came before God in presumed performance of the sacred duties, fire from the Lord consumed Korah and 250 other rebels; the earth also opened her mouth to receive Dathan, Abiram, any of their followers, and their families. (See Numbers 16.)

Even yet the choice of men for sacred calling is of God. He has said, "Touch not mine anointed" (1 Chron. 16:22).

February 17

Moses and Aaron Miss Canaan

Num. 20:12

There is one sad page in the story of the life of Moses. But for one dark moment the record is one of faithful performance before God and of almost infinite patience with a murmuring people.

Shortage of water had brought about another crisis. Again the ungrateful people grumbled to Moses, saying, "Would God that we had died when our brethren died before the Lord!" (v. 3).

God told Moses and Aaron to speak, and water would flow from the rock. They gathered the people before the rock, and Moses shouted, "Hear now, *ye rebels;* must *we* fetch you water out of this rock?" (v. 10, emphasis added). And Moses lifted up his hand and with the rod *smote the rock twice;* and the water came out abundantly.

But alas for Moses and for Aaron, they were told by God

then and there they would not lead Israel into Canaan. The forfeit of that honor was final. Why was the penalty so severe?

Moses reverted to a previous pattern of action. He reasoned, I smote the rock at Rephidim, I will do it the same way now. He did not explicitly obey God. While Moses was not obeying God, he charged the people with rebellion. He did not respect his fellowmen, a fatal fault of those who would be spiritual leaders. He lost control of himself. He acted in anger. He was out of character. Finally, he did not give glory to God. Instead he said, "Must *we* fetch you water out of this rock?"

The humble and obedient give God the glory.

February 18

Look and Live

Num. 21:8

There was no miracle-working power in a serpent of brass. The cure for the deadly sting of the venomed serpent was in willingness to obey God's word. He said, "When he looketh upon it [he] shall live. . . . and it came to pass, that if a serpent had bitten any man, when he beheld the serpent of brass, he lived."

This historic incident in Israel's experience points back to the garden of Eden. It calls attention to the fact that sin is racial as well as personal. Because sin is innate, man turns to sinful practice. "All have sinned, and come short of the glory of God" (Rom. 3:23). A double cure is demanded. Personal sin must be forgiven and sinful nature must be cleansed.

This story of the uplifted serpent of brass points to the uplifted Savior. Jesus said, "As Moses lifted up the serpent in the wilderness, even so must the Son of man be lifted up" (John 3:14). God "hath made him [Christ] to be sin for us, who knew no sin; that we might be made the righteousness of God in him" (2 Cor. 5:21).

Those who were dying of the serpents' stings were healed

46

because they turned in obedience and faith to look at that serpent of brass according to God's prescription for their recovery.

Sinful men of today find pardon and cleansing by voluntary acceptance of Christ as Savior. Their willingness to look to Jesus on the Cross will mean eternal life. The look must be one of contrition and repentance. It must be a look of faith in "nothing less than Jesus' blood and righteousness."

February 19

A Dual Person

Num. 24:10-11

Balaam is one of the most mysterious and contradictory men of the Bible. He showed great reluctance to disobey God. He refused to curse him whom God had blessed. He looked into the future and spoke words that many believed foretold the coming of Messiah. He said, "There shall come a Star out of Jacob, and a Sceptre shall rise out of Israel" (v. 17).

But Balaam was a dual personality. He was double minded and unstable. He did not want to forfeit his relation to God. Yet he wanted to gain the favor of Balak because he was offering him riches and honor. He did what Jesus said none can do: He tried to serve two masters. He knew what he ought to do, but he wanted to possess "the wages of unrighteousness" (2 Pet. 2:15). He had the capability of a prophet of God. But he was known to Balak and the Moabites as a soothsayer.

Balaam found a way to bring a curse on Israel. He told the king to encourage the women at Baal-peor to entice the men of Israel. They did and the men of Israel responded. This brought the wrath of God upon them. Furthermore they turned to idolatrous worship of Baal. As a result 24,000 died in the plague which came as God's judgment upon Israel.

This man of double mind has many counterparts in the church today. Their hearts are divided. They need to be sanctified wholly. There is no duality in a sanctified heart.

47

February 20

The Peril of Partial Obedience

Num. 32:29-30

Israel was near the borders of the Promised Land. They were in undisputed possession of the land called Gilead. It was fertile, well watered, especially adapted for grazing.

The leaders of the tribes of Reuben and Gad looked upon those good pastures with covetous eyes. They proposed to Moses that they be given this area for their inheritance because they had cattle. Moses' answer was, "Shall your brethren go to war, and shall ye sit here?" (v. 6). They then promised to go over Jordan and fight with their brethren in the conquest of Canaan. With that promise given, Moses consented for them to settle their families east of Jordan. As a matter of record they only fractionally fulfilled their promise. Moses had warned them that if they did not keep their word, "Your sin will find you out" (v. 23).

Their request sprang from a wrong motive. The material advantages were uppermost in their thinking: "Your servants have cattle"; "Here is good grass"; and so forth.

They were left outside the intimate fellowship. They were removed from the center of the worship of God.

Their temporary gain turned into eternal loss. Earlier than the other tribes they went after strange gods. And they were the first to be carried into captivity by the Assyrians. They were without the barrier of the Jordan River for defense. Their partial obedience kept them from the greater blessing of full participation in the promises of God. God's best is for those who go all the way.

February 21

God Provides a Refuge

Num. 35:14-15

God is just. The appointment of six cities of refuge is proof that God does condemn the sinner and that He justly provides a place of safety for the guiltless. This is encouragement to all believers that they will receive mercy at the hands of the righteous Judge.

The initiative in providing the cities of refuge was taken by God before the thought ever occurred to man. In like manner the whole scheme of salvation originated in the mind and heart of the Eternal. No sooner had man sinned against God than the purpose of redemption was declared. The prophets foretold it. Angels desired to look into it. Finally Christ Jesus came to declare it.

A corollary of the great truth of God's justice is seen in the fact that in both Old and New Testaments there is an unmistakable distinction between intentional transgressions and involuntary sins of omission or commission. God considers the motive as well as the deed.

These cities of refuge gave no blanket defense to him who fled to them. Each one was protected until his case was heard by the elders and the congregation. Upon establishment of innocence of intentional murder he could remain there in safety. If on hearing his testimony he was judged guilty of murder by intention, he was delivered to the avenger of blood. The cities of refuge were located so as to be accessible to all until justice could be administered.

The crimson Cross is so near by,
Oh, why will ye die?

February 22

Escape from Futility

Deut. 2:3

It was 40 years since Israel had crossed the Red Sea. In the second year they came to Kadesh-barnea. They were only 11 days from Canaan, but their unbelief and disobedience turned 11 days journey into more than 38 years of wandering. It was an exercise in futility. Their movements were probably more or less in a circle. A person lost in trackless waste or wilderness will invariably find himself going round and round. He wears himself out with wearisome travel, but he goes nowhere.

Now the days of judgment were over. Moses records, "The Lord spake unto me, saying, Ye have compassed this mountain long enough: turn you northward." Now they would go toward the land that had been their destination all those 40 years.

How many there are who spend their lives in frustration and futility because they have known the will of God and rebelled against it! If only they would accept God's leadings, they would find themselves on a shining pathway to fulfillment and the land of promise.

Israel now broke out of their syndrome of defeat and confusion. They were on their way again. The hindrances were not all gone, but they were on the path of obedience. They were making progress because they were following God.

February 23
"Hear"

Deut. 6:4-9

To hear means to listen, hearken, obey. It is a clear call to recognize that the Lord our God is one Lord. None are above Him and none are equal to Him. There is no likeness to which He can be compared.

He was not to be worshipped in formal ceremonies or lip service; it was to be from the heart. This word was given in anticipation of the truths spoken by the One like unto Moses centuries later. Jesus said that true worshippers worship the Father "in spirit and in truth: for the Father seeketh such to worship him. God is a Spirit" (John 4:23-24). Hearing and doing is the evidence both of faith and love. "If ye love me, keep my commandments," said Jesus in John 14:15.

When He was asked what is the first and greatest commandment, He gave a direct quotation from this second law. "Thou shalt love the Lord thy God with all thy heart, and with all thy soul, and with all thy mind" (Matt. 22:37).

God is Lord in family life. Teach His words diligently to your children. Teach by example. Teach by frequent repetition.

Teach by keeping these commandments before them, "when thou sittest in thine house, and when thou walkest by the way, and when thou liest down, and when thou risest up." Write them on the posts of thine house and on thy gates.

To those who hear and *obey*, there is a promise. They shall have abundant blessings unearned and undeserved. God will give them rich reward in this life and in heaven to come.

February 24

Building a Home

Deut. 22:8

Building a home is of far greater importance than building a house. The house is for physical protection and comfort. The home is designed for a fortress against evil, a shelter from raging forces of destruction.

It is the climate of a home that is most important. It may be a house that is small, but the spirit should be spacious. The furnishings may be plain, but those who live there may be rich in devotion. The daily food may be simple, but each meal can be a sacramental celebration. The whole of life there may be redeeming because of lofty minds and gracious manners.

The pictures and mottos on the wall, the music, the subjects of conversation at the table, the language used, the look of the eye, the tone of the voice all contribute to the climate.

Weak sentimentalism may say, I love my child too much to discipline him. But true parental love is willing to bear the pain of administering chastening as needed. Submission to rules of conduct begins in childhood.

Integrity is taught by the example of parents. What they do, say, and are is an image that will linger long after the family is scattered.

Prayer and Bible reading are powerful, far out of proportion to the time consumed thereby.

Finally, the climate of a home is enriched and sweetened

by love in action. Love is thoughtful planning to please. It is heard in words of appreciation and praise. It is seen in deeds of kindness.

February 25

The Moment to Decide

Deut. 30:19

The fairness of God's judgment is beyond question. For obedience He promised blessing; for disobedience, He promised cursing. God never deals out half-truths. He states the proposition in such unmistakable clarity that none can misunderstand.

The promise of blessing for obedience and of cursing for disobedience was to be dramatized when Israel had come into the Promised Land. Certain tribes were to stand on Mount Gerizim and the remaining tribes on Mount Ebal. Thus they would face each other across the valley. From Gerizim came the blessing and from Ebal the curse was pronounced. This was to be a continual reminder that God is holy in character and righteous in His judgments. God was fair and Moses was faithful.

God is just the same today. He offers full compensation in this life and the next for obedience. He also issues warnings in His Word to all who are transgressors. Moses called heaven and earth to record that the solemn issues of good and evil, life and death were set forth.

No matter how fair God is in dealing with men and no matter how faithful His servants are, the choice belongs to every individual. Life is blessed or blighted and destiny is determined for all eternity by the choices man makes for himself. He cannot charge God with injustice. Neither can he shunt responsibility to another. "The soul that sinneth, it shall die" (Ezek. 18:4). Because man is born in sin does not mean he must continue in his sin. A Savior has come to save His people from their sins. All who look to Him in contrition and faith will live.

February 26

The Eternal God Thy Refuge

Deut. 33:27

These are among the last recorded words ascribed to Moses. They were addressed to the tribes of Israel and must have been treasured by them. They speak to all believers with reassurance and comfort. The passing of time does not change the God who is love. A farmer noted for his faith in God built a barn; above the roof rose a cupola, atop that was a weather vane, and on it were inscribed in gold letters, "God is love." A skeptic taunted the farmer with this cynical remark, "So your God changes every time the wind does." "No," said the man of faith, "God is love no matter which way the wind blows."

This changeless God of holy love is an ever-present protection for His people. The Psalmist said, "I will say of the Lord, He is my refuge and my fortress: my God; in him will I trust. . . . his truth shall be thy shield and buckler. . . . There shall no evil befall thee, neither shall any plague come nigh thy dwelling. For he shall give his angels charge over thee, to keep thee in all thy ways" (91:2, 4, 10-11).

God is himself the protection given to all who trust in Him. He is also their support. "Underneath are the everlasting arms." They are never too short to reach His children. They are never weary. They are never so overloaded that they cannot bear another burden. The strength of God is unlimited in behalf of those who trust in Him.

February 27

To Pull Down and to Plant

Jer. 1:10

When God called Jeremiah, He said, "I ordained thee a prophet unto the nations." He said, "Ah, Lord God! behold, I cannot speak: for I am a child." But the Lord said, "Say not, I am a child." Jeremiah continues, "Then the Lord put forth his hand, and touched my mouth. And the Lord said unto me, Behold, I have put my words in thy mouth. See, I have this day set thee over the nations and over the kingdoms, to root out, and to pull down, and to destroy, and to throw down, to build, and to plant" (vv. 5-7, 9-10).

Jeremiah accepted his commission with reluctance, as any man called to such an assignment would. He heard the Lord say, "Out of the north an evil shall break forth upon all the inhabitants of the land" (v. 14).

This prophet of doom was to warn the wicked men of his day, people, priests, false prophets, and kings. Nevertheless, God promised restoration. Jeremiah saw a brighter day beyond the dark foreboding. He was to pull down and then to plant and build.

Jeremiah was not obsessed with the negative message. He was a preacher of hope. In honesty he warned of coming judgment as all faithful men must. But in hope he promised, according to God's steadfast love, that there would come the dawn of a better day. Let all God's people tell it as it truly is. But let them see beyond present horizons into the glories of eternal day.

February 28

Yokes of Wood or Iron

Jer. 28:12-13

Jeremiah had proclaimed that Judah would be under the rule of the Chaldeans for 70 years. To illustrate the things he prophesied, he was instructed of God to make yokes of wood— one for Zedekiah, king of Judah, and one for his own neck— as a reminder of what he had announced as the program of God for the immediate future.

Hananiah, one of the false prophets, spoke out. He said, "The word of Jeremiah is false. The yoke of Babylon will be broken in two years."

Hananiah broke the yoke of wood after taking it off the neck of Jeremiah, telling the people that the yoke of Babylon would also be broken. But Jeremiah replied, "Thou hast broken the yokes of wood; but thou shalt make for them yokes of iron."

The yokes of wood spoke of the submission which Jeremiah had recommended. He said that resistance would only mean more severe and cruel bondage. They were to serve the king of Babylon. Remain in this land, continued the prophet, and he will deal more kindly with you. Wait in patience, cooperate with the inevitable. Nurture your faith and hope in God. The day of deliverance will come.

Yet the rebellious people of Jerusalem and Judah listened to the prophet of lies instead of the man who knew and declared the word of God. The iron yoke of Nebuchadnezzar was put upon them. Their country was laid waste, their city was destroyed, their temple was razed to the ground. The king saw his sons slain. His eyes were then blinded. He and many captives were carried to Babylon.

Rebels against God always forge for themselves yokes of iron.

February 29

The New Covenant

Jer. 31:31-34

Jeremiah had seen the failure of national religion. He now proclaimed the doctrine of individual responsibility. From that viewpoint he envisioned the day when a new covenant would replace the old.

The fulfillment would be when the Messiah King had come to establish His spiritual kingdom in the hearts of men. The author of the Epistle to the Hebrews, seeing the first covenant was not without fault, declared the new covenant was now in effect. The new and living way into the holiest had been consecrated for us. Having an High Priest over the house of God, we draw near in full assurance of faith.

The new covenant opened the door for every man to come to God and know Him in personal relationship. A new motive for obedience to the law of God was given to all who believe in Jesus. The laws of the old covenant were based on an arbitrary authority. They were to be obeyed or the penalty was to be administered. Now the law was built into the mind and written on the heart. This provided an inward disposition and desire to do all the known will of God.

Our holy religion is no longer external conformity. It is the expression of our wills to do all God's will because of the renewing of the mind by the Holy Spirit. Inwardness has replaced outward conformity to legal demands. Under the new covenant, to do God's will is a pleasure. Our sufficiency is of God.

March 1
Teach Us to Pray

Luke 11:1

This earnest request was voiced by one disciple. No doubt it expressed the desire of all of them. It was for their sakes but for our good as well.

Jesus had been teaching them to pray by example for a long time. They had observed Him seek the quiet of a desert place to pray. They knew He spent nights in prayer. They probably had seen His countenance change as He prayed. They took note that prayer was the preparation He sought when He was faced with important decisions or great responsibilities. They must have reasoned among themselves that if He, their Lord and Master, needed the renewal, guidance, and strength that prayer afforded, certainly their need was far greater. Could it be that prayerlessness is the explanation for many of the blundering decisions, the poor performance, and embarrassing failures of Christians today?

Wouldn't it behoove us to learn from Jesus to pray with regularity? If prayer becomes a habit of life, God is a never-failing help in time of need. He is there when the emergencies arise. There is automatic appeal to Him, and there is immediate response to an urgent call. In our weakness, He is our strength.

The disciples had awesome respect for their Lord when He was engaged in prayer. It was when He ceased that they made their request. If Christians prayed with greater frequency and with resulting effect on their personalities, wouldn't those who observe that, respect them more?

March 2

A Model for Group Prayer

Luke 11:2a

In response to the request of the disciples, Jesus gave them a model for group praying. It was not a mold into which all their spiritual longings should be cast. It was rather a series of principles by which their thoughts were to be guided as they expressed their yearnings to God.

It is noteworthy that all the pronouns in the request and in the instructions given by the Teacher are plural. It is never "I" or "my," it is always "us" and "our." It is like a family prayer. In his book titled *Quiet Talks on Prayer,* S. D. Gordon points out five different relationships that are included in the Father-concept of God.

He is a concerned Father. He watches over His children. He who notes the sparrow's fall never forgets His child.

God has the tenderness of a compassionate mother. Though a mother forget her own offspring, "yet will I not forget thee," He says (Isa. 49:15).

God is like a confidential friend. Jesus said to His disciples, "Henceforth I call you not servants; for the servant knoweth not what his lord doeth: but I have called you friends; for all things that I have heard of my Father I have made known unto you" (John 15:15). He shares and keeps the sacred trust. A friend loveth at all times.

The disciples' relationship to God is that of a constant lover. There is no fickleness or caprice. He is changeless in His faithfulness.

God is a considerate husband. His love is selfless. He always has forethought for His beloved. On His part, there is no provision for divorcement. Having loved His own, He loved them to the end.

March 3

"Hallowed Be Thy Name"

Luke 11:2b

The lessons Jesus taught His disciples concerning prayer were implicit rather than explicit. He expected them to read between the lines as well as learn the words. There is a principle of reverence which should be observed in approach to God. Those who come to God should come as to the high and holy God who inhabiteth eternity. The teaching of Jesus was in harmony with His practice. When He offered His high-priestly prayer of John 17, He said, "Father, the hour is come; glorify thy Son, that thy Son also may glorify thee" (v. 1).

The great prayers of the Bible are introduced in a similar mood of awe. When Solomon dedicated the Temple, he bowed on his knees and stretched forth his hands toward heaven and said, "Lord God of Israel, there is no God like thee, in heaven above, or on earth beneath" (1 Kings 8:23). The Psalmist began his prayer, "O Lord our Lord, how excellent is thy name in all the earth! who hast set thy glory above the heavens" (8:1). In the only psalm Moses wrote he began, "Lord, thou hast been our dwelling place in all generations. Before the mountains were brought forth, or ever thou hadst formed the earth and the world, even from everlasting to everlasting, thou art God" (90:1-2).

As Paul came to God in prayer, he said, "I bow my knees unto the Father of our Lord Jesus Christ, of whom the whole family in heaven and earth is named" (Eph. 3:14-15).

This reverent approach to God is taught by Jesus in saying, "Hallowed be thy name."

March 4

We Must Learn Submission

Luke 11:2c-d

These two thoughts are so interrelated that they cannot be separated. Jesus came preaching, "The kingdom of heaven is at

58

hand." This was a spiritual kingdom within the hearts of men, which was now present. His reign over all the kingdoms of the earth was to be long postponed. The extension of the kingdom of heaven in the hearts of men was dependent upon their submission to the total will of God. As He bowed in obedience to His Father's will, so His disciples were to learn that perfect submission is perfect delight.

If the will of God is to be done in earth, it must begin in the center of the individual life. No one can have a part in building God's kingdom on the earth until He rules in every kingdom of his heart. Therefore, when we pray, "Thy kingdom come," we must understand we are saying, "Thy will be done in me." Any prayer that does not express or imply that the one who prays is asking according to God's will, is offered in defiance rather than in submission. That kind of prayer does not anticipate an affirmative answer.

If Christ is supreme Ruler in all areas of my life, then He may use me in any way He wills to build His kingdom. Any rebellion, resistance, or reluctance on my part is a discount on my usefulness in bringing in His kingdom, which is righteousness, peace, and joy in the Holy Spirit. *Lord, let in me Thy perfect will be done.*

March 5

We Are Dependent on God

Luke 11:3

This is an appropriate prayer for everyone to offer. It is not only for those who live from hand to mouth, or for those who do not know where the next meal is coming from. It is a reminder that "man shall not live by bread alone, but by every word of God" (4:4). It is He that giveth to all life and breath and all things. "For in him we live, and move, and have our being" (Acts 17:28). In the words of James, "Every good gift and every perfect gift is from above, and cometh down from the Father of lights, with whom is no variableness, neither shadow of turning" (1:17). Without the benevolent gifts of God, no life can be sustained.

Acknowledgment of dependence on God is a stimulant to faith. The supply of all the necessities of life yesterday and today gives confidence for tomorrow. What the future holds may be uncertain, but the One who holds the future is completely dependable. Great is His faithfulness.

There is a faith-inspiring picture frequently seen. It is of an elderly man sitting at his table on which is a loaf of bread and a bowl of milk. His head is bowed in thankfulness to God the Giver. That should inspire all to say or sing:

> *Be present at our table, Lord;*
> *Be here and everywhere adored.*
> *These creatures bless; and grant that we*
> *May feast in paradise with Thee.*

Such dependence, faith, and gratitude will result in a disposition to share our blessings. "It is more blessed to give than to receive" (Acts 20:35).

March 6

To Be Forgiven We Must Forgive

Luke 11:4a

To forgive the offences of others against ourselves may seem impossible. There are circumstances in which that may be true if the grace of God is not considered. Utter and repeated betrayal may be involved. All standards of justice and fairness may have been violated. The human reaction is to revenge and hatred. But Matthew 6 gives specific guidelines. Jesus said, "If ye forgive men their trespasses, your heavenly Father will also forgive you" (v. 14). If God in love is willing to forgive our many sins, our attitude toward those who have transgressed our rights should be that of forgiveness.

A refined woman knelt at an altar of prayer seeking pardon and peace. She told her counselor that she could not forgive a certain person who had been responsible for the murder of her husband and her son. By a technicality of law he was living in freedom and public favor. She asked, "How can I forgive him?" The wise advice given her was, *"You* can't but by God's grace you can." She released her resentment to God, and forgiveness filled her heart for the murderer. And she was forgiven. "If ye forgive not men their trespasses, neither will your Father forgive your trespasses" (v. 15).

Someone may say, "I forgive what another has done to me, but I will not forget." We pray, "Forgive us our debts, as we forgive our debtors" (v. 12). By that petition do we invite God to remember our sins? He had promised to blot them out and to remember them no more forever. He forgives and forgets. Isn't that what His Word teaches us to do?

March 7

The Christian Attitude Toward Temptation

Luke 11:4b

Temptation is the common experience of man. It is inescapable as long as we are in the body. Our society is evil and the tempter is incessantly active. We are better prepared when he comes as a roaring lion. We are more susceptible when a fowler's snare lies along the pathway. And probably his most cunning approach is as an angel of light to deceive the very elect.

The Christian need not live in unprepared innocence. The certainty of temptation is a warning to be prepared to meet the enemy. Jesus taught us to pray, "Lead us not into temptation." That is, Keep us from any voluntary exposure. Help us to keep our guard on duty. Let us be aware. Give us a permanent attitude of resistance. Fortify us in the knowledge of the Word. Sensitize our conscience to discern good and evil by the Holy Spirit. Strengthen our faith and keep our testimony clear and up to date, for we know that we overcome "by the blood of the Lamb, and by the word of [our] testimony" (Rev. 12:11).

Temptation is not sinful if resisted. Eve and Adam were both innocent and pure, yet they were tempted and yielded. Jesus was without sin. He faced the tempter who used against Him all the artillery at his command. He tried every attack but Jesus won the victory. He overcame because His will was fixed to do the will of His Father.

Every tempted soul can defeat the foe. He needs to pray, *Deliver me from evil and reinforce my will to do the will of God.*

March 8

Give God the Glory

Matthew 6:13b

This doxology is not included as a part of the model prayer in Luke's Gospel. Furthermore it is omitted in many of the best translations of Matthew. The reason is that the earliest manuscripts do not include it. It has been suggested that it was added by those who found the prayer ended without a conclusion that would be a proper climax. It is especially appropriate for public or group usage.

There is more in these words than a beautiful conclusion. There is an expression of faith on the part of the one who prays. Adam Clarke comments, "The word itself implies a confident resting of the soul in God with the fullest assurance that all the petitions shall be fulfilled to everyone who prays according to the directions given before by our blessed Lord." All our prayers should rest the case in the wisdom, justice, and faithfulness of our Heavenly Father. Resignation to His will is implied if not expressed.

There is also meaning in these words that demands scrutinizing our motives. Do we pray that we might consume the results in the gratification of our own desires? Selfless motives are important if prayer is to be answered. Here is a revelation of humility. It is a recognition of God's supreme Lordship in our lives, that in Him is perfect wisdom in either giving or withholding and in timing His answer. God's ability and His willingness are completely trusted. The essence of the whole prayer is that God may be glorified.

March 9

Jesus Taught Persistence in Prayer

Luke 11:9

Between the model prayer and the text for today Jesus inserted the parable of the midnight visitor. The evident purpose was to emphasize the importance of persistence in prayer. But there are several points that should not be overlooked. It was a need that gave rise to the request, not simply the gratification of a whimsical desire. It was for another, not for himself, that one neighbor was seeking assistance from the other. He was found in embarrassing circumstances. The midnight traveler was hungry and the hospitable host had no bread. He asked for three loaves. He could not give his guest one without eating with him. Had there been only two, the friend would have discovered there was no more. Three loaves would only meet the minimum necessity.

The request for a loan was definite and specific. Here is a lesson for all who pray. They should not generalize but ask for a well-defined need to be met. God does not mock those who pray. He gives according to the faith of the one who asks. He is all wise; He gives what we ask according to the need, not often more and never less.

Persistence, importunity, shamelessness overcame the sleeping neighbor's reluctance. That is not why God sometimes delays the answer to our prayers. He is ever rich in mercy to all who call upon Him. Persistence is proof of our faith in God's unlimited resources and His goodness in supplying our needs. His timing is always right.

Every one that asketh, receiveth.

March 10

Answers to Prayer Assured

Luke 11:13

Persistent prayer arises out of urgent need. God cares for all His children. He has no pets. That the disciples might know

63

how much God cares, Jesus introduced a comparison which amounts to a contrast between earthly fathers and their Heavenly Father. If the father who is human, evil, with tainted, limited understanding has desire to give to his children, "how much more" does your Heavenly Father care. Furthermore, His resources are unlimited, in bold contrast to the human father's ability. The more the Father in heaven gives, the more there is to give. His gifts are of supreme value. There is a contrast between the bread, fish, and eggs in the examples and the good gifts bestowed out of heaven's superlative riches and abundant supply.

In the comparable passage in Matthew, the assurance is that God will bestow good gifts. In Luke it is more than good gifts, it is the best and greatest Gift, the Holy Spirit. The fulfillment of the Father's promise was near. The infallible character of God is the assurance that those who ask for the Holy Spirit will receive Him in fullness. The response to that prayer is as sure as the need that inspires it.

He who receives the Holy Spirit receives the gifts of the Spirit according to God's infinite wisdom and His sovereign power. Likewise he receives the fruit of the Spirit which is love and all the graces that cluster around it.

As much greater as the Giver, so much greater is the gift. Seek and ye shall find.

March 11

The Continuing Presence of God

Josh. 1:5

Moses, the servant of the Lord, was dead. Joshua had been chosen of God as the succeeding leader of Israel. Moses had given solemn charge to Joshua and had announced his appointment to bring the people into the Promised Land. Joshua had been Moses' minister. He had been with the senior servant of God in the holy mount. He had led Israel in their military engagements.

Joshua was a worthy successor to the incomparable Moses. The one thing that crowned his human qualifications was that he could and did know the continuing presence of God. God said to Joshua, "There shall not any man be able to stand before thee all the days of thy life." Jordan divided for him as the Red Sea divided for Moses. The Lord magnified Joshua in the sight of all Israel.

God gave Joshua an experience like that which He gave Moses at the burning bush. When Joshua was by Jericho, there stood a man near him with a drawn sword in his hand. Joshua asked, "Art thou for us, or for our adversaries?" And he said, "Nay: but as captain of the host of the Lord am I now come." And the Captain said, "Loose thy shoe from off thy foot; for the place whereon thou standest is holy" (5:13-15). This was confirmation of the promise, "As I was with Moses, so I will be with thee." God's presence is for all those who will hear and obey His call to serve.

March 12

The God of Miracles

Josh. 3:17

To accept the idea that there are no miracles is to reject the authenticity of the Bible. The laws and powers of nature are subject to the authority of the Almighty God. He may employ them to accomplish His purpose. This is a miracle.

The ark was the symbol of the presence of God. But the miracle came when the feet of the priests who carried the ark touched the waters. The waters stood in an heap and the whole company crossed over. The obedience of man is a part of the miracle.

God gave directions to the priests and they followed explicitly. The officers gave directives to the people and they also obeyed. They were told to follow the ark as borne by the priests. They also obeyed the more specific instruction to allow a space of more than a half mile between them and the ark. They were to keep a right perspective, with reverence for the emblem of God's presence in deliberate patterns of progress, not in crowding or panic, not so close their vision would be blurred. Faith in God is demonstrated in obedience.

Another order was given. A man from each of the 12 tribes was to take up a stone from the midst of Jordan and carry it to the place where they lodged. There Joshua made a monument to testify to future generations of the miracle their fathers had witnessed. All who see the miracles of God should leave a testimony to their posterity.

March 13

Jericho's Wall Flattened

Josh. 6:20

Israel's victory at Jericho cannot possibly be ascribed to natural causes. It was by the power of God that the walls fell down flat. There were trumpets of rams' horns, vocal cords, and marching feet.

There were some powerful human factors involved. The morale of the whole congregation of Israel was at a high pitch. They had just finished the wilderness experience. They had also witnessed the crossing of the swollen Jordan. The priests, elders, and people were all acting in unison. They had left the complaints and murmurings of the previous generation in the wilderness. They were in one accord. The unbelief and rebellion of their fathers were now replaced by faith and full cooperation with Joshua and with the will of God. No wonder God gave them such signal victory in their first engagement in the conquest of Canaan.

These human elements played a part in the victory at Jericho. But without a demonstration of God's power the walls of Jericho would have stood firm. All the great victories that have been wrought in the long history of God's dealings with man have come to pass because God had people, sometimes many and at other times a few, who were willing and obedient instruments of God's purpose. They have known God's promises. They have responded in faith and loving obedience. God has done the rest. What great things God is eagerly waiting to do today. He "is able to do exceeding abundantly above all that we ask or think, according to the power that worketh in us" (Eph. 3:20).

March 14

The Aftermath of a Great Victory

Josh. 7:5

After the victory at Jericho came the defeat at Ai. There were reasons. First, those men of Israel became overconfident. They sent a few spies to inspect the defences. They recommended that a small contingent of two or three thousand men go up and smite Ai. At the first show of resistance they fled before the men of Ai. Thirty-six men were killed. The effect of this defeat was to cause the hearts of the people to melt and become as water. That was more serious than the lost battle.

The underlying cause of the defeat was that Israel forgot that the victory at Jericho was won by the intervention of God. They therefore went to take Ai in their own strength.

Another reason for the rout was that sin had been committed. The spoils were all to belong to God. They were devoted or consecrated to God. The sin that brought severe punishment to Achan was that he dared take to himself that which God had declared to be His own.

Joshua prayed to God. He received instructions from God. The culprit admitted his guilt. Severe punishment was administered.

God then gave guidance for taking Ai. The victory was gained. Joshua built an altar and worshipped God.

Before another battle Joshua led Israel to Mount Ebal and Mount Gerizim. There the curses and the blessings were repeated as Moses had commanded. The people had learned their lesson. They were ready now to continue the conquest of Canaan.

March 15

"Give Me This Mountain"

Josh. 14:11-12

Caleb was asking that a promise made by Moses, 45 years before, be fulfilled by Joshua. The conquest of Canaan had been successfully accomplished. But there was some difficult mopping up to be done. Around Hebron were some mountain strongholds still held by the Anakims. Caleb asked that this territory be given him.

He was only asking for the signal to be given, for him to clear the area of the defiant and powerful occupants.

The name of Caleb is immortal. Many have read the story of his life with admiration and excitement. Parents have named their sons for him in all the many centuries that have passed.

Caleb is admired because he brought the spirit of his youth to old age. He was 85 now. He was beyond the years for military exploits. But he said, "As my strength was then, even so is my strength now, for war, both to go out, and to come in." At 40 he was a man of faith. Then he was confident that giants would be bread for those who trusted God. He had not changed his mind. He was an old man who kept the spirit of youth. With the daring and faith that had increased with the passing of the years, he rallied his forces and cleared the mountain of all resistance. Hebron was to be his inheritance forever. His descendants were the possessors for centuries to follow.

Thus Caleb made his name memorable. His example has cheered the hearts of millions unto this day.

March 16

God's Promise Fulfilled

Josh. 21:45

"God is not a man, that he should lie" (Num. 23:19). To Abraham God said, "Lift up now thine eyes, and look . . . northward, and southward, and eastward, and westward: for all the land which thou seest, to thee will I give it, and to thy seed for ever" (Gen. 13:14-15). Centuries later God said to Joshua, "Every place that the sole of your foot shall tread upon, that have I given unto you, as I said unto Moses" (Josh. 1:3). God never forgets His promise, and He never fails to keep it. The land God promised Abraham was now subdued. There failed not ought of any good thing which the Lord had spoken unto the house of Israel.

This is the record of faithfulness in that time long ago. Added to it is the promise of a Savior. That, too, came to pass in the fullness of time. Now believing Christians have the promise of His coming again. And God is not slack concerning His promise. We confidently look for a new heaven and a new earth, wherein dwelleth righteousness.

God will keep His promises to all who trust Him.

> *Be still, my soul; thy God doth undertake*
> *To guide the future as He has the past.*
> *Thy hope, thy confidence let nothing shake;*
> *All now mysterious shall be bright at last.*
> *Be still, my soul; the waves and winds still know*
> *His voice who ruled them while He dwelt below.*

> —KATHARINA VON SCHLEGEL (1752)

March 17
The Power of Personal Influence

Josh. 24:14-15

The record of Joshua's life is a blessing to read. He began as Moses' minister; he finished as the servant of the Lord.

Like Moses, he had summoned the people to hear this valedictory message. And like Moses, he set the alternatives clearly before the people. He said, "Now therefore fear the Lord and serve him in sincerity and in truth: and put away the gods which your fathers served on the other side of the flood, and in Egypt; and serve ye the Lord. And if it seem evil unto you to serve the Lord, *choose you this day whom ye will serve.*"

To choose required turning from the strange gods and cleaving to the Lord.

The word of Joshua was that God would not choose for them. They must decide the issue for themselves. He also said, I have made my choice. You must make your own.

What a blessing to have leaders who make right choices and who set an example of faithful obedience before those who look to them for leadership. Joshua's testimony by word and deed was *"As for me and my house, we will serve the Lord."* And the people answered, "God forbid that we should forsake the Lord, to serve other gods . . . The Lord our God will we serve, and his voice will we obey" (vv. 16, 24).

So effective was the message and example of Joshua that Israel served the Lord all the days of the elders that overlived him. What inspiration, strength, and blessing came by the influence of one faithful leader!

March 18

Shamgar Had an Oxgoad

Judg. 3:31

Great victories for a cause that is just do not depend on numbers or powerful weapons so much as they do on men of valor. The Philistines had invaded the land of Israel. They had so frightened the inhabitants that the highways were unoccupied. Travellers walked through byways. But there was one plowman who was not intimidated. His name was Shamgar. As he plowed his field, he became aware that he was surrounded by the ruthless Philistines. He saw no one to come to his aid. Nevertheless he did not flee. He laid a firm hand on his oxgoad.

What chance would one lone man have to withstand 600 men armed and ready to fight? Shamgar was no coward. A spirit of courage and might impelled him. His homeland had been troubled long enough. He seized the only instrument in sight and slew 1 Philistine. But there were 599 more. Every time 1 fell to Shamgar's oxgoad, there was 1 less to slay. His blood ran hot in his veins. His courage rose with danger. The slaughter continued until 600 dead bodies covered the field.

He was a man with a cause, a believer with faith, an Israelite with a brave work to do. The man who sees nothing to fight for may go on perfecting his equipment. He blames poor tools for bad work. Shamgar's oxgoad became an extension of the arm of God. God still makes judges and generals out of plowmen, and apostles out of fishermen.

March 19

"They Came Not to the Help of the Lord"

Judg. 5:23

God's cause never admits of neutrality. Hearts that are true and brave are ready to accept responsibility. They are never too busy. They are willing to do their full share. And if some did not do more than their share, the cause would not prosper, because there are always those who are heedless of God's call.

It is the laggard that suffers the loss. The faithful may win without him, but that does not abate the curse upon him who stays at home and refuses to do his part to win the battle for the Lord and right.

Little is known of Meroz. It is mentioned nowhere else in the sacred history. We only know that the inhabitants were cursed because when the crisis came, they chose to remain safely at home while their fellow countrymen risked their lives to rid the homeland of the menacing foe.

Barak had defeated Jabin's host. Zebulun and Naphtali had jeoparded their lives. God had marshalled the stars in their courses to fight against Sisera. He had fled away to the tent of Jael. While he slept in her tent, she drove a nail in his temple.

Yes, the battle was won without the recreant people of Meroz. But they were cursed. They were never heard of again.

The Church of God is always beleaguered by the forces of evil. Its ultimate victory is not in doubt. But to save ourselves, we must be prepared to help carry the fight for righteousness to the gates of hell.

March 20

A Man plus God

Judg. 6:12-13

There were many things about Gideon that recommended him for the great work God had for him to do.

He was a busy man, threshing wheat. God does not pick a sluggard.

Gideon knew the history of Israel. When the angel of the Lord addressed him, saying, "The Lord is with thee," Gideon replied, "If the Lord be with us, why then is all this befallen us? and where be all his miracles which our fathers told us of . . . ?"

He was a humble man. When the Lord told him he would be the deliverer of his people, Gideon said, "I am the least in my father's house" (v. 15).

Israel was being chastened because they did evil in the sight of the Lord. In the place of the altar of Baal, Gideon built an altar to Israel's God and called it Jehovah-Shalom—"the Lord send peace." Gideon was a man of faith. He said, "I have seen an angel of the Lord face to face" (vv. 24, 22).

The Lord addressed Gideon as a mighty man of valor. He said, "Go in this thy might, and thou shalt save Israel. . . . Surely I will be with thee, and thou shalt smite the Midianites" (vv. 14, 16). In the valley of Jezreel the Spirit of the Lord clothed himself with Gideon. God put on Gideon as a man puts on a garment. The hosts of Midian fled. It is a *man* plus *God* who is adequate.

March 21

Gideon Seeks Assurance

Judg. 6:36-38

Gideon had already proved that he was willing to obey the Lord. But he wanted to remove any possibility that he was acting presumptuously. God is more disposed to use men who seek to know of a certainty that God is calling than those who act impulsively and in haste.

Gideon's technique for gaining assurance was original. He was not doing what he had heard that someone else had done. First, it was that the ground should be dry and the fleece wet. It came out as he had proposed. Then, to be sure, he said let the ground be wet with dew and the fleece dry. It was so. Therefore Gideon pursued the way of obedience in which he had already begun.

Gideon had no open Bible from which he might learn the will of God for him. The voice of the Spirit speaking within him was not his way of life. Therefore God gave him assurance according to his limited understanding.

Many have sought to find confirmation of God's will by adaptation of Gideon's method. They should observe some precautions: Am I willing to do God's will when it is clear to me? Am I now doing all I know I should? Have I searched the Scriptures? Is my proposal such that the answer is predetermined? Is there a reasonable possibility that God can answer either positively or negatively according to His wisdom and His will for me? Gideon's fleece should not be used promiscuously.

March 22

The Chosen Few

Judg. 7:2

Gideon put forth a summons for an army to assemble. Thirty-two thousand responded. God said to Gideon, "The people . . . are too many . . . lest Israel . . . say, Mine own hand hath saved me." Whereupon Gideon told all the fearful to return to their places. More than two-thirds of them went home. One courageous man is worth more than three if two are cowards.

God said there are still too many. The 10,000 were put to a simple test. Those who could watch for the enemy while they drank were worthy soldiers.

73

With his army reduced to 300 men, Gideon needed a stimulant for his faith. He went down near the Midianite camp. They heard one man tell another that in a dream he had seen a loaf of barley bread smite a tent and it fell flat. The interpretation by the second man of the dream's fulfillment in Gideon's impending victory caused Gideon to tell Israel's camp, "Arise, the Lord has delivered the host of Midian into your hand."

He divided his men into three companies of 100 each. He put strange weapons in their hands, a lamp in a pitcher in one hand and a trumpet in the other. Gideon said, "What you see me do, that you shall do." They broke their pitchers, the lights shone, and they blew their trumpets. The host of Midian fled in fear. One hundred and twenty thousand were slain. In their fright and confusion they slew one another. The wicked systems of men will crack and crumble if the children of God will trust and obey. The battle is the Lord's.

March 23

Samson—Superman

Judg. 16:20-21

Samson was a child of promise. He was born to God-fearing parents. He was dedicated to God from his birth. He was born with a destiny to fulfill.

No one can explain with complete satisfaction the mystery of the fall of Samson. His moral weakness is in striking contrast to his physical strength. It is evident that he was a man of undisciplined desires. What he wanted he was determined to have. He saw a woman of the Philistines and desired her to be his wife. Doubtless this was not of God in the sense that He willed it, but He allowed it and overruled it to bring about a confrontation with the Philistines.

When Samson became aware of his great strength, which had been demonstrated in ripping a lion apart, he began to trifle with riddles. He sought revenge by burning fields of corn for personal injuries. To escape a trap into which he had voluntarily entered, he made show of his great strength by carrying away the gates of Gaza.

He was enticed by a treacherous woman. He broke his vow to God. His strength was gone. He knew not that the Lord had departed from him. He was a helpless victim in the hands of his enemies.

That he was able to destroy more of the Philistines in his death than in his life is small compensation for a life of such great possibilities which came so far short of fulfillment. Strength turned to weakness by sin is tragedy unspeakable. Let the strong know their dependence on God.

March 24

Human Nature Demands Authority

Judg. 21:25

Forms of government may be subject to debate. Nevertheless an established government vested with authority is a necessity. When a considerable segment of a given society fails to recognize that their rights end where the other person's rights begin, then statutes for government must be enforced.

In the day of the judges the ideal was that God was the Ruler and that all who were Israelites would keep His commandments. The failure was not with the ideal but in the practice of men. There was no king nor established authority to enforce the laws of the covenant; therefore each man was a law unto himself. He was judge of his own conduct. He "did that which was right in his own eyes." Deplorable degredation was the inevitable consequence.

That the time comes when one must follow the dictates of his conscience is true. The alternative would be rules ad infinitum such as the Pharisees developed, with everyone judging everyone else by his set of rules. Laws and rules are good. They must, however, be enforced by self-discipline. But in the home, the school, the church, or the nation, rules are a necessity.

The rule for a sanctified Christian is the Word of God. The help for obedience is the Spirit of God dwelling in the heart. Then one can say with Paul, "Herein do I exercise myself, to have always a conscience void of offence toward God, and toward men" (Acts 24:16). Psychologists are saying in this day of permissiveness that youth as well as adults are searching for authority administered in love.

March 25

The Loyalty of Love

Ruth 1:16-17

The story of Ruth is one of the most beautiful to be found in all literature. It begins in circumstances of deep sorrow. Death had claimed three husbands in quick succession. To make loneliness more acute, the husbands were migrants in a strange country. There the sons had married. There they were buried. Naomi, the mother-in-law, decided to return to the land of her kindred. The widowed daughters-in-law proposed to go with her. Naomi remonstrated. Orpah consented to remain among her people, whereas Ruth uttered her immortal pledge of loyalty which will be quoted as long as human speech is heard.

It is obvious that Ruth's loyalty was born of pure love. There were no mixed motives. She knew Naomi had no more sons to give her. Furthermore she knew she would find no husband in Israel, for the Hebrew people usually married only those of their own blood. In no way known could the life of Naomi be any other than one of poverty. Ruth made her choice to go with Naomi because she loved her.

Unselfish love never goes unrewarded. Still caring for Naomi, Ruth went into the field to glean. It was in the field of Boaz, a kinsman of Naomi. He had learned what Ruth had done for the sake of her mother-in-law. He must have reasoned, Here is a young woman who has beauty as well as qualities of character that are admirable. Boaz married Ruth.

She became the great-grandmother of David. Of his line Jesus was born to bless the world. The loyalty of love is rewarded.

76

March 26

"Thy Servant Heareth"

1 Sam. 3:10

Hannah, Samuel's devout mother, promised God that if He would give her a man child, she would lend him to the Lord forever. True to her word, she brought the child to Eli the priest. She said, "For this child I prayed; and the Lord hath given me my petition . . . Therefore also I have [returned] him to the Lord; as long as he liveth he shall [belong] to the Lord" (1:27-28). Samuel harmonized his will with his mother's vow. Early he learned to listen to the voice of God speaking to him, and throughout his long life he obeyed.

Samuel continued to live at Shiloh with Eli. When he was still a young lad, he was sleeping but he heard a voice. Thinking it must be Eli speaking, he answered, "Here am I; for thou calledst me" (3:5). Eli told him he had not called. A second and a third time the voice was heard. Eli now suspected that God was speaking. He told Samuel that when he heard the voice again, he should say, "Speak, Lord; for thy servant heareth." Samuel did as Eli instructed him. Whereupon God gave the boy a message of solemn import to the aged priest. When he was pressured to tell all, he did not withhold the truth. It was a shocking pronouncement.

For any man to speak for God he must learn to listen for the message from God.

Throughout his long life Samuel spoke with such authority that he was recognized as both prophet and judge in all Israel. He was a man of God.

March 27

Gracious in Rejection

1 Sam. 12:23

Samuel stands out as one of the most exemplary men of the Bible. After he had anointed and proclaimed Saul as king, Samuel bore his testimony. "I have walked before you from my childhood unto this day. Behold, here I am: . . . whose ox have I taken? . . . or whom have I defrauded? whom have I oppressed? or of whose hand have I received any bribe to blind mine eyes therewith? and I will restore it." And they said, "Thou hast not defrauded us, nor oppressed us, neither hast thou taken aught of any man's hand" (vv. 2-4). In his spirit there was no guile.

What an example for all who are public servants! Samuel goes even farther to prove himself a gracious and faithful servant of God and His people. He knew that he still had a duty to perform and a charge to keep. For the sake of the people whom he had loved and served even after their rejection, Samuel said, "As for me, God forbid that I should sin against the Lord in ceasing to pray for you: but I will teach you the good and the right way." He did teach them and us.

How many persons have served God well until their place of trust and honor has been given to another, then turned bitter. In so doing, they spoil the record, belittle themselves, and dishonor God. Let Samuel's spirit inspire all God's servants to be gracious in rejection.

March 28
A Kingly Fool

1 Sam. 26:21

Saul, Israel's first king, was God's choice from among all the men of Israel. He was anointed and introduced to the people by Samuel. They shouted, "God save the king" (10:24).

Some despised him but he held his peace. After his first military victory, "The people said unto Samuel, Who is he that said, Shall Saul reign over us? bring the men, that we may put them to death. And Saul said, There shall not a man be put to death" (11:12-13).

Eventually another spirit possessed Saul. He became impatient with waiting for Samuel to come to offer the sacrifice to God. Presumptuously he offered the burnt offering. Samuel rebuked Saul, saying, "Thou hast done foolishly: . . . now thy kingdom shall not continue" (13:13-14).

Instead of utterly destroying Amalek as God commanded, he spared the best of the flocks and herds supposedly for a sacrifice to the Lord. Samuel reminded him that obedience is better than sacrifice and informed him that the kingdom would be given to his neighbor. Samuel saw Saul no more.

God told Samuel to anoint David to be king. The Spirit of the Lord departed from Saul, and an evil spirit troubled him. He became insanely jealous of David. He sought to kill him.

Opportunity came for David to slay Saul. He would not stretch forth his hand against the Lord's anointed. Saul, aware of what had happened, said, "I have played *the fool,* and have erred exceedingly." In the home of the witch of Endor, he told the departed Samuel, "God has departed from me" (28:15). He fell down slain on Mount Gilboa. "How are the mighty fallen!" (See 2 Sam. 1:27.)

March 29

Living as a Prince, Dying as a Fool

2 Sam. 3:38, 33

Abner was a man of noble mind and generous spirit. He was Saul's commander in chief. He proved his loyalty to the dead king by identifying himself with his son Ishbosheth. He considered him as rightful heir to the throne of Israel.

David had become king of Judah in Hebron. He grew in strength while Ishbosheth became weaker. Finally their forces met in battle. The men of David under Joab prevailed. Abner fled from the field. Asahel, a brother of Joab, pursued him. Abner thrust him through with his spear and he died.

Abner turned to David and asked for terms of peace. David then ruled a united kingdom.

Jealous Joab proposed a meeting with Abner. He smote Abner and he died.

David wept at the grave. He inquired of his servants, "Know ye not that there is a prince and a great man fallen this day in Israel?" Yet it was David who had asked, "Died Abner as a fool dieth?" How could a man live so well, yet die as a fool?

Abner should have been armed and guarded. His hands were not bound nor his feet in fetters. He faced a deadly foe unnecessarily and unprepared.

They met just outside the gates of Hebron—a city of refuge. Safety was in reach but Abner did not take advantage of it. Multitudes die just outside mercy's door, so near and yet so far.

March 30

Inexhaustible Love

Luke 23:34

The first word to be spoken by Jesus from the Cross is unexpected and amazing. A protest of innocence, a bid for sympathy, a judgment upon those who put Him there might have been understandable. But a prayer for their forgiveness is beyond the comprehension of the finite mind. It is strong proof that He was the Son of God. Those who drove the nails, Pilate who ordered the execution, the Jewish leaders who brought the false accusations, and the frenzied mob who cried, "Crucify him," are the objects of His prayer for pardon. Indeed, all who have despised His offers of mercy, taken His name in vain, and crucified the Son of God afresh, are embraced in His arms of love. "They know not what they do" is not without evidence of His love. It implies that He had placed the most charitable construction possible upon their hateful conduct toward Him. In this, as well as in His prayer for their forgiveness, He is an example to all His followers.

Jesus was not a helpless victim of cruel, envious men. Knowing what awaited Him, "He stedfastly set his face to go to Jerusalem" (9:51). He could have called 12 legions of angels to fight for Him. When He heard the taunt "He saved others; himself he cannot save" (Mark 15:31), He could have come down from the Cross. But He said, "I lay down my life . . . No man taketh it from me, but I lay it down of myself." "Greater love hath no man than this" (John 10:17-18; 15:13).

March 31

With Jesus in Paradise

Luke 23:42-43

Isaiah, describing the death of the Suffering Servant, prophesied, "He was numbered with the transgressors" (53:12). Three men were condemned to die; two were transgressors, the third fulfilled the law. All three were out of harmony with the accepted way of living. Two were below it, One was above it. The two suffered justly; the Third suffered on behalf of the first two and all others in like condemnation.

According to Matthew and Mark, the two robbers joined the frenzied crowd in railing on the Man on the middle cross, which may have been prepared for Barabbas. But repentance came to the one who rebuked the other for having blasphemed the One who hung between them. Possibly he had heard the prayer of Jesus, "Father, forgive them." He turned his face in painful agony toward Jesus and uttered his own prayer with contrition and faith. "Lord, remember me when thou comest into thy kingdom."

Jesus heard his words and read his thoughts. He said, "Verily I say unto thee, To day shalt thou be with me in paradise." He saved one man in the throes of death, that no sinner might despair; and only one, that none might presume.

In this word from the Cross, we learn that those who die trusting in Jesus as Savior enter into a state of blessedness with Him when life ends in death. He is there and that is blessed. Dying in Christ, then, is not a fearsome leap in the dark. Death is the gateway to life.

April 1

The Strong Bond of Love

John 19:26-27

In that dark, lonely hour most of those who had followed Jesus had deserted or were despairing. Of the Twelve, only John was there. As might be expected, His mother stood by. Of the other three women, it is believed one was Mary's sister and another was the wife of the brother of Joseph. There is intimation that John was a cousin of Jesus. All these would then be joined by family ties. They were strong then and always should be. The other Mary was the one who had been forgiven much and therefore loved much. It was a small, select band. It is in life's extremities that true love is demonstrated.

It is in these words of Jesus that humanity is seen at its best. He was completely human in His suffering pain of body and anguish of mind. But in His dying moments His thoughts turned compassionately to His mother in her unspeakable grief. Some have reasoned that Jesus did not early begin His public ministry, which took Him from home, because His earthly foster father had died and His mother needed His support until others were ready to take care of her.

Now the final separation had come. In tenderest tones of love He said, "Woman, behold thy son!" "You can lean on him for support, strength, and comfort." Then to John He gave the solemn charge, "Behold thy mother!" From that hour that disciple took her into his own home.

The grace of God brings out the best of which man is capable.

April 2

That Bitter Cup

Mark 15:34

Possibly no trial common to man is more severe than the feeling of utter loneliness. In such a time, one is tempted to think no one understands or cares. That supreme test came to

Jesus. In that moment the words of the Psalmist which He had learned in His youth came spontaneously from His lips, "My God, my God, why hast thou forsaken me?" Hitherto He had always known the nearness and approval of His Father. Now there was, even if momentarily, a dark wall of separation. No wonder He cried, "Why?"

This was the cup that He had prayed might pass from Him if possible. But if He was to make atonement for sin, He who knew no sin was to become sin for the sinner. This involved that separation from the Father-God while He tasted death for every man. He had accepted that awful hour when He said, "Nevertheless not my will, but thine, be done" (Luke 22:42). That was obedience in superlative cost and painfulness.

There was no resentment or bitterness in this cry of dereliction. It may have been perplexity and amazement. But it was not doubt or surrender. His faith held fast in that darkest hour. It was still, My God! My God! Now it could be written that He "was in all points tempted like as we are, yet without sin" (Heb. 4:15).

All who have been saved unto eternal life should offer a sacrifice of praise that Jesus drained that bitter cup to its dregs.

April 3

The Suffering of Death

John 19:28

In no portion of Scripture is the human and divine nature of Jesus more clearly seen than in the seven words from the Cross. This fifth word is proof that He was truly human. He was famishing with thirst. His flesh was crying out for relief.

Before the ordeal of crucifixion began, He had been offered drugged wine to deaden the pain. He had refused it because He did not want His senses dulled. He had been made a little lower than the angels for the suffering of death. He would face death that had come to man because of the fall of the first Adam, with full awareness of the suffering it brought. Furthermore, He would be an example of courage for those who in the passing of time would be martyrs for His sake. He had said, "The servant is not greater than his lord. If they have persecuted me, they will also persecute you" (John 15:20).

That His thirst was real is not hard to understand. The last food and drink He had taken was at the Last Supper 18 hours earlier. Much had transpired to bring weariness to His body and anguish to His mind. There was the agony in Gethsemane, the betrayal of Judas, the denial of Peter, the trial before the Sanhedrin, the scourging, the walk to Calvary bearing His cross until He fell beneath its weight, the excruciating pain of crucifixion, and the hours of living death under the sweltering sun. His mortal frame wracked with pain called for a small token of relief.

April 4

Perfect Fulfillment

John 19:30

Jesus spoke one word in the Greek language. It is the most meaningful single word ever spoken. To Him it was, no doubt, a sigh of relief. His whole life on earth had been under threat of death. Herod had the boy babies of Bethlehem slain to end a challenge to his reign. Jesus' townspeople sought to hurl Him from the precipice near Nazareth. His critics sought to catch Him in His words that they might have cause to stone Him to death. Now it was all over.

For God and the angels, as well as Satan and all demonic powers to hear, it was a shout of victory. From His rendezvous with Satan in the wilderness all the way to Golgotha, the battle raged between good and evil, between truth and error, between holiness and sin, between Christ and the devil. Now the battle had reached a clashing climax. Christ had won the victory. The Lion of the Tribe of Judah had prevailed.

To all the sons of Adam's race it was the announcement of supreme importance: "It is finished." Prophecies had come to pass. Types were now antitypes. Ceremonies were replaced by reality. Christ's heel was bruised as He hung on the Cross while

84

all hell and wicked men rejoiced. But Satan's head was bruised. Redemption's price was paid. Salvation full and free was offered to whosoever believeth.

That which God foreordained before the foundation of the world was now in full effect. This wonderful stream of salvation would flow into eternity.

April 5

The Prayer of Commitment

Luke 23:46

Jesus offered His own committal prayer. A few hours before, He had looked into the face of His Father to say, "I have glorified thee on the earth: I have finished the work which thou gavest me to do" (John 17:4). The final tests of Gethsemane and Calvary were passed. The separation with its "why?" and the agony with its "thirst" were in the background. The victorious announcement had been made. He was ready to dismiss His spirit. His life had been lived in full harmony with His Father's will. His first recorded word was, "I must be about my Father's business" (Luke 2:49). His whole earthly life had been in a prayerful relationship to His Father. He had been sustained in the assurance of doing the Father's will. Now it was most natural for Him to speak again to the Father in complete confidence, "Into thy hands I commend my spirit."

There was no darkness; all was light. There was no shadow of doubt; there was perfect trust. It was no farce play on the stage of life with the curtain rung down. It had been faith, obedience, and love all the way. It was life at its best. Now it was to be the glory which He had with the Father before the world was.

With the beauty and simplicity of a devoted Son to a faithful, loving Father, Jesus said, "All is in Your hands for safekeeping." In that same sublime assurance Stephen said, "Lord Jesus, receive my spirit" (Acts 7:59). Even so may it be to all who live in God's blessed will.

April 6

Now Is Christ Risen

1 Cor. 15:20

In this chapter Paul does more to illuminate the mysteries of the Resurrection than can be found anywhere else in the inspired writings. First he establishes the fact that Christ rose from the dead. He cites the infallible proof, especially the testimony of those who saw Him, of whom some remained to bear witness. He adds that he had seen Him as one born out of due season. He supports that record with a sound, logical argument which reduces the denial of Christ's resurrection to an absurdity. With that truth affirmed, the apostle concludes that if the dead rise not, then Christ is not risen. "But now is Christ risen from the dead, and become the firstfruits of them that slept." As the first ripened fruit is proof that the full harvest is certain, even so Christ's resurrection is the sure promise that the dead in Christ shall rise.

Paul also answers the question, "With what body do they come?" Since flesh and blood cannot inherit the kingdom of God, it will be a spiritual body. As we have inherited a natural body from Adam, so we shall inherit a spiritual body from Christ. It will be a body like unto His glorified body that He brought from the grave. It will be individually recognizable. "As in Adam all die, even so in Christ shall all be made alive" (v. 22). It is sown a natural body, it is raised a spiritual body on which death shall have no power. "Thanks be to God, which giveth us the victory through our Lord Jesus Christ" (v. 57).

April 7

Jesus the Leader

John 14:12

The prophet Isaiah saw the Messiah as a leader of the people. Jesus fulfilled that ideal as well as all others. As a leader, He completely identified himself with the cause He came to advance. The wisdom of Jesus is seen in the fact that

He advisedly related His work to the passing of time. He knew the task He had come to accomplish would not be done in a few years. He had come to sow the seed. Others would gather the harvest. He laid the foundations. His followers would build the house. He initiated the Kingdom. Its consummation would come when time flows into eternity. His successor would be the Eternal Spirit.

Jesus rested the certainty of the successful outcome of His redeeming work on the identification of himself with the will of His Father in heaven. His purpose was one with the purpose of Almighty God. In such a spirit, the Son of Man came to the end of the days of His flesh. He knew He would die the death of the Cross. But He knew Calvary was not the end. With no misgivings, He committed the eternal truth to His followers and trusted them to proclaim it with the Holy Ghost sent down from heaven. The risen Lord gave them the Great Commission.

"Now unto him that is able to do exceeding abundantly above all that we ask or think, according to the power that worketh in us, unto him be glory in the church by Christ Jesus throughout all ages, world without end. Amen" (Eph. 3: 20-21).

April 8

Joined to Omnipotence

John 14:12-14

As the disciples came near to the time when Jesus would no more be with them, they feared that futility would be their lot. They would face a world with which they could not cope. Jesus reassured them. He said, "He that believeth on me shall do greater works than I have done." This is a mind-boggling statement. How could it be?

The Lord did not stop there. He reinforced His words with a promise that meant their limited, finite power would be joined to the power of God. The connection with omnipotence was made by prayer. It was not prayer on the give-and-take level. It was prayer in the name of Jesus. And that is more than a formula at the end of a list of petitions. To pray in the name of Jesus implies that the one who prays is partaker of the nature of Jesus, and that implies that prayer ends with "the will of the Lord be done." That was the prayer of Jesus. That is the prayer of those who know His name and nature. Then the prayer is answered in making the one who prays a miracle. The believer's life is an extension of Jesus' life. He joins His prayer with that of the believer. He prayed as one who had familiarity and equality with God and perfect access to the resources of heaven.

Faith is voluntary confidence in the ability of God to do what He has promised. "All things are possible to him that believeth."

April 9

The Holy Spirit Glorifies Jesus

John 16:12-14

In giving the Holy Spirit His rightful place, we keep the central focus on Christ. It is He who carries on the work of Jesus as Teacher. The Spirit of Truth is given to guide those who are Christ's, into all truth. Jesus said, "I have yet many things to say unto you, but ye cannot bear them now." He left it to the ministry of the Spirit to illuminate the Word and enlighten the eyes of their understanding. God reveals the things which He hath prepared for them that love Him, by His Spirit. He does not speak of himself. What He hears from the Father is what He speaks. He glorifies Christ.

Peter and Paul are the principal preachers of the Book of Acts. They were inspired to proclaim the gospel. They were Spirit-filled apostles. They set the pattern for preachers in all the Christian centuries. An examination of their sermons will prove that their theme was Jesus Christ and Him crucified. He was to them the risen Lord, exalted to the right hand of God, until He should make His enemies His footstool. Likewise in the Epistles, in all things Christ has the place of preeminence.

W. F. Warren's hymn expresses the truth in beautiful poetry:

I worship Thee, O Holy Ghost.
I love to worship Thee.
My risen Lord for aye were lost
But for Thy company.

. . . .

I worship Thee, O Holy Ghost.
I love to worship Thee.
With Thee each day is Pentecost,
Each night Nativity.

April 10

The Blessed Trinity

John 14:10, 16

The doctrine of the Trinity is woven into the creeds of the evangelical Christian church. They sing as one, "Holy, Holy, Holy! Merciful and Mighty! God in three Persons, blessed Trinity." This doctrine is supported by conclusive evidence in the entire Bible. In no other chapter does it have such clear teaching as in chapter 14 of John's Gospel.

John records Jesus' words, "I and my Father are one" (10: 30). In chapter 14 He amplifies that statement. Jesus said to Thomas, "If ye had known me, ye should have known my Father also." To Philip he said, "He that hath seen me hath seen the Father . . . I am in the Father, and the Father in me" (vv. 7, 9-10). There could be no clearer affirmation that the Father and the Son are one.

Here Jesus also identifies himself with the Holy Spirit. He said, "I will pray the Father, and he shall give you another Comforter, that he may abide with you for ever." The word "another" conveys the meaning of one exactly like the one with you now. Jesus went on to say, "He dwelleth with you, and shall be in you. I will not leave you [orphans]: I will come to you" (vv. 17-18). Which is to say, The Holy Spirit has been with you because of Me. When I am no more with you in visible

89

presence, I will be in you with the Helper. This is "Christ in you, the hope of glory."

> *Hail to the Father,*
> *Hail to the Son,*
> *Hail to the Spirit,*
> *The great Three in One.*

April 11

Father, Glorify Me

John 17:5

The prayer of Jesus as recorded in the 17th chapter of John is the introduction to the priestly ministry of Christ. He has finished His work as Teacher and Prophet. He now begins His intercession before God, and He ever liveth to be our Advocate with the Father. We see Him here in the holy of holies of the new covenant.

In the first eight verses of the chapter, the prayer is that He, the Son, might be glorified with the Father. With intimate expression of filial love and obedience, He reviews the record of His life in the flesh. "I have glorified thee on the earth." The purpose of the Father's sending Him had been successfully accomplished. "I have finished the work thou gavest me to do." Redemption of all who would believe had only to be completed by the giving of His life on rugged Calvary. That hour had come.

"I have manifested thy name [the nature of holiness] unto the men which thou gavest me out of the world. They have . . . beheld My glory, the glory as of the only begotten of the Father, full of grace and truth" (see 1:14). The revelation of God to man was now complete. The light of the glory of God was seen on the face of Jesus Christ. He is like God and God is like Jesus.

Now Jesus asks that the transcendent glory of which He had emptied himself in becoming flesh should be restored to Him. "Glorify thou me . . . with the glory which I had with thee before the world was."

April 12

Sanctify Them

John 17:17

The second division of the prayer of Jesus is for His disciples. It includes verses 9 to 19. His great concern for them is expressed in verse 17. Phillips translates this text, "Make them holy by the Truth for your word is the Truth." Weymouth shows insight to the deeper meaning. He translates verse 17 "Sanctify them" and verse 19 "I consecrate myself." Thus he uses the word in its twofold definition. Jesus was fully aware that those men needed to be cleansed and made holy. To assure that their purification was made possible, He said, "I devote myself to death on the Cross that they might be sanctified."

Jesus knew their lives had been changed by accepting His teaching and by following His example. He said to the Father, "They have kept thy word . . . they are thine . . . I am glorified in them . . . none of them is lost, but the son of perdition . . . they are not of the world, even as I am not of the world."

Yet Jesus knew they were yet carnal. James and John had sought the chief seats in the Kingdom to gratify their personal ambitions. All the others were angry with them. All needed hearts purified by faith.

The One who knew what is in man knew Judas would betray Him, Peter would deny Him, and Thomas would be almost submerged in his doubts. He also knew that by giving His life a sacrifice for sin, the complete cleansing of repentant disciples was within the reach of their faith. God heard His prayer. Their hearts were purified at Pentecost.

April 13

Christ Shares His Glory

John 17:21-22

When Jesus said, "for their sakes," He included His disciples with Him then, and all who should believe in Him through their word. The prayer and the Calvary deed were for their sakes. The third section of the prayer is for the whole company of the redeemed until "all the ransomed church of God be saved to sin no more." The burden of His prayer is amplified in the purpose clauses introduced by the words "that they."

The first is "that they all may be one." It is a prayer for unity of all believers. It is a spiritual unity for which He prays. Being filled with the same Spirit, they would become one fellowship in Christ. It is fellowship among themselves and with Christ the Son and God the Father, one as *they* are one. The second is "that the world may believe." When the world sees Christians living as Jesus taught that they should in the Sermon on the Mount, the world will believe in Jesus. They will see His light and life in those who follow Him.

The third is "that they may behold my glory" (v. 24). They are to see the glory of shared sonship and holy character now. It will be the glory of seeing Him face-to-face and being with Him where He is. "That the love wherewith thou hast loved me may be in them, and I in them" (v. 26). This agape love, which is shed abroad in our hearts, is on display in the lives of those for whom this prayer is answered.

April 14

Fruitful Branches in the Vine

John 15:4

As a branch is joined to the vine by natural growth, so a Christian is joined to Christ by faith. Useless and fruitless as is the branch severed from the vine, so is the Christian who does not abide in Christ. "Without me ye can do nothing" (v. 5).

A condition for continual relation to Christ is fruitfulness. Every branch that beareth not fruit He taketh away. They are gathered with the wicked and cast into everlasting fire. There is no ground for the doctrine of eternal security here.

Fruitfulness is the result of abiding in Christ. As natural as it is for a vine to bear fruit, so it is logical for a Christian in living relation to Christ to bear the fruit of holiness within and righteousness without. As the vine bears grapes, those who are clean through Christ's words bear the fruit of the Spirit, which is love. The loving, obedient Christian has a redeeming influence which results in the salvation of others. This is the secret of a growing church. The fruitful branch is purged. "Now ye are clean through the word which I have spoken unto you," said Jesus. There is no point in arguing for either purging or pruning. Both are necessary that the fruitful branch may bring forth more fruit. The Christian whose heart is pure must be disciplined and chastened. He, accordingly, turns all his life to loving obedience to Christ the Lord. The net return to him is fullness of joy, and to the Christian community healthy growth. All is to the glory of God.

April 15
Friendship with Jesus

John 15:14-15

Love is the strongest bond between persons of moral choice. Personal relationships are easily strained and dissolved without the cement of love. Paul said, "Love is the bond of perfectness." Agape has only one source: "God is love." There is a fusion of love in all God's attributes and acts. Even in His judgments love shines through. "Whom the Lord loveth he chasteneth." Christ's coming and dying is love in action on the highest plane. Greater love hath no man. Jesus said, "As the Father hath loved me, so have I loved you" (v. 9). It was love expressed in total self-giving. Jesus in turn said, "This is my commandment, That ye love one another" (v. 12). Love must be mutual, recip- rocal, to form a perfect bond of union. We love God because He first loved us. Christ loved His own and they responded in love unto death for His sake.

Love binds hearts together, whether it be with husband and wife or among fellow Christians. In the family of God the tie that binds may be stronger than those of kinship. This friendship is voluntary and must be nurtured on purpose.

Friends of Jesus are friends of one another. There is a recognized equity in such a holy relationship. It is a holy partnership.

The reward of such friendship with Christ begins in this life. Jesus said, "Henceforth I call you not servants . . . but . . . friends; for all things that I have heard of my Father I have made known unto you." This blessed and holy communion with Christ and His friends will be continued for ever and ever.

April 16

The Authority of Jesus

John 5:6, 8

Jesus took no pains to refute superstition. His answer was an undeniable miracle. There is no explanation of how Jesus came to be in that place where many seeking healing were gathered. He came to make one man whole. Having accomplished His mission, He was soon lost in the throng. The healed man did not know who Jesus was.

The approach of the Great Physician to the man in need was, "Wilt thou be made whole?" That question related to what the Master would say next. The will to be whole conditioned the response to the command, "Rise, take up thy bed, and walk." The will to believe became actual faith in obedience. The impossible was done. The infirmity of 38 years was gone.

When challenged by the legalistic Jews who reminded him that it was unlawful to carry his bed on the sabbath, the man's reply was, "He that made me whole . . . said unto me, Take up thy bed, and walk" (v. 11). The authority of Jesus was thus established.

Jesus found the man in the Temple where he had gone, no doubt, to offer thanks to God. The Lord of the Sabbath said to him, "Thou art made whole: sin no more, lest a worse thing come unto thee" (v. 14). He reported to the Jews that it was Jesus who had made him whole. They sought to slay Him. His defense was, "My Father worketh hitherto, and I work" (v. 17). God does not withdraw His sustaining power. He will continue His work of healing and redemption.

April 17

The Inward Imperative

John 9:4

Jesus said, "Before Abraham was, *I am*" (8:58). This was the proclamation of His eternal Being. He said, "All power is given unto me in heaven and in earth" (Matt. 28:18). That was to say *I can*. To the leper he said, *"I will;* be thou clean." The impossible was done at His word. But now we hear Jesus say, "I must." This seems out of harmony with His supremacy. What could place Him under compulsion? It was not a will superimposed upon Him, it was the imperative within Him.

It was the awareness of being sent of the Father. He said, "I came down from heaven, not to do mine own will, but the will of him that sent me" (John 6:38). And, "My meat is to do the will of him that sent me" (4:34). In the days of His voluntary humiliation, He was completely submissive to the Father's will. To His disciples He said, "As my Father hath sent me, even so send I you" (20:21). They shared His mission and His compulsion. Furthermore, it was the knowledge that He was in the presence of great human need. Here was a man born blind. It was neither his sin nor that of his parents but that the works of God should be manifest in him. How great our duty to a world lost in sin and darkness!

The final fact that placed Jesus under compulsion was that "the night cometh, when no man can work." For, whether He comes or calls, our time is short. Therefore, we must work while it is day.

April 18

"Now I See"

John 9:5, 25b

The miracle of giving this man sight was not restoration. The sensitive, delicate organ of seeing had never responded to light. This did not perplex Jesus. It afforded Him occasion to prove that He was the Light of the World. Isaiah's prophecy was fulfilled: "The people that walked in darkness have seen a great light" (11:2).

Jesus could have spoken the word and sightless eyes would have been healed. But, that sensible people of all ages might not refuse the means available, He used what was in His reach— spittle, clay, the water in the pool of Siloam. In testimony to his faith, the man born blind obeyed the authoritative word of the Master. "He went . . . and washed, and came seeing." This man had an experience that outran his understanding. He was confronted by unbelieving Jews who sought to shake his testimony. His evasive, fearful parents gave weak support. None of these things moved him. He did not yet know who the Man was who had given him sight; but he could say confidently and fearlessly, "One thing I know, that, whereas I was blind, now I see."

What he knew by experience was preparation for fuller understanding of the doctrine of Christ. While the skeptics did their worst to confuse him, Jesus led him step by step to full faith. He first said, "A man that is called Jesus" had given him sight. Then he said, "He is a prophet." Finally his testimony was clear and certain; he said, "Lord, I believe." And he worshiped Him.

April 19

Blinding Light

John 9:39

It is an apparent contradiction to say that light illuminates and blinds. Yet the proof of it is simple. The sun sheds its radiance over all the earth. Without that light all is darkness. But a few seconds looking at the sun with no protection for the eye will produce temporary blindness; continued, that blindness would be permanent.

Jesus is indeed the Light of the World. "That was the true Light, which lighteth every man that cometh into the world" (1:9). The blind who respond to Him in faith and obedience are made to see. Those who in unbelief reject Him are made blind. The light they have had becomes darkness; and how great is that darkness!

The Jews had unmistakable proof that Jesus had opened the eyes of a man born blind. But their minds were set in prejudice and unbelief. While the blind man that had been healed was led to worship Jesus as Lord, they were saying, "This man is a sinner" (9:24). In simple faith he said, "Since the world began was it not heard that any man opened the eyes of one that was born blind" (v. 32). But with the light of divine revelation shining unto them, they walked in darkness. They were soon saying that He, Jesus, had a devil. Before long, they had crucified Him.

Walking in the light leads to perfect day. Going against light brings blindness and eternal darkness. "This is the condemnation, that light is come into the world, and men loved darkness rather than light, because their deeds were evil" (3:19).

April 20

"Behold How He Loved Him!"

John 11:35-36

A number of explanations of why Jesus wept at the grave of Lazarus have been suggested. It is certain that it was not because He had not been there to heal him. He had said to the disciples that He was glad that He was not there for their sakes, that they might believe.

Possibly His tears were shed in sympathy for Mary and Martha and others who mourned his death. Certainly His was a compassionate spirit. But He knew He would raise Lazarus from the dead.

The remark of the Jews was "Behold how he loved him!" A more plausible reason for the falling tears and groaning spirit of the Master is that He was sorrowful for the fact that He was about to call His friend, whom He loved, back from the better world to this life with its toil and heartache.

There is a difference in the resurrection of Lazarus and

97

that of Jesus, who "being raised from the dead dieth no more" (Rom. 6:9). Jesus had said to Martha, "I am the resurrection, and the life: he that believeth in me, though he were dead, yet shall he live: and [he that] liveth and believeth in me shall never die" (John 11:25-26).

Knowing God and Jesus Christ whom He has sent *is* life eternal.

The resurrection of Lazarus is a preview of what the Lord Jesus Christ will one day do in raising *all* the dead (see 5: 25-29).

April 21

The Good Samaritan

Luke 10:33

In this short story Jesus immortalized a nameless man. In answer to the question "who is my neighbour?" He presented this Samaritan as an ideal. In every detail of the story it is true to life. It shows how true love works. It knows no barriers. It seeks opportunity to manifest itself in action.

The victim was a Jew. The minister of mercy was a Samaritan. There was racial hatred between them. This was but one reason the Samaritan could have offered for passing by as the priest and the Levite had done. Delay on his journey, risk of his own life and property, the drain on his own resources were all disregarded. To him his neighbor was anyone in need. He acted upon the promptings of his heart. His deed was according to the need. Love will make any sacrifice necessity may demand.

This Samaritan looked upon the half-dead man with sympathy. Doubtless he thought, I could be the one lying there naked, bleeding, and half dead. He, in compassion, did all he could do now. And he pledged his help to restore the man to normal self-reliance. He acted in the spirit of the law, not the letter.

Jesus then turned the question on the one who asked it. "[Who] was neighbour unto him that fell among thieves?" The lawyer said, "He that shewed mercy on him." Jesus' final word was to him and all who read the story. "Go, and do thou likewise" (vv. 36-37).

98

April 22

The Lost Sheep

Luke 15:4

Jesus personified the compassion of God. Therefore, despised publicans drew near to hear the gracious words that proceeded from His lips. In contrast, the Pharisees and scribes, encased in their self-righteousness, murmured, "This man receiveth sinners, and eateth with them" (v. 2).

Jesus answered their scornful gibe in three parables which Luke records.

In the first, He reveals what God is like. He said God is like a shepherd. Jesus said, "I am the good shepherd" and "I and my Father are one" (John 10:11, 30). A shepherd might have 100 sheep, but he was quick to recognize it if 1 was missing. Even so God is concerned that man is lost to His loving care and far from the safety of the fold. God made man for himself. Pursuing his own sinful ways, man is lost to God. It is as a mother whose son has gone astray. She has lost part of herself. God, like the mother, yearns for the one that is gone from Him.

Knowing the helplessness of man, God, like the shepherd, seeks the one who is out in the desert, wild and bare. He sent His Son to seek the wanderer. When he is found, the Savior, like a shepherd, takes him in His arms of love with forgiveness and brings him to the fold in restoration to safety and life eternal. The repentance of the sinner is involved, for there is more rejoicing in heaven over 1 sinner who repents than over 99 self-righteous ones who feel no need to repent.

April 23

The Lost Coin

Luke 15:10

In the second parable given in response to the slur cast due to publicans and sinners, Jesus forever condemned any social order based on a caste system. He was more concerned with the insinuation against unfortunate people than with the sarcastic denunciation of himself.

Jesus Christ saw value in every lost son of Adam's race. None were so vile that they could not be redeemed. None were so good that they needed no redemption.

The coin that was lost was not valuable so much because of the metal of which it was made, as it was because of the superscription it bore. Every lost sinner bears the image of his Maker. It may be sadly defaced; nevertheless, the image of God remains, and he is capable of being saved to the uttermost. He is more valuable than all the world.

The coin while lost could not complete the payment of a debt. The woman's need may have intensified the diligence of her search. She lighted her candle, she moved the furniture, she swept the house until she found the lost coin. The Holy Spirit is seeking, searching for lost men. Let every redeemed person offer his help. The longer the sinner is lost, the more unlikely his recovery. The woman of our parable was overjoyed when her search was successful. She could not keep her joy to herself. She called her neighbors and friends to rejoice with her. Let the whole church sing for joy when a sinner has come home. The angels of God rejoice over one sinner who repents.

April 24

The Younger Son

Luke 15:13

This is a story reenacted in every land and told in every language. It is treasured by so many because it is so true to life. This younger son gave full rein to dispositions inherent in every child. His self-will broke out in open rebellion. The restraints of home and parental authority were unbearable. In self-assertion he asked his father for immediate possession of that portion of the estate that would be his. Having won that argument, he declared his life to be his own; he would enjoy his "freedom."

He took his journey into a far country. The distance was

100

not great in miles. But it was far away from the climate of home. Loving discipline was replaced by reckless indulgence. And take note of what he spent! His money came easy, so it was easy to see it melt away. He spent his time, hours, days, years. Character was gone too. Honor, respectability, a good name— priceless values—were treated as rubbish. His father's living was spent. A father has a right to expect that his life will be extended in that of his son. This prodigal wasted what his father had earned and cut short the influence of his good life.

But when he had spent all, in a land of famine, feeding swine, and perishing with hunger, he came to himself. He did repent. He arose and came to his father.

April 25

The Father's Welcome

Luke 15:20

This, the pearl of the parables, reaches its moving climax in the father's welcome to his returning prodigal. Here is divine love in action. This father is representative of the Heavenly Father. He never let die the hope that his son would return. It was the awareness of that love that encouraged the prodigal to say, "I will arise and go to my father." In like manner, God's prevenient grace goes wherever His lost ones go. Except for love that supplies its own motive, the sinner's plight would be hopeless.

After a time, one lone man appeared on the homeward road. There was something familiar in his form and gait. The proud head was bowed, the quick step was slowed. Hope in the father's heart changed to faith and faith to fact. Yes, it was the long-lost son coming home at last. With all the speed with which his aging legs could carry him, the father traversed the distance between them. The loving father met the prodigal son with warm embrace and with a kiss of pardon. The son started to pour out the words he had rehearsed over and over again. He never got to the petition that he might be as a hired servant. The father called to his servants, "Bring the best robe and put a ring on his finger, shoes for his feet. He is a son, not a servant. And kill that calf saved for a sacrifice, and let us eat and be merry. For my son was dead and is alive. He was lost and is found." And they began to be merry (see vv. 22-24).

In like manner, the Heavenly Father forgives and forgets.

April 26

The Elder Brother

Luke 15:28, 31

A casual reading of this classic story might find one wishing it had ended with the gracious welcome of the prodigal son by the father. That would have been the omission of a message to a large segment of the human family. The introduction of the elder brother with his smug protestations of righteousness and his demonstration of envy and pride is to point the finger of divine judgment at the Pharisees and all who would, like them, live in a world with self at the center.

It is probably easier to love the bighearted, glad-handed wastrel than the conceited legalist who knows nothing of the need of the grace of God's forgiving mercy. The one will confess his sin and find pardon and a new life in Christ. The other may feel no need of repentance or forgiveness.

The elder brother was morally upright, industrious, and probably religious. Had that fat calf been offered in a ceremonial sacrifice to God, he would have joined in the formal worship. But he showed no gratitude to his father even though he knew that all the estate was his own. When he worked overtime, it was for himself, and he had no joy in his brother's return and restoration. Instead, he was envious and figured that he should not be given such a welcome.

Jesus is saying that God is like this compassionate father and loves everyone, and that Christ had come to save all the lost, whether prodigal or Pharisee. All are invited to the mercy seat.

April 27

Jesus Passes By

Luke 18:37-38

Double calamity had befallen Bartimaeus. He was blind and he was a beggar. He evidently had heard about Jesus of Nazareth and the miraculous cures that He had brought to unfortunate persons like himself. Hearing a shuffle of feet and a murmur of voices, he asked what it meant. He was told that Jesus of Nazareth passed by. Immediately he recognized his opportunity had come. With clearer understanding than most possessed, he cried, "Jesus, thou son of David, have mercy on me." Those who were in the vanguard rebuked him. Bartimaeus, realizing his golden opportunity was passing, now cried the more, "Thou son of David, have mercy on me."

That cry of desperation mingled with faith reached the ears and heart of the Savior. He stood and, sensing the man needed help, commanded him to be brought unto Him. Many needy ones must have someone to bring them to Jesus. Mark notes that, casting away his garment, he came to Jesus. He threw off all that would hinder him. It was a reminder that everything except faith in Jesus must be left behind.

Jesus asked Bartimaeus, "What wilt thou that I shall do unto thee?" The reply was definite and urgent, "Lord, that I may receive my sight." Jesus responded, "Receive thy sight: thy faith hath saved thee" (vv. 41-42). With poverty and blindness gone, the son of Timaeus followed Jesus, glorifying God. He knew his life was changed by the Savior who was also to be followed as Example and Lord.

April 28

Christ Stills the Storm

Mark 4:41

On the voyage of life, any day may bring unpredictable events. It is important that everyone shall be prepared for the unexpected. The best possible preparation is the assurance that Christ is in calling distance.

A small ship had embarked on the Sea of Galilee to cross to the other side. Soon it was threatened by a great storm. Fortunately, Jesus was on board with the disciples. After a long day, He was sleeping even as the ship was tossed by wind and waves. His consternated disciples awakened Him with the startling words, "Master, carest thou not that we perish?" He arose and rebuked the waves and said to the sea, "Peace, be still." The wind ceased and there was a great calm (vv. 35-39).

From this thrilling story we can gather some helpful inferences. First, we see here convincing evidence of both the humanity and the divinity of Jesus. Being human, He was weary. Therefore, He sought rest in sleep. At the sound of His commanding voice, the wind and the sea obeyed. The disciples said, "What manner of man is this?" He was the God-Man.

A second inference is that Christ permits His disciples to be tested, but is ever present to meet their need in the emergency. Jesus was surprised that with all they had seen, they had no faith. He is always near and can be trusted.

The final conclusion is, Jesus is master of every situation. At His word, the sea was calm and distressing fear was changed to worshipful faith.

April 29

One in a Multitude

Mark 5:30

Jesus was so responsive to human need that multitudes thronged Him. He was on His way to do a deed of mercy for a little girl. A curious crowd pressed upon Him. But among them there was a woman whose need was desperate. She had an affliction that had hindered her for 12 years. She had sought relief from every known source. She had spent all she had. Her sense of need was heightened by the fact that her money was gone, but her nagging, humiliating ailment was not gone. She was timid about coming openly to Jesus, though she believed He could heal her, but she knew contact with Him according

104

to the law would contaminate Him. Therefore, she said, "If I can only touch His clothes, I will be whole. No one need know."

While the crowd was almost smothering Him, she came near enough to touch His garment. Immediately she was healed of her scourge. Jesus knew power had gone out of Him. He asked what to the disciples was a foolish question, "Who touched me?"

The healed woman in fear and trembling told Jesus all the truth. Her desire was born of desperate need. Her faith was simple and voluntary. This made her the one in a multitude who had received the healing power. Jesus, to correct the error of her reasoning, said to her, "Daughter, thy *faith* hath made thee whole; go in peace" (v. 34). He let her and all others know the power that made her whole was in Him, not in His clothes.

April 30

Have Faith in God

Mark 11:20-22

After Palm Sunday, Jesus spent the night in Bethany. It was probably in the home of Mary, Martha, and Lazarus. Early the next morning, in company with the disciples, He was returning to Jerusalem. Not having had breakfast, Jesus was hungry. He saw a fig tree full of leaves. It was such a tree as put on fruit before the leaves appeared. But upon coming near, Jesus found no figs, "nothing but leaves." He said, "No man eat fruit of thee hereafter for ever." The next day as they passed that way, Peter said, "Master, behold, the fig tree which thou cursedst is withered away."

In reply to Peter's pointed remark, Jesus said, "Have faith in God."

An essential element in full faith is the confidence that God's judgments are always good. They are invariably mingled with mercy. To have faith in God is to believe unquestioningly in the wisdom of His providences. The experiences which God determines or permits to come into our lives fall into two classifications, those that are beneficent and those that are adverse.

We handle the first gratefully. The test comes when the contrary winds blow. Only when faith's anchor holds in adversity is it sufficient. God is more real and personal to those who prove Him in severe trial.

One who has vigorous faith believes in the ultimate success of God's great venture in creation and redemption. Creation was not a mistake, and Calvary is not a failure. I will stake my life on the outcome.

May 1

God Speaks

Heb. 1:1-4

No book of the 66 in the Bible opens with more faith-inspiring truth than the Epistle to the Hebrews. It is comparable to Gen. 1:1 or John 1:1. Its ideas are exalted and its language harmonious. It declares that God has spoken to man and that He continues to speak.

Before the prophets came, God spoke by angels to men whose ears were attuned to hear. Three men appeared at Abraham's tent door; two were angels, but the third was the Lord who came in temporary appearance of a man. The Lord in like manner spoke to Moses face-to-face as a man speaks to his friend.

Prophets and angels were used to deliver the message of God in the time of dim and unfolding revelation. That progressive revelation reached its climax when the Word became flesh. Jesus Christ is Heir of all things. By Him worlds were made. He is the effulgence of God's glory and the likeness of His being. He speaks on the most important theme—*salvation*. This is the message of the Eternal Son and Savior. His throne is for ever and ever. The earth shall perish but He remains.

Therefore, we ought to give heed to what we have heard lest the message be lost, as water from a leaking vessel. If the word spoken by angels was steadfast, how shall we escape if we neglect so great salvation? God speaks today by the Holy Spirit and through His Word which is settled forever in heaven. Men must listen and obey.

106

May 2

God and Sinners Reconciled

Heb. 2:9-11

There are words in our Christian vocabulary which reach beyond the rational. *Redemption, incarnation,* and *atonement* belong in that list. They are too fathomless, too lofty, too measureless for the finite mind fully to comprehend. To remove them and their rich meaning from our usage would be to reduce Christianity to a humanitarian system. "Now we have received, not the spirit of the world, but the spirit which is of God; that we might know the things that are freely given to us of God" (1 Cor. 2:12).

God so loved the world that He spared not His own Son but delivered Him up for us all that with Him He might freely give us all things. We see the obedience of Jesus the Son. "He took not on him the nature of angels; but . . . the seed of Abraham" (Heb. 2:16). "It became him, for whom are all things, and by whom are all things," to make the Pioneer of our salvation perfect through suffering. He tasted death for every man.

After the humiliation and the suffering, we see Him crowned with glory and honor. This redemptive act of God in Christ has brought pardon, reconciliation, and sanctification. Sinful man is made partaker of the divine nature because Christ partook of his humanity. "For both he that sanctifieth and they who are sanctified are all of one: for which cause he is not ashamed to call them brethren." It is wonderful to be one of a redeemed society of which God is not ashamed. And we shall share His glory when we sit with Him upon His throne.

May 3

The Christian's Rest

Heb. 4:9

Several versions read that "there remains a Sabbath rest for the people of God." It is the eternal sabbath of love. It is inner calm and peace to be enjoyed even in the stress and pressure of daily toil.

Some have interpreted this as the rest into which the Christian shall enter when he arrives at the end of his earthly journey and enters his eternal home. To be sure, that is included in the promise. But rest is to be known in this life. It comes to final perfection in the life everlasting. The rest we know now is a token of the heavenly rest.

This rest is known to those who, by faith, have been cleansed from all sin. In that glorious purity and fullness of the Spirit the Christian realizes harmony within. The entire personality is blended with the nature and will of God. *O sweet rest!*

This is also the rest of spiritual satisfaction. Want that is a craving for forbidden fruit is gone. Desire for more of God's saving fullness is strong. "Blessed are they which do hunger and thirst after righteousness: for they shall be filled" (Matt. 5:6). "Delight thyself also in the Lord; and he shall give thee the desires of thine heart" (Ps. 37:4).

As Joshua led Israel into the land of abundance and variety, even so Jesus, a greater than Joshua, leads those who will completely obey and fully trust Him into this blessed Sabbath-rest.

May 4

Grace to Help

Heb. 4:14-16

Even the Christian who has entered into the rest of the entirely sanctified must be prepared to meet temptation. He lives in tension and conflict with the world around him. Can he be victorious over temptation? Can he maintain that inward rest even as his soul is searched by the Word of God? In his own strength alone he is a victim of a powerful foe. But he does not need to fear, for he has a great High Priest who has passed into the heavens. By His help he can be more than conqueror.

Our High Priest has perfect access to the God of all grace. He is the coequal Son. He also has complete understanding of our need and perfect sympathy with our vexing situations. He was tempted in all points as we are. His temptations in a typical sense included all of those to which Christians are subjected. Satan appealed to His physical appetite. He tempted Jesus to reach for power over other men even as we are tempted. He was tested at the point of His loyalty to God. These represent all the temptations to which men are exposed. Jesus, our Mediator and Advocate, won the victory by His unwavering obedience to God the Father. Therefore, He is able to sustain those who are tempted.

"Let us therefore come boldly unto the throne of grace, that we may obtain mercy, and find grace to help in time of need." Jesus never fails.

May 5

Costly Obedience

Heb. 5:8-10

At Jesus' baptism the Voice from heaven announced, "This is my beloved Son." His Sonship did not necessarily constitute Jesus as High Priest. This was received by God's appointment. No man becomes a priest by his own choice. Even as God appointed Aaron, so He appointed Jesus.

His priestly intercession began as His last discourse to His disciples reached its climax in the prayer of John's Gospel, chapter 17. He entered much more deeply into His priestly function in Gethsemane when He prayed so earnestly that His sweat was as it were great drops of blood. "Father, if thou be willing, remove this cup from me: nevertheless not my will, but thine, be done" (Luke 22:44, 42). It was a prayer that He might escape the bitter experience of momentary banishment from God. That came when He cried, "My God, my God, why hast thou forsaken me?" (Mark 15:34). His Father did not remove the bitter cup, but He did send angels to minister to Him and give Him strength to drink the cup to its bitter dregs.

To qualify as the Representative of sinful man before a holy God, our High Priest must go all the way in offering His own body on the Cross. This was the only adequate sacrifice. He learned obedience in the things He suffered.

"Obedience which costs extreme suffering takes on a new dimension." Jesus was obedient unto death, even the death of the Cross. "Being made perfect, he became the author of eternal salvation unto all them that obey him."

May 6

Let Us Go On to Maturity

Heb. 6:1-3

These Hebrew Christians had entered a period of stalemate. They had entertained their doubts until their faith was atrophied. The light they had seen had become dim and shadowy.

The Christian life is one of progress. It can never be static or stationary. It is either go on or go back. The apostle who wrote this Epistle was deeply concerned that those to whom he addressed his appeal should go on to full-grown adulthood. They had ceased to grow toward maturity. When they should be teachers, they had need to be taught. They were babes who could only take milk for nourishment. They could not receive or digest strong meat. Because they were living in prolonged infancy, they were unable to discern both good and evil. They confused truth and error.

They, like many modern stunted Christians, wanted teaching and preaching that stirred their emotions rather than truth to enlighten the mind, awaken the conscience, and feed the soul on the strong meat of God's Word. As a result their ethical practice was not in harmony with Christian ideals. They could soon enter a fixed state of moral and spiritual stupidity from which their recovery was increasingly improbable.

From warning and rebuke the apostle who loved them most turned to exhortation and encouragement. He admonished them to recovery from apathy and passivity to active pursuit of perfection. Christian perfection does not imply that the ultimate goal has been reached but that the normal progress toward that goal is now being realized. The goal is Christlikeness.

The Anchor of the Soul

Heb. 6:18-19

Hope is a firm expectation based on solid foundations. Our Christian hope is inspired and supported by God's unchanging Word. Here we are told that God has reinforced His Word by His oath, that by two unchangeable things in which it is impossible for God to lie, we might have strong assurance of the fulfillment of what God had promised. This hope, therefore, is supported by the veracity and character of God himself. To the Christian, nothing could be more certain.

This blessed hope has given sinful men the will to flee for refuge to the offered place of safety. Here is a clear reference to the cities of refuge provided for one responsible for an accidental death under the old covenant. There he was safe from the avenger. Under the new covenant Christ by His death on the Cross provided a refuge for all who would turn to Him in repentance and faith. To Him they have fled for refuge to lay hold on the hope set before them. Those who turn to Him are never rejected.

That hope is an anchor of the soul, sure and steadfast. Weymouth translates those words "an anchor that can neither break nor drag." The figure is of a vessel approaching the desired harbor in a storm. Fearing the possibility of being wrecked on hidden rocks, the master of the ship orders the anchor to be cast. The anchor holds and the cable does not break. The Christian's hope-anchor is as dependable as God's promise and His oath.

Christ Our High Priest Forever

Heb. 7:25-26

The priesthood of all believers in Christ was proclaimed by Martin Luther. This has been an important concept for all Protestants. The validity of that doctrine is conditioned upon the high priesthood of Jesus Christ. All believers have access to

God through His intercession for them. Therefore the priesthood of believers is a corollary of the fundamental doctrine of the high priesthood of Christ.

In this seventh chapter of Hebrews, the author is setting forth the superiority of the priesthood of Christ over that of Aaron. He was made Priest after the power of an endless life. The Psalmist prophesied, "The Lord hath sworn, and will not repent, Thou art a priest for ever after the order of Melchizedek" (110:4). The mysterious king of Salem is a type of the Messiah Priest. He was without predecessor or successor as priest of the Most High God. He was made like unto the Son of God. As our High Priest, Jesus Christ came of no line of priests. He had no ancestors and no descendants. His was an unchangeable priesthood.

The superiority of the priesthood of Christ is also seen in the fact that He did not have reason to make a sacrifice for His own sins. He was "holy, harmless, undefiled, separate from sinners, and made higher than the heavens." Therefore His offering of himself without spot to God was acceptable and adequate.

He saves from the guilt, the power, the stain, and the penalty of sin and finally from its presence. It is eternal salvation. "He ever liveth to make intercession" for us.

May 9

The New Covenant

Heb. 8:6

The first covenant that God made with Israel when He brought them out of Egypt was good, but it was not faultless. Had it been adequate, there would have been no cause for a new covenant. God knew and His chosen people proved by experience that the covenant of law was insufficient to meet the need of the sons of Adam. When God said, "I will make a new covenant with the house of Israel" (v. 8), He made the first old, out of date, obsolete.

The old covenant was like the shadow of a tree cast upon the ground. It was in the shape and appearance of a tree but

112

without substance and reality. It had value to those who would take refuge in it by obedience. That which the new covenant offered in Christ, the Mediator, provided a more excellent ministry than the priests could who served under the law.

The new covenant is better than the old because it is supported by better promises. The old offered those who brought their gifts and sacrifices pardon for inadvertent, unintentional transgressions or omissions. The new covenant offers pardon for the willful sinner.

The old provided ceremonial cleansing for those defiled. It could never make the conscience perfect. The new covenant provided complete cleansing of the conscience from guilt, and the will from rebellion, and the affections from defilement. The old covenant allowed only the high priest to enter the holy of holies. The new covenant opened the holiest to all who enter by faith in Christ.

May 10

Christ Was Once Offered

Heb. 9:27-28

Verse 27 has often been used as a text for an evangelistic sermon on death and the Judgment. That it declares that death for every man is certain and the Judgment inescapable, none can deny. Of these solemn facts all men bad and good need to be reminded. Such interpretation of this text is permissible.

The author, however, primarily was using his knowledge of the fact that death and the Judgment come but once to every man to illustrate the grand truth that when Jesus the Son of God offered His own body on the Cross, He made a sacrifice once for all. No other sacrifice that had ever been made could provide pardon for voluntary transgressions. None could cleanse the conscience or make a heart full of sin pure. All others were typical and prophetic of the great redemption which was finished when Christ gave His life a ransom for all. Previous offerings for sin had their validity verified at Calvary. In one great redemptive deed, Christ became the Sacrifice which provided salvation for all who would receive Him as Savior and Lord.

The sacrifice that Christ made was for all who would in contrition and faith look back to the Lamb of God who suffered death for every man on that dark Friday. The provision He made was universal. All who ever lived and all who would live find Him an adequate Savior. His coming again will be the ultimate salvation of those who look and live. Then He will save the whole creation that groaneth and travaileth in pain together until now. The whole curse of sin will be lifted.

May 11

Perseverance Is Imperative

Heb. 10:35-36

The first and deepest concern of the author of the Epistle to the Hebrews was that those to whom he wrote should go on in the steadfastness of their Christian faith. This concern is expressed repeatedly in such expressions as "Let us hold fast the profession of our faith without wavering" (10:23); "Let us go on unto perfection" (6:1); "Let us run with patience [or perseverance] the race that is set before us" (12:1). Here in this passage he expresses the same idea in the words "Cast not away . . . your confidence."

There is glory in going on. The benefits of the Christian way of life are not all postponed until life after death. Holiness has its own reward. The pure in heart see God and enjoy His blessed fellowship on the journey of life. The Comforter has come. He supplies strength according to His riches in glory by Christ Jesus.

It is all this and heaven too. There will be the abundant entrance into life eternal. The Lord and Judge of all will pronounce that long-anticipated plaudit: "Well done, good and faithful servant . . . enter thou into the joy of thy lord" (Matt. 25:23).

It is said when Spartan mothers sent their sons to battle, they wished them well but said, "Return carrying your shield or be carried on it." The apostle is saying to the Hebrews and all Christians, "To the faithful, God will fulfill His promise. Therefore never be a quitter."

May 12
The Meaning of Faith

Heb. 11:1

"Now faith is a confident assurance of that for which we hope, a conviction of the reality of things we do not see" (Weymouth). "Now faith is being sure of what we hope for and certain of what we do not see" (NIV). Probably in this verse we find the only attempt to set forth the meaning of faith in the Bible. Hope is the feeling that what is desired is possible. Faith is the full persuasion that it is now a fact. What we have taken by faith is now in our possession. Faith in the biblical sense is firm belief in God and that what God has promised, He will perform. "He that cometh to God must believe that he is, and that he is a rewarder of them that diligently seek him" (v. 6). Salvation is received by faith. Until faith has laid firm hold on the word of promise, there can be no answer from God. No other proof can be sought or given save that God has promised.

Why God would give His Son to be the Savior of sinful man; why Christ would die to bring salvation to a rebel race; how the Holy Spirit can convict sinners and lead them to repentance; how He can regenerate the soul of man and make him a new creature—such are all beyond the reach of human reason or intelligence. But all these things become unshakable reality by faith in Christ. By faith heaven becomes a conviction with certainty.

May 13
Ready for the Race

Heb. 12:1

The writers of the New Testament books rather frequently use the contestants in the Olympian races to illustrate the lifestyle of Christians. There are obvious similarities.

Preparation for successful pursuit of the Christian way of life is comparable to the track runner who has hope of winning. He rids himself of every encumbrance. Excess clothing is removed. Furthermore, he has disciplined himself until his weight is conducive to speed and endurance. The admonition in our text calls for these same principles to be observed by those who expect to run the Christian race successfully.

There is the added call to rid oneself of the sin that so easily entangles. It is not one's most persistent weakness. It is obviously something which clings closely, something chronic rather than intermittent. It is the sin that dwells in us. Certainly that sin must be purged if consistent victory is to be known.

The Christian, like the Olympian runner, must show persistence. It is not a short burst of speed. It is an endurance test. Who will be there at the finish? "He that endureth to the end shall be saved" (Matt. 10:22).

There is one point of dissimilarity. Paul said to the Corinthians, "Know ye not that they which run in a race run all, but one receiveth the prize? So run, that ye may obtain" (1 Cor. 9:24).

In the Christian race, everyone who stays in there to the finish receives the prize. Everyone who wins the race is an encouragement to all the others. The prize is eternal life and all the blessedness of heaven.

May 14

The Secret of Constant Victory

Heb. 12:2

There are many factors involved in being a victorious Christian. There is the regular practice of reading God's Word, meditating upon it, and praying. It is a truism that life in the Spirit must be nourished. Faithful attendance upon the means of grace offered by the Church is important. But the one absolute essential is to keep a fixed gaze upon Jesus, the Author and Finisher of our faith.

Jesus is our Example in His total commitment. With Him

there was never a moment to consider any option but to do the will of His Father. As the Cross loomed before Him, He steadfastly set His face to go to Jerusalem. Even in Gethsemane it was "Not my will, but thine." The initial commitment must be irrevocable. It is a start to see the finish, regardless of the cost. The famous preacher Paul Scherer described it as "a commitment that will leave its arithmetic at home." Jesus gave us an example of calm courage and deep, settled peace in spite of hateful scorn by foes and desertion by friends. "Consider him that endured such contradiction of sinners against himself, lest ye be wearied and faint in your minds" (v. 3). Look to anyone else and eventually be disillusioned and disappointed. Look at yourself and succumb to despair.

We are to look to Jesus as the Source of our strength. He lived in joyful anticipation of ultimate victory. Even death on the Cross would climax in resurrection and ascension. He shares His victory with those who look to Him. He is the great Example.

May 15

Discipline Pays Dividends

Heb. 12:5-11

This is one of the many paragraphs in the Bible which must be taken as a whole in order to grasp its full meaning. A single verse does not summarize the truth contained in these seven verses. They all deal with the subject of discipline.

All true disciples accept joyfully the discipline of their Lord. Contrary to what many believe, to be a disciple of Jesus is to discover the only true freedom. The love slave to Christ is truly free. He is gloriously free. This is a dividend of discipline self-imposed.

The one who sees voluntary obedience to Christ as an inspiring challenge also finds that he is qualified for service. In serving God and man he finds supreme joy. To those who accept it as a proof of God's love and a token of sonship,

117

discipline prepares them for the tests that they are sure to meet in life. Discipline builds strength of character.

In the disciplines which God directs, one discovers how great the grace of God truly is. Divine resources are found unlimited. It is God's means of polishing and refining His children. They are partakers of His holiness; they grow in holy character and Christlikeness. Those who accept discipline as from the Lord are prepared to give comfort and encouragement to others in like experiences. Those who rejoice in their trials find victory more thrilling. They are prepared to enjoy heaven more because their capacity for it is greater. God has promised to fill the Christian's life with the peaceable fruit of righteousness.

May 16

We Are Come to Mount Zion

Heb. 12:22-24

Here is a contrast between Mount Sinai and Mount Zion in striking symbols and figures of speech. At Sinai there was darkness; at Zion there is light. At Sinai there was a terrifying tempest; at Zion there are gentle zephyrs bearing good tidings. At Sinai there was the frightening blast of a trumpet; at Zion there is the blessed invitation to draw near. At Sinai there was the threat of death; at Zion there is the promise of forgiveness and life everlasting. Sinai thundered out the law; from Zion the gospel of grace and peace is heralded for whosoever will. At Sinai there were forbidding barriers; at Zion there are outstretched arms of love and mercy.

Thank God that for Christians Sinai is the background while Zion gleams with promise for all time and eternity.

We will come to God the Judge of all. He is a Judge whose holiness is worshipped. In His presence all heads are bowed, all hearts are purged, all wills are obedient.

God is a Judge whose power is infinite. He is able to save to the uttermost.

We come to Jesus the Mediator. "There is one God, and one mediator . . . , the man Christ Jesus" (1 Tim. 2:5).

We are come to the General Assembly and Church of the Firstborn. Here is the holy heavenly fellowship. It is fellowship with God through Christ. It includes myriads of angels and all the spirits of just men made perfect. What a prospect!

May 17

Holiness Required

Heb. 12:14

God is holy. It is certain that a holy God cannot receive unholy persons to himself in complete fellowship. To bridge the chasm of separation, God provided salvation to the uttermost. Therefore all who would be received into that blessed fellowship with God here and hereafter must accept the provision offered and be made pure in God's sight.

A series of warnings cluster around this well-known text. The first is found in verse 13: "Make straight paths for your feet, lest that which is lame be turned out of the way." Model a holy life.

The second warning follows the text in verse 15: "Lest any man fail of the grace of God." Holiness is an aid to steadfastness of purpose. The next warning signal follows immediately: "lest any root of bitterness springing up trouble you, and thereby many be defiled." Bitterness must be uprooted. Entire sanctification purges out the last root of bitterness.

The final warning is lest any trade permanent values for temporary gratification. Holiness is the safeguard to a Christian living in this sinful world.

Holiness is to be possessed by faith now and pursued as a way of life. John Wesley said, "Without holiness no man shall see the Lord. Nothing under heaven can be more sure than this. None shall enjoy the glory of God in heaven but he that bears the image of God on earth. None that is not saved from sin here can be saved from hell hereafter."

May 18

The Unchangeable Person

Heb. 13:8

"Jesus Christ the same yesterday, and to day, and for ever." What He was, He is. What He is, He will always be. He will never be more or less. He will always be the same, unchanging and unchangeable. He dominates the past, the present, and the future.

John's Gospel records Christ speaking of himself in many ways. Jesus declared, "I am the light of the world: he that followeth me shall not walk in darkness" (8:12). He is still the only Light that shatters this world's darkness. To those who know Him there comes no blackout. He said, "I am the bread of life" (6:35). We feed on Him in our hearts by faith day by day. He is the never-failing nourishment for the souls of all who believe. He is the Staff of life.

Jesus also talked about the water of life. "Whosoever drinketh of the water that I shall give him shall never thirst; . . . [it] shall be in him a well of water springing up into everlasting life" (4:14).

Christ asserted, "I am the good shepherd . . . I am the Door by which the sheep may enter and go in and out and find pasture" (10:11, cf. 9).

He later explained, "I am the way, the truth, and the life: no man cometh unto the Father, but by me" (14:6). He remains the only Way to God, the personification of truth. He is the Life eternal.

Jesus reminded His disciples He was their "Master and Lord" (13:13); yet, "I am among you as he that serveth" (Luke 22:27). He washed His disciples' feet and wiped them with a towel. The towel is the symbol of His servanthood. Jesus Christ is the answer to the hopes, the dreams, the longings of men in all ages.

120

May 19

The Continuation of the Life of Christ

Acts 1:1

In the Gospel that bears his name, Luke records the story of the life of Jesus from His birth at Bethlehem until His ascension from Bethany. But to this beloved physician, the story did not end there. It was to be continued by the apostles who received the Holy Spirit.

The first verse of the first chapter of Acts is more than a salutation to Theophilus—the God-lover. Luke makes known that in the former treatise he had reported all that Jesus began both to do and to teach. The teacher gave His lessons by the most effective methods known to man. He used revelation, a divine disclosure of the very being and character of God. He taught by exemplification. He said, "I am the truth." He employed didactic instruction. Seeing the multitude, He opened His mouth and taught them.

The Master conveyed eternal truth by illustration. His parables are classic in their profound simplicity. And this, the Greatest of all instructors, drove home His message and motivated men for heroic action by urgent exhortation. Luke's Gospel also reports all that Jesus did. His miracles attest His divine power.

And now Luke says that was only the beginning. As Jesus had promised, the Spirit came to dwell in His followers of the 1st century and the 20th, and all that may follow. The gospel would still be preached, and the miracles of God's grace would still be seen.

May 20

Jesus' Final Instructions

Acts 1:2

According to Matthew, the last command Jesus gave to His disciples was the Great Commission. "Go ye therefore, and teach all nations" (28:19). Mark phrased it, "Go ye into all the world, and preach the gospel to every creature" (16:15). This means that every true disciple of Christ is obliged to share the Good News. The word of Christ is personal. "Go ye" means me. It is also universal. It is to every creature. It is what we are that speaks most convincingly for our Savior. Our words, our deeds, our shining light speak forth the love and grace of God day by day.

The word "commandments" in our verse for today is variously translated. In some it is "command," in others it is "orders," and still others "instructions." No matter how we read it, the burden is upon us to obey with deep dedication. We cannot truly please our risen Lord if we do not do our best to give as freely as we have received.

But the Master knew that those to whom He committed the task of telling the Good News to all the world were inadequate in their own strength. Therefore, He gave further command that they should not depart from Jerusalem but wait for the promise of the Father. It was the fulfillment of that promise that would provide the adequacy for their assignment. With Him, they would not be wanting in competence, courage, or faithful performance. He said, "The Holy Spirit coming upon you, ye shall be witnesses unto Me" (cf. v. 8).

May 21

"A Cloud Received Him out of Their Sight"

Acts 1:9-11

It is Luke that gives most of the information concerning the ascension of Jesus. He makes it dramatic and vivid. Jesus did not simply disappear while the attention of the disciples was diverted. While they beheld, He was taken up. So concentrated were their thoughts that, when they could no longer see Him, they were still gazing up into heaven.

A cloud received Him out of their sight. That He is absent and yet present is a paradox that captures the mind and imagination of devout believers. He said, "I go away; nevertheless, I will not leave you orphans; I will come to you. . . . And lo, I am with you always, even unto the end of the age" (cf.

122

John 14:18; Matt. 28:20). By spiritual perception He is nearer than sight or sound or touch. Another like himself, the Holy Spirit, with whom He identifies completely, has come to be in you. Jesus is at the right hand of God, but He is here in the reality of a personal companionship.

His promise, "I will come again," was confirmed by angelic witnesses. They said, "This same Jesus, which is taken up from you into heaven, shall so come in like manner as ye have seen him go into heaven." They gave no intimation of when, but they did give assurance that He would come again personally, visibly, and gloriously.

Implied in the word of those heavenly messengers was the command of their Lord, "Occupy till I come" (Luke 19:13). The fields are white unto harvest.

May 22

Preparation for Pentecost

Acts 1:14

The first step in preparation for a personal Pentecost is always obedience to God's known will. The disciples had heard Jesus say, "Wait for the promise of the Father" (v. 4). To that command they gave diligent heed. There was an appointed time on God's calendar. It was to be on the great feast day to relate the future to the past and to facilitate the rapid spread of the gospel to the uttermost part of the earth. In this instance, there was a time elapse necessary. This is not the case since the Spirit descended on that historic day. The only time appointed now is that required for the preparation of the individual to receive the fullness of the Spirit.

For that purpose the time was occupied by those gathered in the Upper Room. They continued in prayer and supplication until their spirits were completely blended and until their dominant desire was for the coming of the promised Comforter. Supplication means prayer with earnest pleading. All their carnal and worldly desires were now submerged. In a post-Pentecost plea Charles Wesley cried:

Oh, that the fire from heaven might fall,
And all my dross consume.
Come, Holy Ghost, for Thee I call;
Spirit of burning, come.

Those present in that Upper Room prayed until their consecration reached the depth of total and final commitment to the will of God.

They continued in supplication until their faith became expectation for immediate fulfillment. They were all filled with the Holy Spirit.

May 23

"Judas by Transgression Fell"

Acts 1:25

Why did Jesus choose Judas as one of the 12 apostles? Did He not know that according to prophecy he would be a traitor? It seems clear that Jesus chose Judas because He loved him and believed he had the possibility of being a faithful disciple. Jesus wanted all to know that His love reached out to the unfortunate as well as to the more respectable and well-mannered persons like John the Beloved.

There is evidence that Jesus showed special favor to Judas. He carried the bag. At the Last Supper He sat near Jesus. When the Master said, "One of you shall betray me," the identification came when Jesus gave the sop to Judas. This was a token of love for the one to whom it was given. When Judas led the soldiers to take Him, Jesus addressed the traitor as "friend."

How could Judas do such a dark deed to a friend who had shown him such love? Doubtless he had a good beginning; he was chosen and commissioned as were the rest of the Twelve. But a sinful heart had not been cleansed. The old temptation to love money was not resisted. He made his deal with the chief priests and captains. He was the traitor, and he was a suicide. He went to the place of his own choice. He remains a solemn reminder that all who know Christ should appropriate His sanctifying grace and find victory over indwelling sin.

May 24
"What Meaneth This?"

Acts 2:12

The outpouring of the Holy Spirit on the Day of Pentecost came at the time of the Feast of Weeks. The Jews commemorated the giving of the law at Mount Sinai in this, the second great feast in their calendar of events. On the Day of Pentecost there were unusual phenomena of nature, even as there were when the law was given. At Sinai there were thunders, lightnings, a thick cloud upon the mount, and the voice of the trumpet exceeding loud. At Pentecost, there were the sound from heaven as a rushing mighty wind, cloven tongues like as of fire, and the speaking in other languages. These great manifestations of God's presence and power were accompanied by inaugural displays that were never repeated. If the law needed no further attestation, much less the coming of the Spirit, who bears His own witness to the hearts of those who receive Him.

What meaneth this sound from heaven, as of a rushing mighty wind? All know that there is power in the wind. The power of the Spirit is displayed in the transformation of the lives of men. They are made new creatures. Without the wind of the Spirit, the Church is like a vessel at sea caught in a dead calm. The winds of the Spirit are blowing. Let us lift our sails to take advantage of their power.

May 25

"My Spirit upon All Flesh"

Acts 2:17

Joel prophesied, "It shall come to pass." Peter said, "This is that which was spoken by the prophet Joel." The prophet foresaw it hundreds of years before. Peter witnessed the fulfillment on the Day of Pentecost. In the intervening centuries Jewish exclusiveness had drawn hard lines. The Jews seemed to misunderstand God's promise to Abraham. Instead of hearing, "In thy seed shall all the nations of the earth be blessed" (Gen. 22:18), they conceived the idea that God had said, "In *thee,* shall all *thy seed* be blessed." In Jesus' day the concept of exclusiveness had grown until all except Abraham's seed according to the flesh were Gentile dogs.

On the Day of Pentecost the Spirit was poured out upon all flesh. The barriers were removed. "The promise," said Peter, "is unto you, and to your children, and to all that are afar off, even as many as the Lord our God shall call" (v. 39).

The limits were all self-imposed. The availability was universal. The reception was by the willing and the believing. The word of Joel had come to pass. All could now enter the glorious Church which Christ loved and gave himself to sanctify. By the Spirit's coming and abiding, all could "put on the new man, which is renewed in knowledge after the image of him that created him" (Col. 3:10). "To God be the glory; great things He hath done."

May 26

"In the Last Days"

Acts 2:17

The Spirit of God is as perpetual in His availability as He is universal. "Last days," in this case, includes all the days of the gospel age from the descent of the Holy Spirit on the Day of Pentecost until "the Lord himself shall descend from heaven with a shout, with the voice of the archangel, and with the trump of God" (1 Thess. 4:16). The Holy Spirit came to make Christians adequate to meet the demands of their untoward generation. The history of the victorious Church is in fact the biography of Spirit-filled men. Where there has been failure, it has been because men have not opened their hearts to the incoming of the Holy Spirit. They have depended upon their resources and their skills rather than on the Spirit of God who had been promised by the Father.

In this age men stand amazed at the marvels that have been done because the atom has been split and nuclear energy has been released. The spiritual equivalent is in the power of the Spirit. To all who will come to God with openness to receive and readiness to be used, the gift of the Holy Spirit will be bestowed. They cannot manipulate the Spirit of God to do their will. But they can yield themselves to the Spirit to perform God's will. The maximum accomplishment in the work of God is by total yieldedness to the control of the Spirit. By giving His wisdom, man understands what the will of God is; and in His power the work is done.

May 27

The Spirit and the Word

Acts 2:37, 41

The solid content of Peter's sermon on the Day of Pentecost is from the word spoken by holy men who were moved by the Spirit of God. The main body of his sermon deals with the doctrine of Christ, which is according to the word spoken by the Psalmist David, who was indeed a prophet. His conclusion was, "Therefore let all the house of Israel know assuredly, that God hath made that same Jesus, whom ye have crucified, both Lord and Christ" (v. 36).

Those who heard were pricked in their hearts and said to Peter and the rest of the apostles, "Men and brethren, what shall we do?" In answer to their question, Peter said unto them, "Repent, and be baptized every one of you in the name of Jesus Christ for the remission of sins, and ye shall receive the gift of the Holy Spirit" (cf. v. 38). The Word declared in the power of the Spirit will invariably produce conviction for sin. The letter of the Word without the Spirit may sound only as cliches or platitudes. The Word is the Sword of the Spirit.

Modern believers are amazed at the results of that sermon preached by Peter on the Day of Pentecost. The same day there were added unto them about 3,000 souls. What a harvest for one sermon! Of course, there were other forces at work. Nevertheless, let those who are engaged in the great business of evangelism take heart. Your labor is not in vain in the Lord.

May 28

"They Continued Stedfastly"

Acts 2:42

It is often said that a good beginning is half the battle. However true that may be, without steadfast continuation the victory is never won. A vital, heartwarming experience of salvation is important, but the follow-through is the final proof. Those converts had the stuff of which martyrs are made. They had the character of true soldiers of the Cross. They made their choice forever.

These new Christians gave all their successors a pattern of practice to follow. Their faith was proved in their faithfulness. New converts who are in earnest always come back for more. They like the sincere milk of the Word. They are soon able to digest the strong meat as well. From infancy they go on to maturity.

These learners fell in love with their teachers, the apostles. They knew there was mutual encouragement and strength in togetherness. They needed the others and the others needed them. How true it is in every age! The Church is indeed a fellowship. Christians sit together in heavenly places. This holy comradeship came to its highest, richest meaning when they broke bread together. They shared that experience around the table of the Lord. The holy sacrament stimulated memory of Calvary and deepened their gratitude for the sacrifice that their Lord had made for them. It inspired their hope that He would fulfil His promise to come again and receive them unto himself.

These disciplined followers of the risen Lord were strengthened every time they sought the place of prayer. There they drew from the unlimited resources of grace.

May 29

Such as I Have, I Give

Acts 3:6

Peter and John were filled with the Spirit. The love of God was shed abroad in their hearts. This meant that in their souls was an overflowing compassion for all their fellowmen. The greater the need of a brother man, the greater was their compassion for him.

The love these apostles had for God is seen in the fact that they went up to the Temple at the hour of prayer. Faithfulness in prayer is always a measure of Christian devotion. Peter and John demonstrated their love for their neighbor, a lame beggar.

These Christians, lately filled with the Holy Spirit, had compassion on the impotent man. Peter said, "Silver and gold have I none; but such as I have give I thee." It is axiomatic that what one does not have he cannot give. It is equally true that what one does possess, he is obliged to share. The experience of the Spirit's fullness gave these men something far better than material riches. They knew they had found the secret of a life of wholeness. In strong faith Peter said, "In the name of Jesus Christ of Nazareth rise up and walk." Immediately the cripple's feet and ankle bones received strength. He leaped and walked and praised God.

To give of that we have is an expression of gratitude to our Heavenly Father who has given so lavishly to us. It is a token effort to pay our debt to our fellowman. And not to be forgotten is the fact that giving is a condition for continual receiving and growing.

May 30

They Suffered Shame for His Name

Acts 5:41-42

The advice of Gamaliel, as measured by its effect, was good, but not good enough. To adopt the wait-and-see policy under such circumstances was a compromise. What a great leader he would have been had he taken his stand for Christ and called upon all members of the council to do likewise! His counsel may have saved the lives of the apostles, but it did not save their hides. They beat them and let them go.

It is not Gamaliel who is the hero here. It is those who could take the disgrace and suffering and rejoice that they were counted worthy to suffer shame for Jesus' sake. They, no doubt, recalled the last beatitude spoken by the One they had seen crucified. His word was a prophecy as well as a blessing. "Blessed are ye, when men shall revile you, and persecute you . . . Rejoice, and be exceeding glad: for great is your reward in heaven" (Matt. 5:11-12). As did the Master, so did the servant. They were triumphant in suffering. They magnified the grace of God.

Peter's words, written years after, are the more meaningful because they have the added richness which could only be the result of his own experience. He wrote, "Who is he that will harm you, if ye be followers of that which is good? But and if ye suffer for righteousness' sake, happy are ye . . . For it is better, if the will of God be so, that ye suffer for well doing, than for evil doing" (1 Pet. 3:13-14, 17).

Those men of courage were not only conquerors, they were *more than conquerors!*

May 31

Irresistible Grace

Acts 6:8, 10

Some manuscripts and many translations have "grace" instead of "faith" in verse 8. Since grace comes by faith, it is reasonable to assume that if Stephen had grace, it was because he had faith. That God had bestowed on him abundant grace is seen clearly in his conduct in the fierce trial through which he passed. When he was falsely charged with blasphemy as he sat before the council, his face shone as if it had been the face of an angel (v. 15).

That Stephen was full of grace is further evident by his prayer while angry witnesses hurled stones upon his body. Being full of the Holy Spirit, he said, "Lord Jesus, receive my spirit" That is quite like the last words of Jesus from the Cross: "Father, into thy hands I commend my spirit." Then, kneeling down as the last death-dealing stone was hurled, Stephen echoed the prayer of Jesus for those who crucified Him. "Lord, lay not this sin to their charge" is divinely like "Father, forgive them; for they know not what they do" (7:59-60; Luke 23:46, 34). This was the secret of the power with which he spake. What he said was reenforced by the grace which was so beautifully shining in his life. To grace was added wisdom. Stephen was not an apostle; he was a layman.

That God would ever save men against their will is incredible. But it is certain that the Word, spoken under the anointing of God's Spirit by one whose life is full of grace and his words with wisdom, will produce conviction.

June 1

Spirit-guided

Acts 8:29

God's directives are sometimes mysterious. Philip had been used of God to bring about a great revival in Samaria. The people with one accord gave heed to the things he spoke. Miracles of healing were numerous, and unclean spirits came out of those who were possessed with them. No wonder there was great joy in that city.

The work of Philip had been observed and approved by Peter and John, and the believers had received the Holy Spirit. As this great awakening reached its climax, a strange leading of the Spirit came to Philip. The angel of the Lord spoke to him, saying, "Arise and go toward the south unto the way that goeth down from Jerusalem unto Gaza, which is desert."

God had a reason for sending Philip on this mission. There was a man with a hungry heart and an eager mind to learn, who met with Philip as if by appointment. His interest in the faith had been awakened, but he was going home without his questions answered or his heart satisfied.

Philip was given a specific command to join himself to the Ethiopian's chariot. Philip took in the situation at a glance. Even the portion of Scripture which the stranger was reading fitted the occasion perfectly. From Isaiah 53 Philip preached unto him Jesus. The conversion took place, the eager mind was convinced, and the hungry heart satisfied. He was baptized. God's purpose was accomplished. The man of Ethiopia went home to proclaim his faith.

June 2

Vision and Providence

Acts 10:17-18

Peter was deeply grounded in the prejudice of the Jews. He heard the risen Lord say, "Ye shall be witnesses unto me both in Jerusalem, and in all Judaea, and in Samaria, and unto the uttermost part of the earth" (1:8). He had received the Holy Spirit in fullness on the Day of Pentecost. The housetop experience made him ready to share the gospel with Gentiles.

About noon Peter went up to the housetop to pray. As he prayed, he fell asleep. A sheet was let down from heaven. In it were all manner of fourfooted beasts (including swine), wild beasts (also forbidden), creeping things, and fowls of the air. And there came a voice saying, "Rise, Peter; kill, and eat." He protested, "Not so, Lord; for I have never eaten anything that is common or unclean." The Voice said, "What God hath cleansed, that call not thou common" (vv. 13-15).

To help Peter understand and obey the vision he had seen, and while he was considering its meaning, the Spirit said, "Three men seek thee, Peter. . . . Go with them, doubting nothing: for I have sent them" (vv. 19-20). Peter would have been mystified by the vision but for the fact that it was matched by a providential call to go to preach the gospel to the Gentiles. It took the vision to make Peter willing. It took the open door to make the vision more than a baffling dream. That was the final confirmation of the call.

June 3

God Answers the Cry of a Hungry Heart

Acts 10:34-35

Cornelius was an exceptional man. It is evident that exposure to the religion of the Hebrews had convinced him that their God was far superior to the deities his fellow countrymen worshiped. How far he had gone in his identification is not known. He was a devout man of prayer; he feared God with all his house. He had led his family in worship; he accepted the responsibility of his stewardship. He gave much alms to the people; he had a commendable social concern.

With all this to be said in favor of Cornelius, he was not a Christian. He was walking in all the light he had received. He had a heart reaching out for a more perfect knowledge of God.

As Cornelius prayed, an angel of God came to him and told him to send to Joppa and call for Simon Peter who should tell him what he ought to do. The response was immediate. When Peter came, he declared Jesus to be Lord of all. He preached Christ crucified and risen from the dead. He declared that through His name whosoever believeth shall receive remission of sins. With open mind and believing heart Cornelius and his household received Jesus Christ as Savior and Lord while Peter preached.

Before he had finished speaking, the Holy Spirit fell on all that heard the word. Time elapse is not an important factor in God's dealings with those who have yearning hearts. He waits to satisfy the hungry soul with forgiveness and His Spirit's abiding fullness.

June 4

Goodness Is Winsome

Acts 11:24

Goodness is the most important characteristic of one who would be a soul winner. Intelligence is desirable; goodness is indispensable. Learning can be and should be a valuable aid to effective witnessing for Christ. Prepared men have been greatly used of God to lead multitudes to Christ. Paul was such a man. But if the leaders of thought and action had not had their satellites in men of modest intellect and limited talents, their labors could not have been so fruitful.

Paul was the outstanding evangelist of the first-century Church. Yet he needed Barnabas, who was a good man, full of the Holy Spirit and faith. His goodness was the fruit of the Spirit. It was transparent holiness. His motivation was selfless. His love was unmixed. Much people were added to the Lord.

Barnabas, "Son of Encouragement," sold his land that those in need might share his possessions. When Saul was under suspicion, it was Barnabas who befriended him until he was accepted. He rejoiced when he saw the grace of God in the disciples at Antioch. He exhorted them to cleave unto the Lord.

This Son of Encouragement knew the Church needed a wiser man than he to lead on to stronger faith and expansion. Therefore, he departed to seek Saul; and when he had found him, he brought him to Antioch where for a year they assembled with the church. Converts need to be taught as well as to be saved. The Church today needs men of the intellect of Paul, and it needs men of the goodness of Barnabas.

June 5

The Disciples Called Christians

Acts 11:26

The word "Christian" is used so naturally to identify the followers of Christ today that we are prone to think the Early Church bore that name. But as a matter of fact, many years had passed before that title was used. And it is of interest to note that the word "Christian" occurs only three times in the entire New Testament.

Whence came this name? It did not arise among the hostile Jews. They scornfully called the believers Nazarenes. Some would suggest that the name was given out of the necessity of designating a growing group of people who were drawn together by a common interest, like a political party.

134

There is good reason to believe, however, that it was Barnabas and Paul who by divine inspiration began to call the disciples Christians. Isn't it heartwarming to believe that this name was chosen of God because those believers, "saints" as they were called among themselves, were such disciplined followers of Jesus Christ that God himself described them as Christians. God saw in those disciples men and women who would live like Jesus lived. They were adorned with the fruit of the Holy Spirit. As Jesus was "the Anointed One," so they would be anointed with the Holy Spirit. They were not called "Jesus People," they were called Christians. If they suffered as Christians, they would glorify God in their suffering even as Christ had suffered. What a world this would be if all who bear that name were worthy of it!

June 6

The Beginning of Worldwide Mission

Acts 13:2-4a

The time had come for action in obedience to the Great Commission. The risen Lord had said, "Go ye into all the world, and preach the gospel to every creature" (Mark 16:15). Just before He ascended into heaven, He promised power to witness in Jerusalem and all Judea and Samaria and unto the uttermost part of the earth. The message was clear and the power was adequate. The first steps had been taken. The open doors nearby had been entered. Now it was imperative that the greater adventure should be undertaken. The work in Antioch was established. There were capable men to carry on there. This was to be the base from which the worldwide outreach should be launched.

The choice of Barnabas and Paul was of God. The Holy Spirit said, "Separate me Barnabas and Saul for the work whereunto I have called them." It was the Holy Spirit who communicated the knowledge of their call to the church. The listening church confirms the choice of God. The called ones respond in eager obedience. There was no protest or hesitation

135

on the part of Barnabas and Paul. They were ready to hazard their lives for the name of the Lord Jesus Christ.

Being sent forth by the Holy Spirit, they were guided to the right places. When they arrived, the Holy Spirit had preceded them. He was there with them. He ordered their departure for the next appointment. When they left, He went with them, but He also remained to carry on the work.

June 7

Where the Spirit of the Lord Is, There Is Peace

Acts 15:25, 28

A burning issue had arisen in the Infant Church. The success of the evangelistic mission had brought about a disagreement. Many Gentiles were being converted to Christ. Some Jewish Christians, zealous for the law, took it upon themselves to promote the teaching that, for Gentiles to be included in the Church, they must be circumcised and obey the law of Moses. Self-appointed representatives went to Antioch and beyond to bring the Church into line.

Paul and Barnabas resisted the legalistic Pharisees. It was decided they should go to Jerusalem to submit the matter to the apostles and elders of the Church. The missionaries declared what God had done with them. Peter, being present, spoke on behalf of liberty for the Gentile Christians. He testified to what had happened under his ministry in the house of Cornelius a great while ago. They had received the Holy Spirit and their hearts were purified by faith. "We believe that through the grace of the Lord Jesus Christ we shall be saved, even as they" (v. 11).

In unity of spirit a decision was reached. James said this occurred when they were assembled in one accord, and it seemed good to the Holy Ghost and to us. This Spirit-inspired decision saved the Church of Jesus Christ from being another Judaistic sect such as the Pharisees. It gave a pattern of liberty in unity. It has been the inspiration for the motto, "In essentials unity, in nonessentials liberty, in all things charity."

June 8

Sanctified Disagreement

Acts 15:39-40

As certain as sanctified Christians are human, they will have differences. It is probable that they will have agreement on fundamental issues. But in personal and practical matters, they may differ frequently.

Barnabas had been a great friend to Paul, who recognized his benefactor gratefully. Their labors and journeys had been abundant and rewarding. They seemed to complement one another. Hardship and persecution had only drawn them closer together.

The time came, however, when they took opposite positions about a point of personal concern. They were about to begin a second missionary journey. The question arose whether John Mark should accompany them. For some reason, he had turned back on the previous tour of duty. Paul thought he should not be given opportunity to go again. Barnabas urged that John Mark, his cousin, should have a second chance. They were firm in their views. They went different directions. but their devotion to the Lord and His calling was constant.

It seems certain that Barnabas was right in the end. Paul came to the admission long after the separation. He said, "Take Mark, and bring him with thee: for he is profitable to me for the ministry" (2 Tim. 4:11). Love and patience usually win.

The best part of the story is that there were two missionary adventures instead of one. Both were fruitful. Wherein God does not rule, He overrules to gain the glory.

June 9

The Haves and the Have Nots

Acts 16:9-10

To those who are led of the Holy Spirit, closed doors mean other doors will open. God does not lead to frustration. Faith may be tested by delays, but God will show the way. Paul and his companions had Asia in view. The Holy Spirit forbade them. The obvious alternative was Bithynia. The Holy Spirit did not allow them to enter. For a brief time they traveled, not knowing their eventual destination. Then came the vision in the night. A man of Macedonia was pleading, "Come over and help us."

That was the call of desperate need. With confidence, Paul and his coworkers concluded that this was the open door of great opportunity. They knew now why the other doors were closed to them. Their confidence was so firm that even many stripes and the dark inner prison did not cause them to doubt the Macedonian call.

The pronouns of verse 10 have a deeper meaning than that Luke had joined the team at Troas. *Us* and *them* identifies the haves and the have nots. All of *us* who have the gospel are called to give it to *them* who have it not. If we fail, then they will die in the darkness. Not all can be full-time missionaries at home or abroad. But all who cannot go can send. There is a task for everyone who sees the vision and hears the cry of need. We, the haves, know the answer. We are debtors.

June 10

Voluntary Praise

Acts 16:25-26

Prayer and praise belong together. Prayer produces praise. It is an appropriate part of prayer. It is also an expression of faith that prayer is heard and answered. Without praise, prayer can easily turn into a way of just getting what we ask.

The prayer of Paul and Silas was mingled with praise to God. Their adverse circumstance had not turned them to self-pity. They were believing that God would turn their persecution into victory for the cause for which they had come to Philippi. At midnight, in the inner prison, with feet in stocks, lying on their bruised and bleeding backs, they prayed and sang praise to God. That was voluntary praise. It did not come from an ecstatic emotion. It was not a part of a planned service of praise and worship. It was praise when and where such song could be least expected.

Paul and Silas believed steadfastly that they were there by God's providence. They made the best of the situation. I can imagine they sang at least the first verse of the 27th psalm. "The Lord is my light and my salvation; whom shall I fear? the Lord is the strength of my life; of whom shall I be afraid?" They were not careful to subdue their voices. The prisoners heard them sing and God heard them pray. They did not pray for an earthquake; the earthquake was God's idea. And it did more than bring release to God's servants. It resulted in a church made up of the elite, wealthy Lydia; the jailor and his family; and a slave girl. All classes were included.

June 11

The Entrance of the Word

Acts 17:11-12a

The Psalmist spoke for men of all generations when he said, "The entrance of thy words giveth light" (119:130). The greatest hindrance to the success of the gospel has always been closed minds. Whenever the Good News has penetrated the shield of prejudice, it has won the day.

Many Jews in Thessalonica reached their negative conclusions because their minds were made up before they ever heard the message. Paul "reasoned with them out of the Scriptures, opening and alleging, that Christ must needs have suffered, and risen again from the dead; and that this Jesus, whom I preach unto you, is Christ" (vv. 2-3). And some believed. But the Jews which believed not aroused the rabble. They set the city in an uproar. They expelled the preachers, but they did not destroy the faith of those who believed unto salvation.

Upon his arrival in Berea, Paul found even the Jews were more open-minded. "They received the word with all readiness of mind, and searched the scriptures daily, whether those things were so." Therefore many of them believed. At no time in the history of Christianity has the gospel message received universal acceptance. But to those of receptive mind it has been the power of God unto salvation. The seed that falls on the good ground of an open mind bears blessed fruit in transformed lives.

Prejudice is aggressive and destructive. The Jews of Thessalonica went to Berea and stirred up the people. They rejected light and sought to blind the eyes of others too.

June 12

The God Unknown

Acts 17:23

In some respects the conditions under which Paul preached in Athens were widely different than those in which we preach today. In other respects there are striking similarities. He stood before the supreme court of that ancient city famed for its literature, its superior intelligence, and its great philosophers. He preached to people who worshiped in temples dedicated to the pagan deities of Greek mythology and to those whose gods were made of wood, stone, gold, or silver by men's hands. Paul took his text from one of their altars which bore the inscription "To the Unknown God." He said, "This God whom you acknowledge is unknown to you; He is the One I declare unto you."

In an enlightened civilization, idols made by human hands are scorned. Science has swept away the myths by which the Athenians were enthralled. We preach in churches dedicated to the worship of the God of whom Paul preached. He is spiritual, not material. He is the One who gives to all life and breath and all things.

There are many members of Christian churches, however, who worship a God unknown. Their religion is a formal profession. They have no personal knowledge of God. They are conformed to this world. Their ethical practice is in bold contradiction to the teachings of Jesus. Their faith does not go beyond the acceptance of pious platitudes and meaningless cliches.

Paul declared to the Athenians that God is "not far from every one of us: for in him we live, and move, and have our being" (vv. 27-28). This faith we declare today.

140

June 13

God's Word of Encouragement

Acts 18:9-10

There was a great work to be done in Corinth. It was a city steeped in sin. Its pagan temples were centers of vice. Its population was cultured but corrupt. Paul had come with the message of redemption through faith in Christ. He was starting to see some fruit for his labors.

It was then God spoke to Paul by a vision in the night, saying, "Be not afraid, but speak, and hold not thy peace: for I am with thee, and no man shall set on thee to hurt thee: for I have much people in this city." God did not say the victory would be easily won. But He did promise Paul protection and a harvest of souls. The voice of God to Paul was the deciding factor. The result was a strong, continuing church in that place of such great need.

It may be said that it proved to be a problem church. The problems gave Paul occasion to deal with them for the benefit of that church and all that have ever been.

Consider how impoverished we would be if we were without the 13th chapter of 1 Corinthians with its praise of love, or the 15th with its great argument for the resurrection. Then consider the loss if we had not the message of consolation, comfort, and assurance contained in 2 Corinthians. God spoke to Paul and he obeyed.

June 14

The Word of God Is Powerful

Acts 19:20

In Ephesus, Paul confronted almost every conceivable form of opposition. There was the great temple dedicated to the worship of Diana. The Ephesians assumed all Asia and the world worshiped their goddess. Those committed to false gods are seldom easy to change.

The Jews, with their deep-seated prejudices, were there too. Paul preached to them until many were hardened.

The Greek intellectuals were there. Paul believed that the gospel would stand all the tests that human intelligence could propose. Therefore he taught daily in the school of Tyrannus for two years.

Those who sought in hypocrisy to counterfeit the gospel that Paul preached were there. The pretenders fled, naked and wounded.

Those obsessed with love of material prosperity were there. Those who turned to Christ brought their curious arts and books together and burned them. Demetrius and the idol makers saw their craft in danger. They started an uproar and a riot involving a multitude.

It was in that situation that Paul preached. Upon arrival in Ephesus he found certain disciples who knew only John's baptism. Paul preached Christ unto them. They were baptized in the name of the Lord Jesus. Then Paul laid his hands on them and the Holy Spirit came on them. All the men were about 12.

Through 12 Spirit-filled men the Word of God mightily grew and prevailed. "This continued [for] two years; so that all they which dwelt in Asia heard the word of the Lord Jesus, both Jews and Greeks" (v. 10). A few can become a multitude.

June 15

Bound in Spirit

Acts 20:22-23

A few times in a life span the Spirit-filled, Spirit-led Christian may feel that he must obey the mandate of the Spirit within, even if no man approves. Paul was listening to the Spirit of God. The result was a strong conviction which compelled him to obey. His will was to do the will of God at all cost.

All he had received was by the grace of God. Therefore, he must give as he had received. The compulsion within the mind and soul of the apostle was the command of love. He said, "The love of Christ compelled me." It was akin to the word of Jesus, "I must work the works of him that sent me" (John 9:4). That inward imperative is deep within the soul of all committed Christians. Entire sanctification means total obedience to the Father's will.

Neither Paul nor you nor I can see all that obedience includes. But obedience is unquestioning. Paul said, "[I do not know] the things that shall befall me [in Jerusalem]: save that the Holy Spirit witnesseth in every city, saying that bonds and afflictions abide me. But none of these things move me, neither count I my life dear unto myself, so that I may finish my course with joy."

"None of these things" included bonds and afflictions, silver or gold, the advice and pleading of his friends. To their entreaty he replied, "I am ready not to be bound only, but also to die at Jerusalem for the name of the Lord Jesus" (21:13).

June 16

Injurious Surmises

Acts 21:28-29

Paul was in Jerusalem for the last time. The brethren received him gladly, but the problem was how to handle the report that he was preaching that Jews as well as Gentiles did not need to have their male children circumcised or keep the law of Moses.

The apostle produced the proof that he did walk orderly himself and called upon all Jews to do likewise. But the Jews of Asia stirred up all the people and laid hands on Paul. They cried out, "Men of Israel, help: This is the man, that teacheth all men every where against the people, and the law, and this place: and further brought Greeks also into the temple, and hath polluted this holy place."

Their accusation was based on a *supposition*. They had seen Paul with Trophimus, an Ephesian, on the streets of Jerusalem and supposed he had taken him into the Temple. For such surmised offence they sought to kill Paul.

The hostile mob was incited to violence by a supposition.

There is no way to measure or estimate the damage that has come to the lives of Christians and the Church because people have based their conclusions on injurious surmises. Paul's life would have been snuffed out by the angry mob without a shred of evidence against him, had not God come to his rescue by the intervention of the Roman occupation army. Many good people have suffered character assassination by reports based on suppositions.

June 17

A Christian Citizen

Acts 22:24-28

Paul's claim of Roman citizenship was both valid and valuable. The Sacred Record does not reveal how it came about, but his own testimony was never refuted or even questioned. He could say, "I was born free."

Paul did not necessarily believe that all the Roman government did was in accord with God's will. He did believe that cooperation with the inevitable was the better part of wisdom. Such reasoning underlies the doctrine of Paul as expressed in Rom. 13:1. He wrote, "Let every soul be subject unto the higher powers. For there is no power but of God: the powers that be are ordained of God."

There is no proof that Paul believed the emperor or his representatives were just in all their administration of government. But he was a loyal subject. Therefore, he believed and preached that all who enjoyed the rights of citizenship should accept the duties of citizens. To Timothy he wrote, "I exhort therefore, that, first of all, supplications, prayers, intercessions, and giving of thanks, be made for all men; for kings, and for all that are in authority" (1 Tim. 2:1-2). With such an attitude the apostle had a right to claim protection, justice, and courteous treatment from Roman officials; and he received those considerations on many occasions.

Christian citizenship calls for obedience to law. Let no Christian minimize the value of citizenship in a nation which is pledged to ideals of liberty and justice for all.

144

June 18

A Christian Under Provocation

Acts 23:1-5

By birth, by training, and by conviction Paul was a zealous Pharisee. When he became a Christian, he was no less zealous than he had been before. Having rescued Paul from the infuriated mob that would have killed him, the chief captain learned that he was a Roman. Therefore he sought to give Paul a fair hearing before his accusers. He was called before the Sanhedrin.

Paul bore a sincere, humble, and inoffensive testimony to any with open mind. The command that he be smitten on the mouth came as a shocking order from the high priest. Paul's retort is understandable even though inappropriate. His pronouncement was deserved and it came to pass as he said. Ananias was deposed not long after this incident and assassinated by Jewish zealots a few years later.

The exact meaning of Paul's response to the protest of the bystanders is not clear. It seems probably that what he meant was, "I spoke in haste and was unconscious for the moment that I was speaking to the representative of God." He acknowledged that he knew what was written (Exod. 22:28). In a becoming manner, he admitted his error without denying the truth of what he said.

All this is to remind all Christians that the best of men in moments of provocation may speak, in haste, words that may need forgiveness by God and man. Holiness of heart does not imply perfect control at all times. It does mean humility of spirit and readiness to admit wrong.

June 19

Convicted but Not Converted

Acts 24:25

Felix was unfit to be a judge of men. He was without any sense of moral values. In his private life, he was ruled by his sensuous passions. He had enticed Drusilla when she was

145

another man's wife. He was a favor-courting politician, willing to do the Jews a pleasure to gain their good will. His leniency to Paul was an admission that there was no serious charge against him. The worst transgression for a man in public service is willingness to be bought. Felix was not only ready to accept bribes, he sought the chance to do so.

When Paul stood before Felix as an accused prisoner, he made his own defense, of necessity. In that testimony he wove in a word which stung the dormant conscience of the governor. He said, "Herein do I exercise myself, to have always a conscience void of offence toward God, and toward men" (v. 16). Felix must have winced when he heard those pungent words.

Paul came to grips with the seared conscience of the governor. He did not make direct charges against him by calling out the sins of which he was guilty. But he did what must be done if sinful men are to be slain with conviction. "He reasoned of righteousness, temperance, and judgment to come."

Felix procrastinated. He missed his moment for action. He called Paul again and again, but for ulterior motives. He never repented. He suffered loss of honor, position, and his soul.

June 20

God's Overruling Providence

Acts 25:10-12

The risen Christ told Paul, "I have appeared unto thee for this purpose, to make thee a minister and a witness" (26:16). Even as He made known His purpose, He gave also a promise to deliver him from the people (the Jews) and from the Gentiles. Whenever God makes known His purpose, He always gives a promise. As completely as anyone yields his will to God's purpose, so completely does God keep His promise. Paul fully obeyed the heavenly vision; therefore, God kept His promise.

While in Jerusalem with the threat of death hanging over him, in the night the Lord stood by him and said, "Be of good cheer, Paul: for as thou hast testified of me in Jerusalem, so must thou bear witness also at Rome" (23:11). Thus was God's purpose and God's promise reaffirmed. Paul knew his work was not done.

Both Felix and Festus evaded their responsibility to set Paul free even though they knew there were no valid charges against him. Therefore, when Paul saw his opportunity to get to Rome had come, he said, "I stand at Caesar's judgment seat, where I ought to be judged . . . I appeal unto Caesar." Again he was claiming his rights as a Roman citizen. Festus, knowing that he had shirked his duty, had no choice but to say, "Hast thou appealed to Caesar? unto Caesar shalt thou go." Both the purpose and the promise of God were fulfilled. The servant and prisoner of Christ was soon on his way to Rome.

June 21

Consider the Goads

Acts 26:14

It is the Holy Spirit who convicts men of sin. Nevertheless the Spirit uses various means to goad the conscience of man.

Some contend that the conversion of Saul was an instantaneous act of God without preliminary preparation. Others believe that God had been dealing with him for some time, especially during the desert journey from Jerusalem to Damascus. The isolation of the desert was conducive to reflection. And now came this blinding light, this voice from heaven, this searching question from Jesus of Nazareth. This was but the climax of what had been surging through the soul of a man who was honest even though mistaken.

Saul knew the Law. He also knew it was inadequate. It is possible that Saul had some time seen Jesus when He was on earth. He could not forget what he saw and heard. It is almost certain that he had heard the advice of Gamaliel when he said to the council, "Take heed to yourselves what ye intend to do as touching these men. . . . for if . . . this work . . . be of God,

147

ye cannot overthrow it" (5:35, 38-39). Saul must have reasoned, If Gamaliel is right, I am wrong. Saul had seen the Christians suffer shame for Jesus' name. At least he had seen Stephen die while he consented to his death. That radiant face and that prayer were impossible to forget. These goads helped bring to a climax the work of God's Spirit, and the raging enemy of Christ and the Christians surrendered, saying, "Lord, what wilt thou have me to do?" (9:6).

June 22

Treacherous Winds

Acts 27:13-14

Paul was now on board ship as a prisoner ticketed for Rome. The ship had arrived at a place called The Fair Havens. Paul counselled the centurion to winter there. But on a day "when the south wind blew softly," they weighed anchor and set sail. Often a season of bad weather is preceded by a day that seems especially fair. Similar times occur when worldly-minded people are led to launch their lives on a course that seems sure to lead to fame and fortune.

Those in charge of Paul's ship sought to sail close to the shore of Crete to play it safe. This too is a pattern often followed by those of world-ward disposition. None take the path that leads to hell as a voluntary choice. C. S. Lewis has said, "It does not matter how small the sins are, provided their cumulative effect is to edge the man away from the Light into Nothing. Murder is no better than cards, if cards can do the trick. Indeed the safest way to hell is the gradual one."

Everyone knows a fair, warm day may precede a stormy blast. The ship had not gone far until there arose a tempestuous wind. Fearing that ever-present peril of sailing near shore, Luke records that they lowered the sails "and so were driven." The ship was at the mercy of the raging sea. How many have sailed from the fair haven when the south wind blew softly and have been caught in the merciless storm, driven beyond control!

148

June 23

God Is Present in the Storm

Acts 27:21-25

For many days the storm had been raging. With neither sun nor stars to guide them, the crew and all the passengers were gripped with fear and stricken with seasickness. They were fasting, and Paul was praying. God heard and answered his prayer with such assurance that Paul began again to speak to the crewmen. He had heard words of good cheer from God. He wanted them to believe in his God whom he served. It was not for himself alone that he had prayed and received an answer. He had prayed that all 276 on board the ship would be spared, and God had given him assurance that not one should be lost, only the ship.

Paul's faith shines out clear and strong while the storm is still raging. Fair-weather Christians are hardly worthy of the name. It takes no faith to believe when all signs are favorable. Paul declared his faith to all who heard him. "Wherefore, sirs, be of good cheer: for I believe God, that it shall be even as it was told me."

From that time fellow prisoners, passengers, and crew stood in awe and listened to the man who showed no sign of fear. Then the prisoner advised all to eat some food, and he took bread and gave thanks to God. When he demonstrated his faith by eating, they were all of good cheer and began to eat. The next day they all escaped safe to land. Faith is the victory!

June 24

Thanksgiving Inspires Courage

Acts 28:15

Mighty conquerors had returned to Rome over the Appian Way, bringing captives as proof of their triumphs. Now a prisoner came who was the greatest conqueror of them all. In fact, he was more than conqueror. Their works have perished and their names are forgotten. The work of Paul the prisoner lives on. He is immortal. "He belongs to the ages."

Paul probably had misgivings about the reception which would be given him in Rome. How his heart must have leaped for joy when the first welcoming delegation met him 40 or more miles away from the city and again when a second group came at least 30 miles on foot to bid him welcome.

Such heartwarming demonstrations caused the great apostle to give thanks to God. He had been delivered from death in the sea. The sting of a deadly serpent had been made a witness to barbarous people. The healing, helping ministry along the way was reassurance that God was with him. And now seeing friendly faces and feeling the warmth of kindred spirits opened up a fountain of thanksgiving in his soul.

Gratitude for past and present blessings always inspires courage for the conflicts of the tomorrows. Paul, under guard, dwelt two whole years in his own hired house and received all that came unto him. His guards and attendants heard, believed, and gave the message to others even in the palace. Centuries later, Christianity became the religion of the Empire. The prisoner was at last the conqueror.

June 25

Scarlet Sins—White as Snow

Isa. 1:18

In the meaning of the name Isaiah, "the eternal God is salvation," is found the theme of his prophecy. There are stern pronouncements of judgment. But George L. Robinson wrote, "Isaiah never promised a woe without adding a corresponding promise."

The earlier verses of this chapter lodge solemn indictment against Israel. Isaiah declared God's message, "I have nourished and brought up children, and they have rebelled against me. . . . they have forsaken the Lord, they have provoked the Holy One of Israel unto anger . . . Why should ye be stricken any more? Ye will revolt more and more . . . Except . . . [for] a very small remnant, we should have been as Sodom" (2, 4-5, 9).

Having described their moral degeneracy, Isaiah points up the futility of their formal religious ceremonies and sacrifices. God, according to the prophet, was saying, "To what purpose is the multitude of your sacrifices unto me? . . . when ye spread forth your hands, I will hide mine eyes from you: yea, when ye make many prayers, I will not hear" (11, 15). The temple-treading priests shared the rebuke of the Holy One of Israel. He calls upon all to put away the evil of their doings and learn to do well.

To all God gives a blessed invitation. "Come now, and let us reason together." Then follows the great promise of salvation. "Though your sins be as scarlet, they shall be as white as snow; though they be red like crimson, they shall be as wool."

Thank God for this foregleam of the gospel. It is the message for this day.

June 26

Isaiah's Vision of God

Isa. 6:1

The God of Isaiah's vision was transcendent. He was high and lifted up. He was exalted above the heavens. Before His throne the seraphim bowed in reverence with wings covering their faces. They realized their creaturehood and covered their feet in humility. They acknowledged their submission, for they were poised ready to fly in obedience to the will of their Creator. The Lord of Hosts inhabits eternity. The heaven of heavens cannot contain Him. The whole earth is full of His glory. "The heavens declare the glory of God; and the firmament sheweth his handywork. Day unto day uttereth speech, and night unto night sheweth knowledge" (Ps. 19:1-2).

The God Isaiah saw was immanent. He was active in the affairs of men and nations. It was in the year King Uzziah died that Isaiah saw the Lord. The prophet had great respect for the king who had ruled so long and so well. But he saw that same king stricken with leprosy because his heart was lifted up with pride. Uzziah in human frailty had fallen and was dead.

God was alive, infallible, active, and ruling in the life of the nation. God is today the supreme Ruler. His kingdom of righteousness shall prevail.

The God of Isaiah's vision was holy. The seraphim sang in antiphonal choirs, "Holy, holy, holy is the Lord of hosts." Isaiah was a new man. The vision transformed Isaiah. He saw God and he saw himself. His "Woe is me!" is followed by "Here am I." It is ever thus.

June 27

The Prophet Sees Himself

Isa. 6:5

He who stands to preach to others should understand himself. It is still more important to see himself as God sees him. For a man of God the searchlight turned upon himself is the way to self-discovery.

The revelation came to Isaiah when he saw the holiness of God. If such blinding vision of the holy God is not given to men in general, there is a revelation of God in Jesus, "the Word made flesh." In Him we see the glory of God's holy being. Isaiah saw himself against the backdrop of God's holiness. I see my true self as I stand beside the one perfect Man, the Man Christ Jesus.

In the presence of the splendid whiteness of the holy God the prophet cried, "Woe is me! for I am . . . a man of unclean lips, and I dwell in the midst of a people of unclean lips." When one has seen his own woeful uncleanness, he can in humble honesty say, "I am undone . . . and I dwell in the midst of a people of unclean lips."

It was not defilement by contamination from the society of which he was a member. His uncleanness was not acquired by a contagion. It came spueing out of the depth of his own inner foulness. He was confessing the sin that dwelt within him. Jeremiah bewailed, "The heart is deceitful above all things . . . who can know it?" (17:9). Before the cure for the sinful nature is known, the depth of one's own depravity must be realized and confessed.

June 28

The Purifying Fire

Isa. 6:6-7

God does not leave a yearning soul under the woe of condemnation. When he confesses his sinfulness, God soon shows him that there is cleansing by His refining fire. God sent one of the singing seraphs with a live coal in his hand which he had taken with the tongs from off the altar. He laid it upon Isaiah's mouth, saying, "Lo, this hath touched thy lips; and thine iniquity is taken away, and thy sin purged."

Isaiah lived in advance of his day. Pentecost was yet to come in fulfillment of prophecy. Nevertheless, Isaiah's vision of the grace of God so inspired his faith that he reached up and touched the faith line. His iniquity was taken away and his sin purged.

This experience of total cleansing is the universal need of man. It is provided through the Blood that was shed on Calvary. It is effected by the coming of the Holy Spirit who is like fire. It was a special dispensation to Isaiah. It is for us all today.

Some may suppose that the fullness of the sanctifying Spirit is given to those who have a distinctive calling and service to perform. But everyone from master to servant is defiled by inward sin and has need of cleansing, that he may fill his place in life to the glory of God. Then let him reach out to receive what God will give by the ministry of His Spirit— a heart cleansed from all sin and filled with love divine.

June 29

Obedient to God's Call

Isa. 6:8

Having seen the adequacy of the grace of God to meet his own deep need, it was natural that the prophet should behold the world of sinful men around him. Therefore Isaiah heard the voice of the Lord saying, "Whom shall I send, and who will go for us?" The spontaneous reply was "Here am I; send me." This is the invariable response of a Spirit-filled Christian. There is always a readiness to fill the place God has for him. This strong impulse will need to be directed into service according to God's will. Then opportunity and capability will harmonize in complete fulfillment.

God made it clear to Isaiah that he was to perform his duty faithfully regardless of whether his message was received or rejected. Faithful performance does not imply that there will be universal acceptance. Even Jesus "came unto his own, and his own received him not" (John 1:11).

Isaiah, like many given a crushing burden, said, "Lord, how long?" The reply was, in substance, as long as there is anyone to whom to preach. Even total rejection did not bring release from the divine commission. There is no point at which a soldier of the Cross can surrender.

Nevertheless God did not leave Isaiah. He promised the return and restoration of a remnant. God will always have a people. Your labor is not in vain in the Lord.

June 30

The Way of Holiness

Isa. 35:8

In the Book of Isaiah is found some of the most inspiring and beautiful poetry that has ever been written. One of his greatest poems is the 35th chapter. In it Isaiah sees the fulfillment of the promises made to the patriarchs, God's people dwelling in peaceful habitations in a land prosperous and productive. His vision is far more glorious than anything history records in that restoration.

Christ ushered in an era in which the eyes of the blind were opened, the ears of the deaf were unstopped, the lame leaped, and the tongue of the dumb sang. In His continuing kingdom on earth He cast up an highway over which His sanctified people would journey to the land of pure delight.

154

Pilgrims enter this higher way of holiness by making a full and final consecration of all they have and are to the fulfillment of God's perfect will in them. They pursue the way with a dependable sense of direction. They are not lured to the byways and detours by the siren song of worldly pleasure. They have blessed assurance of protection from contamination by the unclean and from ravenous beasts that lurk along the way.

Those who travel this way of holiness are under compulsion of a mission. There is a vast, howling wilderness of sin to subdue. There is a barren desert to reclaim from the power of evil. Christ can and will make all things new. These pilgrims will come to their eternal home with songs of everlasting joy upon their heads. They shall be home with the Lord forever.

July 1

"Comfort Ye My People"

Isa. 40:1

The first section of the Book of Isaiah is primarily a message of judgment with promises of salvation. The second section is a message of comfort with words of warning.

Here this man of far vision is promising a better day for God's covenant people. Their warfare would be accomplished and their iniquity pardoned. That they had received of the Lord's hand double for all their sins is illustrated by an ancient custom among debtors and creditors. One caught with debts too many and too great for him to pay, might post a list of his obligations. This was in effect a plea for mercy. His creditor or a benevolent friend might see his plight. He could fold the sheet on which the list was written, thus covering the debts, and sign a promise to pay all. Isaiah was proclaiming pardon for the sins of a penitent people. This is what God has done for all contrite, believing sinners. "Jesus paid it all."

Isaiah also proclaimed comfort by his declaration that "the word of our God shall stand for ever" (v. 8). There is no fickleness or caprice with God. He is not like the grass that withers or the flower that fades.

155

Again the prophet speaks comfort: "He shall feed his flock like a shepherd: he shall gather the lambs with his arm, and carry them in his bosom, and shall gently lead those that are with young" (v. 11). The Almighty Creator is at the same time the tender, compassionate Shepherd. He leads and feeds the flock.

July 2

Strength Increased

Isa. 40:31

The greatness of God is beyond human understanding. The mind of man is incapable of spanning eternity. The omnipotence of God is beyond the comprehension of the finite mind. Man has limited creativity. God is Creator of earth and all that lives upon it. This is the work of God's fingers, and by His will all is kept in perfect balance. Without His supervision and support there would be total chaos.

This God, infinite in wisdom, eternal in being, almighty in power, has knowledge and love of all the more than 4 billion persons who live on this planet. There is no searching of His understanding.

He understands when all others misunderstand. He knows our weakness, our failure, our burden, yea, all our need. He passes over our mistakes and pardons our sins. He never grows tired nor does He sleep. His ears are never closed to our call. His loving heart is always inclined to compassion, mercy, and love.

God is never weary with our coming to Him with our problems. He wants His children to be men in understanding, but He delights to have them depend on Him. "He giveth power to the faint; and to them that have no might he increaseth strength" (v. 29).

The secret of receiving His strength is in waiting upon the Lord, waiting in full readiness to obey His voice when He speaks. All who wait will have strength to "mount up with wings as eagles"; to "run, and not be weary"; to "walk, and not faint."

156

July 3

The Vindication of the Righteous

Isa. 54:17

The righteous servant of God is indestructible. His vindication by a holy God is as certain as the chastisement of the transgressor. Those who devise evil against him will either be turned to confusion or changed into defenders.

This does not mean that the righteous man is never misunderstood or that he will never be outnumbered and defeated. Jesus said, "The servant is not greater than his lord. If they have persecuted me, they will also persecute you" (John 15:20). The righteous servant of God is sure to clash swords with evildoers in an ungodly society. He cannot escape the battle, and in the moment of conflict he may suffer defeat and humiliation. Nevertheless, in the final showdown, right will triumph over wrong. The righteous man takes more comfort in his defeat than he would in sharing the temporary victory of wrongdoers. The cause for which he gave his life will win the decision at the bar of the infallible Judge.

Jesus Christ, the personification of truth and goodness, died at the hands of evil accusers and a cringing coward, but the grave could not keep its prey. He arose from the dead. He will pronounce righteous judgment: "Depart from me," and "Come, ye blessed of my Father" (Matt. 25:41, 34).

God has promised to deliver the righteous from the strife of tongues. They may not always exercise perfect judgment, and they may err in practice; but they live with a clear conscience, which in itself is sweet consolation. Their defense is sure.

July 4

The Secret of Peace and Power

Isa. 48:18

At Sinai God began to make the chosen family into a nation. He said, "Keep my covenant, then ye shall be a [special] treasure unto me above all people." The people answered, "All

157

that the Lord hath spoken we will do" (Exod. 19:5, 8). God spoke the terms of the covenant—the Ten Commandments.

In the text for today Isaiah gives a reminder of the covenant. Through nearly six centuries Israel had transgressed times without number. These solemn words of the prophet recall the warning of Moses. He said, "If thou shalt hearken diligently unto the voice of the Lord thy God, to observe and to do all his commandments . . . [he] will set thee on high above all nations of the earth . . . But . . . if thou wilt not hearken unto . . . his commandments . . . curses shall come upon thee" (Deut. 28:1, 15).

Here then is warning of judgment as well as a reminder of the covenant.

When Abraham Lincoln was on his way to Washington for his first inauguration, he paused in Trenton, N.J., to make an address. His subject was "Almost a Chosen Nation." The United States of America and any other nation that will accept the Ten Commandments can be almost a chosen nation. The peril of any country is the enemy within. Obedience to God's commandments promises peace like a river and righteousness like the waves of the sea.

This word of the prophet is a lament. "O that thou hadst." It is like Jesus' lament over Jerusalem: "If thou hadst known . . . the things which belong unto thy peace!" (Luke 19:42).

July 5

The Gospel According to Isaiah

Isa. 55:1

Isaiah has been called the gospel prophet. It is true that in his message he anticipated the Good News of the New Testament. In the 55th chapter he proclaims the principles of the evangelical faith. It is a universal invitation. It is without money and without price.

In describing the Suffering Servant and what He provided by His death on the Cross, the prophet said, "He was wounded for our transgressions, he was bruised for our iniquities: the

158

chastisement of our peace was upon him; and with his stripes we are healed" (53:5). A well-known scholar has said, "The profoundest remarks upon the meaning of Calvary are not to be found in the New Testament." Truly they are in the 53rd chapter of Isaiah.

Another great evangelical truth is announced in our text. "Come ye to the waters . . . come ye, buy, and eat; yea, come, buy wine and milk." In Isaiah's prophecy water is always a symbol of God's presence. His invitation is to come and drink of that life-giving stream of salvation. A drink from this fountain that never runs dry will bring new life and complete cleansing of the sin-filled heart of man.

Milk is for nourishment. The newborn grow thereby. They come to maturity in Christlikeness.

Wine is to gladden the spirit of man. The gospel helps him carry his cross with a smile.

The gospel preached by Isaiah was also evangelistic. He called upon those who heard, to seek the Lord *now*. Those who respond receive mercy and abundant pardon.

The gospel of Isaiah is both evangelical and evangelistic.

July 6

Messiah Is Come

Isa. 61:1

Of whom does the prophet speak? Jesus gives the answer in Luke 4:21-22: "This day is this scripture fulfilled in your ears. And all bare him witness, and wondered at the gracious words which proceeded out of his mouth."

It was the Lord God who had sent Him. And the Spirit was upon Him. The divine attestation to His Sonship and His anointing had come unmistakably at His baptism by John. The Holy Spirit had descended upon Him in bodily shape like a dove, and a voice from heaven said, "Thou art my beloved Son; in thee I am well pleased" (Luke 3:22). He had also passed the crucial test in the fierce conflict with Satan in the wilderness. Now in supreme confidence He could say, "The Lord

God hath anointed me," which was equivalent to saying, I am the Messiah, the Christ, sent from God.

Jesus came to fulfill a mission. He was the Savior, the answer to man's universal cry. Isaiah gave a preview in outline of what the ministry of the Messiah would be.

He did preach the gospel to the poor. He set the example for the Church to follow in all ages. Her mission is to the needy, the brokenhearted, the imprisoned, the enslaved. Jesus and those He chooses are to proclaim that the year of jubilee has come. It is the day of grace, the time of God's favor. This is the era of God's acceptance of unworthy men. The year of the redeemed has come.

July 7

Son of Man

Ezek. 2:1-2

When God addressed Ezekiel, He called him "Son of man." His name means "one whom God sustains," an appropriate designation for one whose message was directed to the "rebellious house of Israel." God told him that their faces were like flint but that He would make his face as adamant. Ezekiel was called to preach whether they would hear or forbear.

Ezekiel testified, "The heavens were opened, and I saw visions of God" (1:1). If he had not had a personal encounter with God, he could only speak as a man to other men. But Ezekiel could say, "Thus saith the Lord."

Ezekiel also said, "The spirit entered into me when he spake unto me, and set me upon my feet, that I heard him that spake unto me." He was full of divine energy. In the power of the Spirit, he spoke with authority.

God said also to Ezekiel, "Eat this roll, and go speak unto the house of Israel." The prophet responded, "Then did I eat it" (3:1, 3). He who speaks the word must digest it, assimilate it, and live it.

Ezekiel went to the captives. "I sat where they sat" (3:15). He identified himself with the people to whom he was sent. He listened in silence. He heard their confession and complaints. He assessed their attitudes. If the teachers and preachers today know firsthand the sins, the sorrows, the commitments, and the protests of those to whom they minister, their message will be relevant.

The Spirit entered into the prophet, saying, "Go, shut thyself within thine house" (3:24). There, alone, he heard God speak. Therefore he had a message from God.

July 8

"Ye Shall Be Clean"

Ezek. 36:25-27

Here is the greatest promise in the Book of Ezekiel. The prophet is speaking directly of the cleansing of those who would return to the land that had been promised to their fathers. They were to be cleansed from their filthiness and their idols.

But the complete fulfillment of this great prophecy came only when Messiah came. It is the promise of a double cure for sin.

A new heart is promised. The stony heart defiled by sin was to be taken away and a new heart given. Ezekiel prophesied the new birth, of which Jesus spoke to Nicodemus, saying "Ye must be born again" (John 3:7). Paul wrote, "If any man be in Christ, he is a new creature: old things are passed away; behold, all things are become new" (2 Cor. 5:17).

A new spirit within is also promised. It is cleansing of the polluted nature of man. Adam Clarke comments, "It is the truly cleansing water; the influences of the Holy Spirit typified by water; whose property is to cleanse, whiten, purify, refresh, render healthy and fruitful." With the cleansing comes the new spirit. "I will put my spirit within you, and cause you to walk in my statutes, and ye shall keep my judgments, and do them." Again quoting Adam Clarke, "Here is the salvation that is the birthright of every *Christian believer: the complete destruction of all sin in the soul, and the complete renewal of the heart;* no *sin* having any place *within,* and no *unrighteousness* having and place *without.*"

July 9

The Healing Waters

Ezek. 47:12

The contents of these 12 verses of the 47th chapter of Ezekiel are capable of differing interpretations. Those who would literalize must certainly acknowledge that there are some problems hard to solve. Adam Clarke offers four different possibilities. The one he seems to favor has much support from biblical scholars and from reason. This flowing stream of water is to be understood spiritually or typically. It shows the effusion of light and salvation by the outpouring of the Spirit of God under the gospel dispensation by which the knowledge of God spread throughout the earth. Therefore, this river that was small in its beginning became wider and deeper until the whole earth received blessing.

The stream had its source in the Temple which to believers in our time is the Church of Jesus Christ. It flows past the altar of sacrifice. It reaches into the desert areas of the world. There are the unbelieving and impenitent who will not receive the redeeming grace of God. Universal salvation is not promised, but abundant and eternal life is for whosoever believeth. There is forgiveness, cleansing, and wholeness for everyone.

There will be by-products of this mighty river of divine grace. By the river on this side and on that side shall grow all trees for food. And the fruit shall be for meat and the leaf thereof for medicine.

Where the healing waters flow, there is health and light. There is peace, hope, and love. There is life instead of death.

July 10

Self-discipline Pays Dividends

Dan. 1:8

Daniel and his three companions were far removed from parents and teachers who had instructed them in the faith and ethics of the Hebrews. They had been chosen to stand in the

162

king's palace and to learn his language and to do his bidding. They could lose his favor and their heads. They were offered the delicacies that came from the king's table. How could temptation to forget their early training, accept their fate, and make the most of it have been stronger? "But Daniel purposed in his heart that he would not defile himself with the portion of the king's meat, nor with the wine which he drank." There can be no doubt that his fellow captives held to the same convictions. It was a firm decision not to compromise.

It is possible for parents of our day to build into the character of their offspring some ideals, some steadfastness of purpose that will help them to stand for right and for the faith of their fathers. But the fathers and mothers must themselves be godly examples. Smoking, tippling, trifling-in-sex, lying, cheating, Sabbath-breaking parents do not rear their posterity to be loyal to biblical standards of conduct.

The firm but courteous refusal of Daniel and his compatriots was honored. They stood before the king fairer and fatter than all their fellows. Self-discipline still brings health, wisdom, and character; also, the confidence of men and the blessing of God.

July 11

Faith Tried by Fire

Dan. 3:16-18

Faith that depends upon the outcome of any contingency is mere speculation. True faith is unshaken confidence in God no matter what happens in the course of human events. The testimony to their faith by Shadrach, Meshach, and Abednego is in the words "But if not." They were saying, "No matter what the outcome of this ordeal by fire, we believe God."

Such unconditional belief in God never misses the reward. This illustrious trio were cast bound into a fire so hot it destroyed those who threw them in. The fire only burned the bonds. The haughty, furious king beheld a sight which brought him to his feet in astonishment, saying, "Did not we cast three men bound into the midst of the fire?" Receiving an affirmative answer, he said, "Lo, I see *four men loose,* walking in the midst of the fire, and *they have* no hurt; and the form of the fourth is like the Son of God." To the men in the furnace the king called, "Ye servants of the most high God, come forth" (vv. 24-26). Before, he was demanding they do homage to the golden image he had set up. All the officials and advisers to the king saw these men upon whom the fire had no power.

Now the king blessed God who delivered his servants; and he made a decree of condemnation upon anyone who should speak against the God of the Hebrews, "because there is no other God that can deliver after this sort" (v. 29). And the king promoted them.

July 12
"As He Did Aforetime"

Dan. 6:10

Daniel was not praying to his God in defiance of the edict of the king. Rather, he was doing what he had done with consistent regularity. Opening his window toward Jerusalem and bowing on his knees was proof that his faith was in the God of Israel.

He was not frantically praying in a crisis. He did not ask God to do to his enemies what they had plotted to do to him. He did not even ask God to deliver him from the den of lions. He was simply keeping up his daily devotions. If men have practiced prayer daily, it is a natural pattern of life. Grace for the trial is ministered of God to those who call in the moment of stress. The constant relation to the Heavenly Father guarantees all-sufficient grace in time of need.

Because Daniel was prayed up to date, he faced the ordeal of the lions' den calmly. He knew God was faithful. No matter what the ravenous beasts might do to him, it was well with his soul. Because this true and faithful servant of the Most High God had so consistently practiced the presence of God,

He was with him in the lions' den. Daniel did not gleefully rejoice when those who planned his ruin were the ones who provided a feast for the hungry lions. His reward came when King Darius said, "I make a decree, That in every dominion of my kingdom men tremble and fear before the God of Daniel" (v. 26).

July 13

A Man Greatly Beloved

Dan. 10:18-19

Daniel had been under a heavy burden for three full weeks. A heavenly messenger now addressed him as a man greatly beloved. Peace and strength flowed into his entire being.

Daniel had been given extraordinary wisdom. One king after another acclaimed his superiority, but he knew his dependence was upon God. He was preferred among the presidents and the princes because an excellent spirit was found in him.

Daniel was found faithful in all his duties. When those jealous officers of King Darius sought occasion to destroy him, the only complaint they could find against him was concerning his God.

Daniel did not gain the confidence of kings and the acknowledgment of faithfulness by his foes by clever evasions of the truth. He told King Nebuchadnezzar that the interpretation of his dream was what he could wish for his enemies. "They shall drive thee from men, and thy dwelling shall be with the beasts of the field, and they shall make thee to eat grass as oxen, and they shall wet thee with the dew of heaven, . . . till thou know that the most High ruleth in the kingdom of men" (4:25). He did not hesitate to say to Belshazzar, "Thou art weighed in the balances, and art found wanting. Thy kingdom is divided, and given to the Medes and Persians" (5:27-28).

Men of wisdom and humility whose only fault is concerning the law of their God, men of impeccable integrity, are still men greatly beloved.

July 14

"The Wise Shall Understand"

Dan. 12:10

Daniel was the most farseeing of all the prophets. It is clear that he saw visions of things to come to pass in the time of the end. These things have been given of God for a purpose. God has a design that is according to His sovereign will and His inscrutable wisdom. Many of those who have sought to literalize and specify times and seasons have been proven wrong. Those who have confessed their lack of knowledge, as well as those who have professed to know, will have complete understanding when we know as we are known.

Daniel said, "I heard, but I understood not: then said I, O my Lord, what shall be the end of these things? And he said, Go thy way, Daniel: for the words are closed up and sealed till the time of the end. . . . Blessed is he that waiteth" (vv. 8-9, 12).

But the purpose of God for those whom He has chosen is clear beyond a doubt. "Many shall be purified, and made white, and tried." God is preparing a people for himself who shall glorify Him in this life and enjoy His presence and fellowship forever. This is God's eternal purpose which He purposed in Christ Jesus.

God delights in a people who have proved themselves in the days of testing. Those who are Christ's know that in the furnace of fire there is grace to overcome. The trial develops strength of character and prepares for a fruitful ministry of encouragement to others. "The wise shall understand."

July 15

Love Is Reciprocal

Hos. 14:4

As God had taken His chosen people to himself, in like manner Hosea had in love taken Gomer into the exclusive covenant of marriage. As the awareness of the infidelity of his wife grew upon him, his love for her was tinged with unspeakable grief. But that love mingled with sadness never turned to bitterness and hatred. It was constant love that would not consent to give the unfaithful wife up to her adulterous lovers.

Gomer, in degredation, was taken to the slave market to be sold to the highest bidder. The husband of her youth was among those who were present for the auction. Hosea must have seen something familiar and something yet to love beneath the disheveled appearance of the woman offered for sale. In the hope and faith that restoration to virtue and beauty was possible, the lawful husband bought Gomer for what amounted to the price of a slave. After a proper time of purification, the prophet took his erring wife back to share his life and love forever.

Since God is holy, He could not condone sin. Nevertheless, He is the God of steadfast love. Therefore, to the sinning nation He would show mercy. From His heart overflowing with love came the grief-laden lament, "How shall I give thee up, Ephraim?" (11:8); and later came the promise, "I will heal their backsliding, I will love them freely."

Hosea is the prophet of grace. He proclaimed that God in holy love offers pardon to every penitent sinner.

July 16

Joel's Trumpet Blast

Joel 2:1 and 15

Joel's dominant theme was "The Day of the Lord." To him, the judgment was in its finality for an appointed time, but it was also a reality in God's day-by-day administration of justice. There is a harvest that follows the sowing in swift succession.

Joel cried, "Blow ye the trumpet in Zion, and sound an alarm in my holy mountain . . . for the day of the Lord cometh, for it is nigh at hand." The punishment that was to be inflicted by enemies was in fact permitted of God to bring His own people to repentance.

Joel for this cause said, "Therefore also now, saith the Lord, Turn ye even to me with all your heart . . . and rend your

167

heart, and not your garments, and turn unto the Lord your God . . . Who knoweth if he will return and repent, and leave a blessing behind him . . . ?" (vv. 12-14).

That such a dispensation of mercy might be realized, Joel sounded another trumpet call to assemble the people for fasting and prayer. The priests and the ministers were to weep between the porch and the altar. The prophet asked, "Wherefore should they say . . . Where is their God?" (v. 17).

Finally, Joel opens the door of hope. His trumpet sounds a note of promise. He says, "Fear not, O land; be glad and rejoice: for the Lord will do great things. . . . And ye shall know that I am in the midst of Israel, and that I am the Lord your God, and none else: and my people shall never be ashamed" (vv. 21, 27).

America, it is time to pray.

July 17

The Righteous Eat Their Fruit Also

Amos 9:14

Amos offered restoration and ample reward to all who kept the faith. "They shall build the waste cities, and inhabit them; and they shall plant vineyards, and drink the wine thereof; they shall also make gardens, and eat the fruit of them."

There is a day-by-day reward for the righteous. Satan never misses a payday. God is a more just and generous Master. He gives to him who labors in His vineyard all he earns and adds the generous portion that is bestowed by abundant grace.

Amos said, "Thus saith the Lord unto the house of Israel, Seek ye me, and ye shall live" (5:4). It is in this life also that the righteous are blessed. The life God promises is worth the living. For everything given up to walk with Him, treasures of far greater value are received.

At the end of every day there is blessed rest and assurance that the next day will be a continuation of the journey toward the ever more alluring goal. Life is never dull; it is full of exciting

168

adventure with the One who grows sweeter with every passing day.

When we have gone the last mile of the journey, the Companion who has made the path shine brighter unto the perfect day will say, "Inherit the kingdom prepared for you from the foundation of the world" (Matt. 25:34).

There will be an eternity to spend in the presence of the One with whom we have made the journey. Heaven above is a continuation of our heaven on earth.

July 18

God Watches Over His Own

1 Kings 17:13

The widow had told him that she was gathering two sticks to make a fire to prepare for herself and her son a morsel of bread with the last bit of meal and oil she had. Then they would die. But Elijah said, "Make me thereof a little cake *first.*" God had sent him with the word "I have commanded a widow woman there to sustain thee" (v. 9). He added to his request, "After make for thee and for thy son. For thus saith the Lord God of Israel, The barrel of meal shall not waste, neither shall the cruse of oil fail, until the day that the Lord sendeth rain."

The widow could have refused to give God's prophet what he asked. If she had, she and her son would have eaten that last meager meal and starved. The faith of Elijah stimulated her faith. She believed and obeyed. Therefore she fed the prophet and God supplied her need. Better be poor in resources and rich in faith than to be a millionaire without faith in God.

Because the widow believed and obeyed, she saw God in miracle-working power in the crisis which followed. Her son sickened and died. But God's man was there to pray for him, and he was restored to life and health. Those who trust and obey God can depend upon His faithfulness in all the succeeding crises of life. "He hath said, I will never leave thee, nor forsake thee" (Heb. 13:5).

169

July 19

God Answers

1 Kings 18:24

In the dramatic contest on Mount Carmel the fact that God answered the prayer of Elijah is the central focus. Those false prophets of Baal had everything in their favor, humanly speaking. There were many of them. Elijah was alone. They were in public favor. The God of Elijah had been rejected by the king and the masses. The most natural thing for Baal to do would be to answer by fire, for sun worship was included in this idolatry. For the God of Elijah to answer by fire was supernatural.

Elijah gave the contestants all day to cry, "O Baal, hear us," but there was no voice nor any answer. When the day was spent, Elijah quickly and confidently prepared the altar of 12 stones, 1 for each of the tribes of Israel, thus testifying to his faith in the God of his fathers. He laid the wood in order and placed the sacrifice upon it. Elijah ordered the altar with the wood and the sacrifice to be drenched with 12 barrels of water. He prayed a prayer of few words; it probably took him about 30 seconds to utter it. Then the fire fell and consumed the sacrifice. The people fell on their faces and said, "The Lord, he is the God" (v. 39).

The gods of the false prophets were silent because they were nonexistent. The God of Elijah answered because he is the living God. The God of Elijah lives and answers prayer.

July 20

Depression After Triumph

1 Kings 19:4

Elijah's great victory on Mount Carmel had lifted his spirit to the highest ecstasy. He prayed and there was sound of abundance of rain. As Ahab's chariot raced toward Jezreel, Elijah girded himself and ran before the king. No doubt Elijah thought a total victory had been won. But disillusionment awaited him. He learned that all the false prophets had not showed on Mount Carmel, that Jezebel had threatened his life, and that Ahab had been only superficially influenced. It was natural his spirit should sag after expending his vital energies so lavishly. No wonder he fled for his life.

Elijah is like the normal man in his flight to safety. From Beersheba he went a day's journey to a place of complete solitude. He knew he needed to be alone. His depression was so acute he sat under a broom tree and prayed to die. God had not forsaken His valiant servant. He knew Elijah needed rest for his exhausted body and a ministry of comfort for his depressed spirit.

While the lonesome prophet slept, an angel touched him and said, "Arise and eat." Elijah looked and there God provided a cake and a cruse of water. He ate and drank and lay down again to sleep. God knew what a weary, spent, and hungry man needed. He is the same today.

Elijah was no coward. After his strength and faith were renewed, he delivered another message of death and doom from God to Ahab and Jezebel. The steel in his blood and bone had returned.

July 21

"A Still Small Voice"

1 Kings 19:11-12

Elijah was not yet ready for the new battles he was to face. From the broom tree a day's journey from Beersheba he journeyed another 175 miles to Horeb. He went in the strength God had given him for 40 days and 40 nights.

Elijah was to have a meeting with God. God said to him, "Go forth, and stand upon the mount before the Lord." A strong wind rent the mountains; after the wind came an earthquake; after the earthquake, a fire; and after the fire, a still small voice. When Elijah heard the still small voice, he wrapped his face in his mantle in awesome reverence. God said, "What doest thou here, Elijah?" He replied, "I have been very jealous for the Lord God of hosts: because the children of Israel have forsaken thy covenant, thrown down thine altar; and slain thy prophets . . . and I, even I only, am left; and they seek my life, to take it away" (vv. 13-14).

God said, "Go, anoint Elisha to be prophet in your place. He shall carry on My work when you are gone." Then came a rebuke for Elijah and the pessimists for all time, and reassurance to those who believe God is still alive. God said, "I have yet 7,000 in Israel all the knees of which have not bowed unto Baal." There is salt in the earth, and a light shines in a dark world. God has not surrendered to evil.

July 22
A Plowman Becomes a Prophet

1 Kings 19:19

Elijah had an order from God to anoint Elisha to be prophet in his place. But Elisha must have had a word from the Lord too. If he hadn't, how would he have understood the strange action of Elijah? He might have reasoned, What does this weird act of the passing prophet mean? All Elijah had done was to pass in silence and throw his mantle on the shoulders of the plowman. God had so prepared the mind and spirit of Elisha that he knew this was confirmation of the call which had been ringing in his ears for many days.

Therefore the response was immediate and positive. He ran after Elijah. His request for a delay was not for postponement to an indefinite time. It was only to pay proper respect to parents, to set things in order on the farm, and bid his friends an affectionate farewell. Elijah accepted his terms without hesitation.

To Elisha it was no opportunity to procrastinate. He took action at once to accept the call of God. His commitment to the call was total and final. He said, I'll not need my oxen any more; I'll kill them, cook the meat, and make a feast for my

172

friends to announce to them that I'm leaving to respond to the will of God. And I will not be back. He used the yoke and the plow to make a fire and cook the meat for the feast. He left nothing to which to return. To him there was no turning back.

July 23

There Were Days of Preparation

2 Kings 2:9-12

Elisha arose and went after Elijah and ministered unto him.

The time for Elijah's translation was approaching. At Gilgal, Elijah said, "Tarry here, I pray thee; for the Lord hath sent me to Bethel." Elisha replied, "As the Lord liveth, and as thy soul liveth, I will not leave thee" (2:2). Gilgal means "round like a circle." Those who linger there go in circles all their lives.

At Bethel, Elijah again invited Elisha to tarry. He made the same reply. Bethel, the house of God, is not a residence. It is a place to go for worship. They two went to Jericho. Again Elisha was admonished to linger at Jericho, the City of Palms, a pleasure resort. He refused. They came to Jordan. Elijah wrapped his mantle together and smote the waters, and they parted and the two went over on dry ground.

The moments were tense with excitement. Elijah said to Elisha, "Ask what I shall do for thee, before I be taken away from thee." He replied, "Let a double portion of thy spirit be upon me." Elijah answered, "Thou hast asked a hard thing: . . . if thou see me when I am taken from thee, it shall be so."

Then came the final test. Swiftly a chariot and horses of fire passed between them as a distraction of the fixed gaze of Elisha. In spite of the swift-passing chariot Elisha's eyes were glued to Elijah. He saw his master go. Elijah's mantle fell at Elisha's feet.

July 24

The Prophet's Call Confirmed

2 Kings 2:13-14

The first time Elijah's mantle fell on the shoulders of Elisha, it was the confirmation of his call to be a prophet. Now the mantle falls again as Elijah was caught up into heaven. Elisha believed his request for the double portion was granted. With the mantle he smote the waters, saying, "Where is the Lord God of Elijah?" The waters parted and Elisha went over. The sons of the prophets at Jericho said, "The spirit of Elijah doth rest on Elisha."

Here was evidence that the power of God is not confined to one man or one generation of men. The enduement of God's Spirit is available to those who will completely dedicate their lives to the service of God.

Elisha was no duplicate of Elijah. But the mighty moving of God's Spirit in the ministry of the successor was no less convincing than it had been in the predecessor; He makes men adequate in their day.

Elisha knew that his master was gone, but he knew God was not gone. He was with him even as He had been with Elijah. Those students in Elijah's school were not sure where their master was gone. They wanted to send out a search party to seek for Elijah. Elisha said, "Ye shall not send." But when they insisted, he let them go to satisfy their questioning minds. They searched in vain for three days. Now they were convinced. God has the answer for *honest* questions in any generation.

July 25

Man's Reception
Conditions God's Giving

2 Kings 4:6

A young man in preparation for the prophetic office died, leaving his widow with his debts and two sons. A creditor was about to take the boys into slavery to satisfy his claims against the husband. This was legal in that day. They would continue in slavery until the year of jubilee.

The mother made her plight known to Elisha. Elisha said to the mother, "What do you have in the house?" She replied, "A pot of oil is all I have." Elisha said, "Go, borrow vessels from all your neighbors; borrow not a few. Then go into your house and shut the door and pour the oil from your pot into those vessels." The widow in simple faith and obedience followed the instructions of the prophet. When there were no more containers to receive it, "the oil stayed." It was enough to pay the creditors and enough to sustain her and her sons.

God is generous in giving. "Giving does not impoverish Him nor withholding make Him rich." Nevertheless man must have the faith to obey and to receive, or the bounty of God is withheld. If there is desire for saving grace, it is abundant and free. If there is hunger and thirst for righteousness, there is satisfying fullness. If there is faith for ability to do God's work, He is able to do exceeding abundantly above all we ask or think. Receiving is a condition for God's giving.

July 26

Contagious Holiness

2 Kings 4:8-9

There is attractiveness in the person who is holy. The profession of holiness may lead to a rigid sanctity that can become pharisaical and judgmental. This explains why some groups of so-called holiness people have remained small and ingrown. In their determined dedication to outward conformity they have not manifested the spirit of holiness. There is strength, beauty, and charisma in the sanctified, Spirit-filled Christian.

In the beginning of their acquaintance Elisha was a casual visitor in the home of the woman of Shunem. As his pauses to eat bread became more regular, the Shunammite woman said to her husband, "Behold now, I perceive that this is an holy man of God, which passeth by us continually."

175

They prepared a little room to be the prophet's chamber. In appreciation for this hospitality Elisha sought to do something for his benefactors. The prophet announced that according to the time of life she should embrace a son. The son was born and grew into youthful years. One day as he was in the field with the reapers, he apparently had a sunstroke and died.

Knowing that the man of God who had promised her the son could help her now, the Shunammite woman reported the child's death to Elisha. Elisha hurried to the home. By the miracle-working power of God the son was restored to life. The presence of God in a holy life produces charm and becoming grace. There is also power to do the impossible when the occasion demands it. Holiness works.

July 27

Honesty Rewarded by a Miracle

2 Kings 6:5-6

Elisha had succeeded Elijah as head of the schools of the prophets. Evidently one of them had outgrown its quarters. The students proposed to go to Jordan and take every man a beam and build an adequate place. They believed it would be a task soon accomplished if all did his share of the work. Elisha gave orders for them to proceed with the plan. And when invited, he went with them.

As one of the students was felling a beam, the axe head fell into the water. It appeared to be beyond recovery. The young man was consternated. His anxiety was greater, for he said, "Alas, master! for it was borrowed." It would have been bad enough to lose his own axe. But to lose a borrowed tool was far worse. It could not be returned to the owner. Those who borrow, whether an axe or a book, should, in good conscience, return the same to the lender.

Elisha inquired where the axe head had been lost. Then in a simple act of faith he threw a stick into the water, and the iron did swim. It is not the nature of iron to float. But God did the

176

miracle to relieve the stricken conscience of a man who knew what he had borrowed should be returned to the owner.

God will always approve and bless that person who keeps a clean, clear conscience.

July 28

Invisible Defenders

2 Kings 6:17

The Syrians were sending guerilla bands across Israel's borders to plunder and harass. Their plans were known and their purpose thwarted over and over again. The king became suspicious that a traitor was revealing his strategy to the king of Israel. Upon inquiry he was told that there was a prophet in Israel who told his king "the words that thou speakest in thy bedchamber" (v. 12).

Whereupon the king of Syria sent an army to fetch one bald-headed prophet. They located Elisha in Dothan. A great host with horses and chariots surrounded the city under cover of darkness. Early in the morning Elisha's servant discovered them. He cried, "Alas, my master! how shall we do?" The prophet replied, "Fear not: for they that be with us are more than they that be with them." The man of God then prayed, "Lord, I pray thee, open his eyes, that he may see." The servant saw the mountain was full of horses and chariots of fire round about Elisha. God's people are safe in His keeping.

God smote the Syrian army with blindness. Elisha led them into Samaria and delivered them into the hands of the king of Israel. The king asked if they should be slain. The prophet said, "Give them food to eat and send them away." The prophet's advice was followed, and that ended the guerilla raids along the Syrian-Israel border for a long time.

Here is a lesson all Christians need to learn. "Be not overcome of evil, but overcome evil with good" (Rom. 12:21). There are invisible defenders against evil powers.

177

July 29

Plenty in the Midst of Famine

2 Kings 7:9

Famine had come to Samaria not because of drought but because an army had besieged the city and cut off all sources of supply. The situation was so desperate that two mothers had agreed that on a certain day the infant son of one of them would be boiled and eaten, and the next day the son of the other mother would provide their food in like manner. In these unbelievable circumstances Elisha the prophet, whose head had been threatened, confidently prophesied, "To morrow about this time shall a measure of fine flour be sold for a shekel, and two measures of barley for a shekel, in the gate of Samaria."

This announcement was received with scornful pessimism. One lord who served the king asked, "If the Lord would make windows in heaven, might this thing be?" (vv. 1-2).

Four lepers facing death decided to risk a visit to the camp of the hostile Syrian army. When they came to the camp, they found it deserted. The army had heard a great noise of chariots and horses which the Lord had sent. Supposing the king of Israel had hired the Hittites and Egyptians to come upon them, they fled in haste and confusion.

The lepers feasted until they were awakened to their moral responsibility to share the good news. They therefore went and called the porters of the city, who told it to the king's household; whereupon the people went and spoiled the tents of the Syrians.

The prophecy of Elisha literally came to pass. Even in times of God's righteous judgment He is pleased to show mercy.

July 30

A Contrast in Strength and Weakness

2 Kings 13:18

Strength and *weakness* are relative terms. A weak, vacillating man who stands among the strong is seen at his worst. In this story we see the aged prophet sick unto death. Elisha would be expected to appear frail and trembling, and the king strong and vital. But in terms of moral and spiritual stamina, the king is weak, the prophet is strong.

The king had no understanding of the meaning of the great drama in which he was a principal actor. He did what he was told to do with indifference. He was like a child at play. He had no great moral indignation against the enemies of God. Mention of the Syrians should have set him on fire. Instead he stroked the ground casually three times and stopped. He should have smitten the ground with all his might five or six times. He had no passionate dedication to his task. He enjoyed the honor of being king but had no real concern for the welfare of the nation. He would settle for partial rather than demand total victory. He was sentimental, shedding crocodile tears. He was insincere, prattling pious words as a lip service.

See the contrast in the aged dying prophet. His voice is strong and vibrant. His hand on the king's hand is firm. His indignation kindled at the halfhearted performance of Joash. He was faithful in every detail to the last. This was what made him stand out as a strong man among the strong.

July 31

Good Men Do Sicken and Die

2 Kings 13:14

Elijah was taken up in a whirlwind. Elisha died the common death of all men. If any man could earn escape from sickness and death, Elisha earned that distinction. On his deathbed he was characterized as "the man of God." Elisha died and they buried him.

It must be concluded that Elisha was the typical man. Elijah was the exception. Sickness is no proof that a person is unrighteous. Some of the most promising men of God have died in their thirties, such as Henry Martyn, Frederick W. Robertson, and Percy Ainsworth; some even in their late twenties, such as David Brainerd, Robert Murray McCheyne, and Jim Elliot. They, like John the Baptist, were as burning and shining lights. They lived brilliantly but briefly. Some good men live longer to get their work done. Elisha seems to have lived well and for a normal span. How long? is not the question, but How well?

There will be a twofold immortality. The Psalmist said, "Mark the perfect man, and behold the upright: for the end of that man is peace" (37:37).

For all such there is the blessed rest that shall never end.

There is also the continuing influence of a holy life. After Elisha was buried, the Moabites invaded the land. As they were burying a man, they spied a band of men. In haste they cast the body into the sepulchre of Elisha. When he touched the bones of Elisha, he revived and stood upon his feet.

There is power in the memory of a true man of God. "He being dead yet speaketh" (Heb. 11:4).

August 1

Jesus Teaching Disciples

Matt. 5:1-2

In Matthew, chapters 5—7 are commonly called the Sermon on the Mount. According to Matthew the Great Commission is, "Go ye therefore, and teach all nations . . . teaching them to observe all things whatsoever I have commanded you" (28:19-20).

Preaching is no substitute for teaching. They complement each other, and for every preacher there needs to be many teachers. In this respect as well as all others Jesus is the prime Example.

It is obvious that Jesus had called at least 4 of His 12 disciples not long before He went up into the mountain and opened His mouth and taught them. There are those who time this discourse after He had spent the night in prayer and called the Twelve.

What the Ten Commandments were to the chosen nation under the old covenant, this Sermon on the Mount is to all disciples of Christ. It is different but it does not abrogate one item in the Decalogue. It deals not in particulars but in principles. It is the Magna Carta of the Kingdom. Its greatest

180

demands should be laid on the conscience of all Christians. It is not futuristic. It is the criterion for ethical practice in this day of grace. The Holy Spirit has come to make it possible for Christians to live by these precepts. The Master dealt with ideals and attitudes. He offered remedies for heart diseases in order that His followers might bear the fruit of the Spirit and thus prove to all who observe their lives that they have been redeemed.

August 2

Blessed Are the Humble

Matt. 5:3

Most of the reliable translations of the Beatitudes keep the word "blessed." Some have chosen the word "happy." But that does not express the deep, rich meaning of the blessedness which Jesus pronounced upon those who possessed the qualities described in these benedictions.

Jesus begins with an appropriate thought. He offers blessing to those who have true humility. The Goodspeed translation is, "Blessed are those who feel their spiritual need." This opens the door of the kingdom of heaven to the contrite sinner. He may enter that door forgiven if he will confess his guilt, admit that he has no merit to offer, plead only for mercy, and accept the free gift of grace. It is the poor in spirit who are blessed.

This blessedness is for those who put no confidence in their worldly possessions. Jesus said, "It is easier for a camel to go through the eye of a needle, than for a rich man to enter into the kingdom of God." He added, "With men this is impossible; but with God all things are possible" (19:24, 26). A miracle? Yes, but possible by the power of God's indwelling Spirit. A man can be rich in material substance and yet poor in spirit and enjoy the blessedness of the kingdom of heaven.

This is the blessedness of total dependence upon God. We are wholly dependent on Him for life and breath and all the joys we have. Blessed forgiveness. Blessed humility. Blessed dependence on God. Blessed assurance in the kingdom of heaven.

181

August 3
Blessed Mourning

Matt. 5:4

The first and second beatitudes are similar in meaning but not identical. In a sense the conscientious Christian continues to mourn. He is continually aware of how far short of being a Christlike person he is and how much he misses perfect performance of the full will of God. He is determined to reach for the higher and better things offered him by the grace of God. He prays earnestly that he may more nearly approximate the ideal which he sees in Jesus.

This mourning does not leave the Christian in a state of melancholy. The blessedness that Jesus promises enables him to lift his head and let his voice be heard in jubilant song. "Weeping may endure for a night, but joy cometh in the morning" (Ps. 30:5). The Holy Spirit gives assurance of forgiveness and the comfort of communion. This is the blessedness of those who mourn in Zion.

Jesus, according to John, said, "Your sorrow shall be turned into joy. . . . your joy no man taketh from you" (16:20, 22).

No honest, serious-minded Christian can say that the normal Christian lives in an ecstasy of joy perpetually. Many things which are an inescapable part of life stab the heart with pain. There are clouds of darkness which are as real as the sunshine. If they do not come to one, they do come to another. This is why Paul admonished, "Rejoice with them that do rejoice, and weep with them that weep" (Rom. 12:15). Nevertheless, the dominant note in the song of the Christian is joy.

August 4
The Inheritance of the Meek

Matt. 5:5

Who is meek? It is not the person who in pretence downgrades himself in a mock humility. He is not negative in the estimate of himself. He does not think more highly of himself than he ought to think. He thinks soberly. He has faith in God, in his fellowman, and in himself.

The meek person is not spineless. He is not a doormat for other people to walk on. He may not fight for his own rights, but he will stand up for the cause that is just. And he will insist that others shall have "fair and reasonable consideration." It is written in the Book of Numbers, "(Now the man Moses was very meek, above all the men which were upon the face of the earth)" (12:3). Would Pharaoh have considered Moses "spineless"?

Jesus said of himself, "I am meek and lowly in heart" (11:29). The Pharisees would not have described Him as fearful and cringing.

What then is meekness? It is submission to the will of God. Why was Moses so fearless when he stood before Pharaoh? It was because he had heard God speak to him.

How could Jesus yield to the designs of the enemies of God and man? It was because He could say, "I came down from heaven, not to do mine own will, but the will of him that sent me" (John 6:38).

The meek shall inherit the earth. They do not need to fight for it. Because they have done the will of God, it is theirs now in spiritual possession. Theirs will be the new heaven and the new earth wherein dwelleth righteousness.

August 5

Satisfied

Matt. 5:6

Hunger and thirst are natural cravings of the body. The satisfaction of these longings is necessary to life. Other desires can be disciplined in postponement, but without food to eat and drink to quench thirst, the body cannot live for any extended period of time. The Master Teacher here compounded hunger and thirst to emphasize the spiritual appetite of the soul of man for righteousness. Man was made for God, and he is never satisfied until he finds God in full salvation. He was

183

made in the image of God, and his life is empty until that image is restored in righteousness and true holiness.

This want in the soul of man is implanted there by God himself, and He is not the author of any human desire without making provision for its possible fulfillment. Therefore what man longs for is righteousness, and with that righteousness he shall be filled. He shall be saturated with righteousness. It is not only righteousness in outward conduct but also righteousness in character. That is holiness.

The new man in Christ is satisfied. He is filled with righteousness. But he must feed on the bread from heaven day by day. One may eat a palate-pleasing menu of delicious food. The next day he will be hungry again.

The yearning of the heart of man is for the righteousness of God by faith through Christ. Peace and rest and love are obtained now by faith. The Christlikeness for which the soul longs is an attainment. God does give completeness and satisfaction.

August 6

The Quality of Mercy

Matt. 5:7

"Blessed are the merciful: for they shall obtain mercy." This makes the clear inference that to receive mercy one must be merciful. Jesus said, "If ye forgive men their trespasses, your heavenly Father will also forgive you: but if ye forgive not men their trespasses, neither will your Father forgive your trespasses" (6:14-15). Stronger still is the application of the story of the servant who was forgiven a large debt because he was contrite but who demanded of a fellow servant that he pay his small indebtedness to him and cast him into prison till he should pay all. When the lord of both servants heard what the unmerciful servant had done, he revoked his forgiveness and delivered the merciless servant to the tormentors until he paid his great debt in full. Jesus said, "So likewise shall my heavenly Father do also unto you, if ye *from your hearts* forgive not every one his brother their trespasses" (18:35). The inescapable conclusion is if we expect mercy from God, we must show mercy to our fellowmen, especially to those who have trespassed against us.

Mercy is defined as compassionate forbearance toward an offender. The deed, even if committed in malice, is to be forgiven and wiped from the record. The offender is in standing as he was before the offence was committed. God's merciful forgiveness should be the measure of ours. He forgives and forgets. William Barclay says forgiveness means to get inside the other person and see as he sees.

August 7

The Beatific Vision

Matt. 5:8

Purity of heart has been defined as singleness of mind. That would be the mind of Christ. Another has said, "Heart purity is to will one thing"; that would be to will the will of God. In other words, heart purity is deliverance from double-mindedness as the cause for instability.

Absent then from the pure heart is all rebellion of the will and all the works of the flesh. There is nothing left in it that is contrary to the nature and love of God.

The heart that is cleansed is simultaneously filled with the Holy Spirit. This certainly means that the fruit of the Spirit is manifest in the life. That fruit is love, pure and perfect love.

"Blessed are the pure in heart: for they shall see God." This blessedness begins in this life in the Spirit. God is seen in the wonders of His creation. He is seen in His self-revelation in His inspired Word. He is seen in the face of Jesus Christ, the Word made flesh. He is seen in the lives of His holy people. He is seen also in the wisdom and graciousness of His providences. All things work together for good. Finally, Christ will be seen

Face to face! O blissful moment!
Face to face—to see and know;

185

Face to face with my Redeemer,
Jesus Christ, who loves me so.

Face to face I shall behold Him,
Far beyond the starry sky;
Face to face in all His glory,
I shall see Him by and by!

August 8

Children of God

Matt. 5:9

Those who make peace must have received peace. One who is condemned by feelings of guilt or who has inward turmoil and conflict certainly cannot lead others to peace. Those who are justified by faith have peace with God. He has made peace by the blood of the Cross. He imparts the peace that passeth understanding to the pardoned sinner. As the very God of peace He gives tranquility. When the sanctifying Savior fills the heart with the Holy Spirit, His presence keeps the peace that arbitrates all conflicts within.

Jesus offered His peace as His legacy to His followers. He said, "Peace I leave with you, my peace I give unto you . . . Let not your heart be troubled, neither let it be afraid" (John 14:27). This is the portion of God's redeemed people. Those who know that peace can be peacemakers among their fellows. Surface storms may come, but Jesus is near to speak peace. Then there is a great calm.

Jesus pronounced a particular blessing upon the peacemakers: "They shall be called the children of God." They are God's children, not because He is the maker of us all, but because they bear a definite likeness to God. The quarrelsome disturbers of the peace in the body politic or in the Church have no likeness to God or His Son. All the true children of the Heavenly Father are peacemakers. They have peace and they diffuse peace. They put out the fires of envy, jealousy, hatred, and covetousness. They are pourers of oil on the troubled waters of contention and strife.

August 9

"Be Exceeding Glad"

Matt. 5:10-12

The blessedness of persecution is limited to those within a well-defined circle. The center of the circle is the truism that persecution, to be blessed, must be for Jesus' sake. The evil charged against the one persecuted must be false. And it must be for righteousness. It cannot be for open, brazen defiance of civil law enacted for the protection of loyal subjects. It cannot be for eccentric teachings designed to arouse the rabble. Neither can it be for freakish notions of our own. Much of what is called "persecution" is self-inflicted in order to have cause for self-pity with the hope of gaining sympathy.

Jesus said persecution was inescapable in this world. He said, "If the world hate you, ye know that it hated me before it hated you. . . . Remember the word that I said unto you, The servant is not greater than his lord. If they have persecuted me, they will also persecute you" (John 15:18, 20).

The secret of victory is in looking unto Jesus who, for the joy set before Him, endured the Cross, scorning the shame.

There are compensations for persecution in this life. There is the joy of identification with the apostles and prophets and more especially with Jesus. There is the result that by it the Church is purified as by fire. There is the assurance that the sincere and devout will join us, for "the blood of the martyrs is the seed of the Church." There is also the eternal reward. Paul wrote, "If we suffer [with Christ], we shall also reign with him" (2 Tim. 2:12).

August 10

Christian Influence

Matt. 5:13

God promised Abraham that his seed should be blessed and that all families of the earth should be blessed through him. Jesus began His ministry by pronouncing blessing upon those who were His disciples. The next word spoken by Him was an extension of His influence through their lives to all the world. He said, "Ye are the salt of the earth . . . Ye are the light of the world."

Salt penetrates. It touches every particle of the food to which it is applied. To the one who accepts Christ as Savior every area of his personality is transformed.

Salt preserves. Before refrigeration it was a principal means of keeping food from spoiling. Christian influence in the world is what salt is to food. In the society of today, corrupted by evil, life would be intolerable but for the redeeming effect of vital, life-changing Christianity. God destroyed Sodom because of moral decay. The sins of Sodom are at work today. It is the presence of millions of righteous people which saves our generation from the judgment of the God who can only do right.

Salt savors. It makes food palatable. Our holy faith adds zest to life. It saves from tasteless monotony. It changes the routine of life from boredom to exciting pleasure.

Salt can lose its saltness. Religion can also deteriorate into lifeless creeds and meaningless formalities. It can so blend with the world that its distinctives are lost and its redeeming influence forfeited.

August 11

Christians as Rainbows

Matt. 5:14-16

The effect of salt is inward. Light shines outward. The working of salt is invisible. A light shining is seen by all. Salt conditions character. The light points up good works.

John records Jesus as saying, "As long as I am in the world, I am the light of the world" (9:5). Here He is saying to His disciples, "Ye are the light of the world." It is often said that those who believe in Jesus and are redeemed by His grace, reflect the life of Jesus in a dark world like the moon reflects the light of the sun when it is unseen in the night. It would be better to say the Christian refracts the light that shone in the person of Christ, as a ray of light shining through a glass prism

188

is bent in another direction and is diffused in all the beautiful colors of the rainbow. The same effect is seen when the sun's rays shine through the rain. A bow of varied colors spans the sky.

Reflected light shines on the object but does not change it. The refracted light of Christ shines through a human personality, transforms and transfigures it. It is then diffused in the good works of kind and gracious deeds, which spring from thoughts of love.

The candle that gives light is consumed by the burning. So the Christian offers his life as a living sacrifice to give light in a dark world.

Let your light so shine before men that they may see.

August 12
The Righteousness God Approves

Matt. 5:20

The righteousness of the Pharisees was not easy. They made rigid demands of themselves. Being hard on themselves made them harsh with others. They kept the letter of the law religiously, but they nullified its spirit by their multiplied traditions.

In the remaining part of this chapter Jesus sets forth the qualities that shine out in the Christian whose righteousness God approves. His demands are greater than those of the law. Obedience to the spirit of the law is more important than conformity to the letter. Inward holiness, spiritual wholeness and health must be the mainspring of outward righteousness.

God is concerned with attitudes as well as actions, thoughts as much as words, being more than doing. God looks on the heart. To Him covetousness is as bad as stealing. One who hates his brother is a murderer. An estrangement from a brother will bring separation from God until reconciliation restores peace and good will. A lustful look united with willful intentions is adultery.

The multiplying of words or use of oaths does not cover deceit. Commitment to principles of public justice does not open the door to revengeful action. To love one's friend is natural; to love his enemy is supernatural. Turning the other cheek, giving one's coat as well as his shirt, going the second mile is to live in the spirit of the law which Christ fulfilled. His grace is sufficient.

Perfection is the aim of the Christian; that is to be understood as perfection in love.

August 13
Save for Keeps

Matt. 6:21

Martin Luther said, "What a man loves, that is his God." A pertinent question for all to ponder is, "What is your life center?" If our affections are set on things on the earth, the material and temporal values, then we are earthbound creatures. All such live for this brief span. They take no thought for eternity. Jesus taught that man is a being destined to live forever. Life on earth is brief at the longest. Man's true self will live forever. His well-being in the endless existence depends upon his choice between alternatives here. The shortsighted man who lives for the present gathers only such treasures as thieves can steal, moths can destroy, or time corrode. It is certain he cannot take them beyond the grave.

In contrast, the one who sets his affections on things above is making his investments in values of which he can never be deprived. He has "an inheritance incorruptible, and undefiled, and that fadeth not away" (1 Pet. 1:4). The direction of his gaze is upward. His life is elevated. His eternal destiny is heaven. His total life purpose is to serve his generation and to glorify God.

To the earthbound slave, life is emptiness. Eternity will be a misery without mercy and a memory of torment without comfort. How different the one who lives with eternity's values in view. He lives in the blessedness of present fulfillment and the assurance that eye hath not seen nor ear heard the things that God hath prepared for him. What he gives is what he keeps.

190

August 14

20/20 Vision

Matt. 6:22-23

The lamp of the body is the eye. The ability to see aids every function and movement of the body. It enhances the enjoyment of all other sense stimulants. The fragrance of the flower, the exhilaration of music, the taste of food, the exciting touch of a loving hand are all appreciated by the contribution made by seeing. Any defect of the eye is therefore a handicap to the entire life of the person.

All of this is a parable of what spiritual vision is to the soul. A clear, straight vision of spiritual verities is the guide to holiness of heart and life. The want of it leads to a distortion in character and abortive conduct.

Sin in the heart blurs the sight of the spiritual eye. When it takes root in the will and results in rebellion and transgression, it may become total blindness. How great is that darkness! The consequence is a life of groping in fear to eternal night.

Even to the soul benighted by generations of living in darkness, God in mercy directs a ray of light. Response in obedience will bring increasing light that may lead to bright day.

Those surrounded by the light of glorious revelation who will walk in the light, need not lose their way or fall victim to the snares and pitfalls laid for their destruction. Rather, they, by obedience to the light, may find cleansing from sin which heals the defects of the spiritual eye and brings an illumination on the path that shines more and more unto the perfect day.

August 15

One Master

Matt. 6:24

Jesus did not hold an earned Ph.D. in psychology. John said of Him, however, that He "needed not that any should testify of man: for he knew what was in man" (2:25). The psychoanalyst will draw a consultee into conversation and

191

eventually render an opinion as to his mental soundness. Jesus had the ability to look through a person. He never employed the professional tricks to uncover the hidden thoughts and intents of the mind. His unerring insight made it possible to prescribe effective cures for distraught and guilt-ridden souls.

A well-known psychiatrist said not long ago that if people would accept the principles set forth in the Bible, most of those of his profession could close their offices.

No one would deny that the dictum of our text for today is psychologically sound. Anyone who has ever tried to serve two masters has discovered that the result was double-mindedness and split personality. This word of the Master Teacher has the sanction of psychology as well as the authority of divine inspiration. To all such, inner conflict and frustration are inescapable.

Serving two masters rules out the possibility of maximum achievement because the drive of a master passion is cancelled. The best that can be expected is mediocrity.

The alternatives Jesus cited were God and money. He said everyone must decide who his master will be. Will it be the material or the spiritual, the temporal or the eternal? John said, "The world passeth away, and the lust thereof: but he that doeth the will of God abideth forever" (1 John 2:17).

August 16

Life's Highest Priority

Matt. 6:33

All normal persons are reaching for a goal. If that is not true, life becomes static. There is no excitement in a standstill. The once challenging prospect may have come to fulfillment; but if it has, the horizon has moved further out. The lure of adventure remains.

What one seeks determines what he is. If it be sensual gratification, he becomes bestial. If it is money, he tends toward that which is hard and metallic. If it be the wisdom of this world, he will be a lopsided freak. If he will seek to know God and His righteousness, he can enjoy pleasure with no dregs of

192

regret. He can enjoy prosperity and glorify God with his wealth. He can put life together with wisdom from above. He can realize the chief end of man which is to glorify God here and enjoy Him forever.

Entrance to the Kingdom is by way of the new birth. Jesus said to Nicodemus, "Verily, verily, I say unto thee, Except a man be born again, he cannot see the kingdom of God" (John 3:3). "The natural man receiveth not the things of the Spirit of God . . . they are spiritually discerned" (1 Cor. 2:14).

The kingdom of heaven must be established in man's soul. The King must occupy the throne room. Total submission to the will of the King makes His Lordship a delightful experience. His subjects are love-slaves forever. Christ is in the control tower. Perfect submission is perfect delight.

Seek heavenly things and all earthly good will be added. "Grace is the way to glory; holiness is the way to happiness." If God is first, He will supply all the needed things.

August 17

The Strait Gate and the Narrow Way

Matt. 7:13-14

"The strait gate" is the entrance to the narrow way that leads to life. It is clear to the searching mind and devout spirit that Jesus intended His hearers to understand that the strait gate is described in verse 12: "Therefore all things whatsoever ye would that men should do to you, do ye even so to them: for this is the law and the prophets." This is an all-inclusive summary of the law given by God to Moses and of the exposition of that law by the prophets.

We call it the golden rule. If men would live by this pattern of conduct, they would need no other rules to guide them. Doing to others as we would have them do to us would certainly include all the commandments in the Decalogue. It would mean the gate is smaller and the way narrower than any set of rules ever conceived by man could make them. This is a concept found in the ethical ideals of many nations. Jesus summed them all and expressed the thought more clearly than has ever been done.

This requirement for even entering the narrow way is far more penetrating and exacting than the law, with all the added traditions, had been. It begins in the heart from which all action flows. It goes beyond habits and attitudes. It plumbs the springs of life. It discerns the thoughts and intents of the inmost being. It deals with motives.

Do men take liberties because grace abounds? The expectations of the gospel of grace are much greater than the demands of the law.

August 18
The Fruit Identifies the Tree

Matt. 7:19-20

The nature of the tree is known by the fruit it bears. Grapes do not grow on thorns or figs on thistles. "Even so every good tree bringeth forth good fruit; but a corrupt tree bringeth forth evil fruit" (v. 17). The mask of hypocrisy can be worn only temporarily. It will soon be torn away, and the true character of lying prophets, would-be teachers, and false witnesses will be known.

To a trained horticulturist trees can be classified at sight. He would know an apple tree would not bear peaches. But to even a casual observer the tree is known by the time the fruit appears. Nature does not contradict itself.

The soundness of the tree is also known by the quality of the fruit. "A good tree cannot bring forth evil fruit, neither can a corrupt tree bring forth good fruit" (v. 18). The tree that is decayed at the heart can only produce defective fruit. A sound tree will produce fruit that will bear inspection. It is clear that Jesus was teaching that character can be known by the outward evidence of words and deeds. Inward corruption will soon be revealed by outward action, while holiness within will shine out in truthfulness, righteousness, and deeds of love and kindness.

This does not form a basis for premature conclusions as to the trustworthiness of persons. Nor does it give liberty for one to pronounce judgment on another. The pure in heart leave judgment to God, but they can tell the difference between those who are true or false.

August 19

The Test of Discipleship

Matt. 7:21

A disciple is a follower of Christ. In particular, he follows Christ in doing the Father's will. The test of discipleship is not in word but in deed. One may know the will of God well enough to preach it; but if he is not a doer of the Word, he deceives himself. Paul acknowledged he could preach to others and be cast away.

Jesus allowed that there would be many who would say, "Have we not exorcised demons and done miracles in thy name?" But He would say to them, "I never knew you: depart from me" (see vv. 22-23). Adam Clarke comments, "United with Christ all is heaven; separated from Him all is hell."

Followers of Christ are not identified by their pious words or benevolent works but by active obedience to all God's will known to them. Many will be saved who have had limited light and walked in it, while many whose conduct was better will be lost because they had light they did not obey.

The presence of the Temple was not a saving factor to the people of Jeremiah's day. They profaned the Temple of God in their transgression of the covenant. They were carried into captivity, and the house of God was plundered. The church building is a sacred place, and membership in the church is good. Nevertheless, church members cannot cloak their disobedience to God in pious platitudes and pretentious offerings. There is a path that leads from the altar of the church to separation from Christ in eternity's night.

195

August 20

The Wise Builder

Matt. 7:24

Jesus had amplified and applied the law and the prophets in this imperishable message. The summation is a vivid illustration. It is truth simple enough for a child to understand. It was so penetrating and so profound that the people who heard were astonished at His teachings. He taught them as one having authority and not in the threadbare cliches the scribes employed.

A wise man who builds his house for permanence gives serious consideration to the foundation. He then proceeds to erect the superstructure of quality materials that will endure in spite of all the destructive forces in the natural world. Those who build temporary dwellings to be used for a single season may locate them on a sandy shore and use cheap substitutes for their shelter.

The person who builds his life for eternity chooses Christ, the Rock of Ages, as the foundation that cannot be shaken by cloudbursts or hurricanes or earthquakes. "Other foundation can no man lay than that is laid, which is Jesus Christ" (1 Cor. 3:11).

The wise builder of character and destiny structures his life according to the teachings of Jesus. To Timothy, Paul wrote, "The foundation of God standeth sure, having this seal, The Lord knoweth them that are his. And, Let everyone that nameth the name of Christ depart from iniquity" (2 Tim. 2:19). Let nothing be built into that house in which one will live for time and eternity that Jesus has condemned. Let all that He has approved be chosen and cherished in the day-by-day progress of the building.

August 21

"If Thou Wilt"

Matt. 8:2-3

Here was a man who was fully persuaded that Jesus could heal him of leprosy. His faith was not conditional. He believed

Paul identifies this inherent sinfulness as the carnal mind. He also uses the term "flesh," the corrupt nature. He names "the works of the flesh" as "adultery, fornication, uncleanness, lasciviousness, idolatry, witchcraft, hatred, variance, emulations, wrath, strife, seditions, heresies, envyings, murders, drunkenness, revellings" (Gal. 5:19-21). He makes it clear that these are the traits of unregenerate man. He also gives the unmistakable impression that regeneration brings this disposition under the influence of the Spirit of Christ. To describe the state of the unsanctified Christian, he said, "Walk in the Spirit, and ye shall not fulfil the lust of the flesh. For the flesh lusteth against the Spirit, and the Spirit against the flesh: and these are contrary the one to the other: so that ye cannot do the things that ye would. . . . And they that are Christ's have crucified the flesh with the affections and lusts" (Gal. 5:16-17, 24).

This sinful nature Paul calls the body of sin, that must be destroyed or extirpated or pulled up by the roots. It was potentially crucified with Christ on the Cross. It is purposefully done in justification which proceeds to sanctification. It is actually done in an act of complete cleansing, a second crisis experience.

September 4

Freedom from Sin

Rom. 6:22

The sinner is a slave to sin. He is led captive by the devil at his will. His will is rebellious. He is missing the mark because his aim is wrong. It is not inadvertent error. It is voluntary transgression. The justified Christian has received pardon for sins committed, and the sinful nature within him has been brought into subjection. Sin no longer reigns. The grace of God abounds. The question "Are we to make provision for a single act of sin?" is answered with, "May it never be" (see vv. 1-2).

The sanctified Christian has yielded his members in obedience to God. His heart has been cleansed from all that is contrary to the will of God. In him sin not only does not reign, it does not remain. He has reckoned himself "dead indeed unto sin, but alive unto God through Jesus Christ our Lord" (v. 11). He therefore enjoys freedom from sin. This is the only complete freedom known to mortal man. His will being to do the will of God, he is in loving obedience free to do as he pleases. His pleasure is in perfect submission to God. He is free from sin's enslavement. He is free from guilt. "There is therefore now no condemnation . . . For the law of the Spirit of life in Christ Jesus hath made [him] free from the law of sin and death" (8:1-2). "Now being made free from sin, and become servants to God, ye have your fruit unto holiness, and the end everlasting life. . . . the gift of God is eternal life through Jesus Christ our Lord" (6:22-23).

September 5
The Spirit Himself

Rom. 8:16

The Holy Spirit is a person. The text should read, "The Spirit *him*self beareth witness with our spirit, that we are the children of God." He is a person, not an influence. He testifies to our sonship. We are all God's creatures, but we are not all God's sons until we are born again. The Spirit bears witness to our adoption into the family of God.

By the ministry of the Holy Spirit, we receive the *assurance* that we are the children of God. Questions as to our salvation are answered affirmatively. Doubts are gone. John Wesley defined the witness of the Spirit this way: "The testimony of the Spirit of God is an inward impression on the soul whereby this Spirit of God directly witnesses to my spirit that I am a child of God, that Jesus Christ hath saved me and given himself for me; and that my sins are blotted out and I, even I, am reconciled to God."

The Holy Spirit witnesses to sanctification even as He does to salvation.

The Spirit of God also gives the Christian *guidance*. "For

208

as many as are led by the Spirit of God, they are the sons of God" (v. 14). "If we live in the Spirit, let us also walk in the Spirit" (Gal. 5:25). We are not groping our way through life's perplexities. We hear a voice saying, "This is the way, walk ye in it" (Isa. 30:21). Those who are the children of God have an *inheritance*. They are "heirs of God, and joint-heirs with Christ" (v. 17).

September 6

According to His Purpose

Rom. 8:28

The sovereignty of God underlies the truth of this text. This doctrine is stressed more by those who make much of election, but it is believed by all Christians. God's will is supreme. He rules in the world of nature. What He does not determine, He directs. What He does not prevent, He permits. He guides the destiny of nations. He will ultimately make the wrath of men to praise Him. The Captain is still on the bridge. In personal affairs, wherein God does not rule, He overrules for my good and for His glory.

There is an inclusiveness about this word of comfort and assurance. "All things" takes in the manifold blessings of God for which one is spontaneously grateful, but included are life's adversities too. It does not say, All things separately are good. A different translation is, "We know that in everything God works for good." It is when the whole design of God is seen that we find all has been for good. God's chastisements are not pleasurable, but they are for the good of His children.

There is an exclusiveness in this declaration of faith too. It is with those who love Him, those who in response to God's love have faith that works by love in complete obedience. It is to those who are called according to His purpose. The purpose of God is revealed in the next verse: "For whom he did foreknow, he also did predestinate to be conformed to the image of his Son."

209

September 7

Security in Christ

Rom. 8:35

Those who believe in freedom of the will may have failed to magnify the grace of God. He "is able to keep" those who continue in the love of God and present them "faultless before the presence of his glory with exceeding joy" (Jude 24).

For the security of the believer there is every possible assurance. "If God be for us, who can be against us?" To prove that He is for us, God "spared not his own Son, but delivered him up for us all, [then] how shall he not with him also freely give us all things?" (vv. 31-32). He will give us the helmet of salvation to guard our minds from evil thoughts and error. He will give the breastplate of righteousness to protect our affections from the contamination of sensuous desires and worldly ambitions. He will give us the shield of faith by which we can quench all the fiery darts of the wicked. God is for us and no foe can penetrate the fortification with which He surrounds us.

"Christ . . . is even at the right hand of God, who also maketh intercession for us" (v. 34). It is not temporary or intermittent prayer on our behalf. "He ever liveth to make intercession for" His own (Heb. 7:25).

Christ's love reaches to us under all the testing circumstances of life. No authority can cancel it; no barrier can hinder it; no darkness can obscure it. He whose will is fixed in God's will cannot be separated from the love of Christ. We are more than conquerors. There are reserve forces we have not called up, and they will never be inadequate.

September 8

A Living Sacrifice

Rom. 12:1

This is Paul's appeal to the Christians at Rome, and everywhere for all time, to offer themselves to God in total consecration. The basis of his exhortation is the mercies of God. They are extolled in verse 33 in chapter 11: "O the depth of the riches both of the wisdom and knowledge of God! how unsearchable are his judgments, and his ways past finding out!" Consecration to the service of God, to be used for His glory, was to be in grateful recognition of the great salvation offered in the sacrifice of Jesus Christ on the Cross. "How much I owe for love divine; How much I owe that Christ is mine."

The apostle not only refers in this text to the profound truth he has proclaimed in the preceding chapters, but he also introduces an allusion to the whole burnt offering presented to God under the Levitical order of worship. This signified that, in accepting God's mercy, a pledge was given that the whole of life was subject to God's known will. The burnt offering was entirely consumed. Nothing was saved from the fire.

Paul uses this as an illustration to persuade Christians who have been redeemed, to present their whole personality to God. This was to be done in an act of full and final commitment to God as a logical response to His infinite love and mercy. Your body is to be the temple of the Holy Spirit. Your whole being is "consumed on God's altar of service."

September 9
The Perfect Will of God

Rom. 12:2

When Paul said, *"Present* your bodies a living sacrifice," he used the aorist tense of the verb. It was an act to be done at a given point in time. That was total consecration to be proved in performance. This must be a dedication kept up to date at all times. It is an attitude of mind and will, permanently determined. It is singleness of mind—the mind that was in Christ Jesus.

Such a state of mind will be reflected in one's manner of life. He will not be conformed. The manners of the worldly-minded are not the model for Christians. As if by a powerful explosion they have been loosened from the spirit and practice of mankind unredeemed. Phillips' translation is, "Don't let the

211

world around you squeeze you into its own mold, but let God remold your minds from within." It is not simply deliverance from the old way of life, it is a life made completely new. It is remade in the likeness of Christ. It is from within outward. What God does within has a glorious manifestation without.

The challenge to this new man is to "prove what is that good, and acceptable, and perfect, will of God." It is good in the sight of God, and man realizes his highest good. It is acceptable to God and acceptable to the Christian with no reservations. It is perfect obedience and perfect delight. It is likeness to Christ who came to do His Father's will. Sanctification is the acceptance of God's perfect will.

September 10

The Manners of the Sanctified

Rom. 12:3

The most adequate handbook of Christian ethics is the Sermon on the Mount. The precepts found in Romans chapters 12—13 are in many instances parallel to those Jesus taught. In both, we find infallible guidelines for Christian conduct. Those who stand under the banner of "Holiness unto the Lord" should give thoughtful attention to them.

Paul points up the ideals for the sanctified in every relationship of life. Toward God he is to be aglow with the Spirit, serving the Lord. He is to be instant in prayer. Toward himself he is to think soberly. His service, according to his gifts, must be in humility. Brotherly love is the touchstone of his attitude toward his fellow Christians, in honor preferring one another. He is to show charity toward those in need and be given to hospitality. He reaches out with empathy to all who either rejoice or weep.

Toward all men he is never to return evil for evil, but to provide things honest. He is to love his neighbors as himself and, as much as lieth in him, live peaceably with all.

Vengeance is never to be taken out of God's hands. The sanctified Christian is to bless those who curse him, give food

212

and drink to his enemy when he is hungry and thirsty. He will overcome evil with good.

He renders honor to whom honor is due. He owes no man anything but love and thus fulfills the law. He has put on the armor of light, walking honestly as in the day. In short, he has put on the Lord Jesus Christ.

September 11
Things That Make for Peace

Rom. 14:19

Paul in his testimony before Agrippa said, "After the most straitest sect of our religion I lived a Pharisee" (Acts 26:5). He used a double superlative to describe the legalism of the sect to which he belonged. He knew legalism was not the answer to the permissiveness of the pagan world which brought them to the depth of degradation described in Rom. 1:18 and following. When self-appointed Pharisees who believed in Jesus rose up to demand that Gentile Christians must be circumcised and keep the law of Moses, Paul withstood them. How good it was for the Christian Church that he did. That party in the Church almost completely vanished. The Church grew rapidly among Gentiles. The Judaizers phased out.

Nevertheless, Paul knew that salvation by grace alone and by faith alone did not give believers license to disregard the commandments of God. In 13:9-10 he declared that all the law "is briefly comprehended in this saying, namely, Thou shalt love thy neighbour as thyself. . . . therefore love is the fulfilling of the law." None can live according to this royal law and transgress any of the commands of the Decalogue.

Therefore Paul says in substance in this chapter, Do not sit in judgment one of another; do not offend your conscience or that of your brother; do not be a stumbling block to a weaker brother; do not cause division. "The kingdom of God is not meat and drink; but righteousness, and peace, and joy in the Holy Ghost" (v. 17).

213

September 12

Called to Be Saints

1 Cor. 1:2

Paul made an artful approach to the Corinthian church. He had been the founder of the Christian society there. He knew the character of the city and its people. It was cosmopolitan. The elite were there, and slaves were there with a wide variety in between. As was the city, so was the church. Paul knew that there were serious problems in the church and that he must deal with them in candor. Possibly the Corinthian church is more typical of churches as we know them than we are willing to admit. In most churches there is a cross section of society. It should be so. A class-conscious church is lacking something in compassion and concern for humanity's great need. In most churches there are problems with which spiritual leaders must deal.

Paul, in a skillful approach, made no reference to these distinctions or their existing problems. He wanted the congregation's acceptance and their confidence. Therefore, he addressed them as "sanctified" persons, "called to be saints."

The Corinthian populace were so sensuous and corrupt in morals that such persons were said to be Corinthianized. Those to whom Paul addressed his epistle were called out of that context of living. They were to be saints, holy men and women. They were no longer sinners. They were saved by the grace of the Lord Jesus Christ. As redeemed sinners, the work of sanctification had begun in them. They were worshippers of Jesus Christ who desired to be like Him. They were worthy to have the blessings of grace and peace pronounced upon them.

September 13

"Are Ye Not Carnal . . . ?"

1 Cor. 3:3

Very soon Paul came to grips with the problem of divisions among the Corinthian Christians. He had had a reliable report of their infightings. He called them contentious. He reminded them straight off that Christ is not divided and that He is central in the gospel message. He said, "Of him are ye in Christ Jesus, who of God is made unto us wisdom, and righteousness, and sanctification, and redemption" (1:30). He further impressed upon them that "the natural man receiveth not the things of the Spirit of God . . . because they are spiritually discerned. . . . But we have the mind of Christ" (2:14, 16).

With that fundamental truth in mind he now, in chapter 3, lays his finger on the root of the problem. Still addressing them as brethren, thus disarming them and recognizing the genuineness of their conversion, the apostle begins, "I could not speak unto you as unto spiritual, but as unto carnal, even as unto babes in Christ." Note that they were in Christ but they were still babes in Him.

There were three traits of mind that identified them as carnal. (1) They had infantile appetites. They had to be fed with milk and not with meat. (2) They had unholy attitudes. "For whereas there is among you envying, and strife, and divisions, are ye not carnal, and walk as men?" (3) They had superficial loyalties. "One saith, I am of Paul; and another, I am of Apollos; are ye not carnal?" (v. 4).

He declares Christ to be the Foundation and the Holy Spirit in them, as God's temples, the Agent of their sanctification in the truth.

September 14

Concerning Spiritual Gifts

1 Cor. 12:1

Ignorance concerning spiritual gifts is widespread. It is important, therefore, that teaching on the subject should be clear. The Holy Spirit in fullness is promised to all Christian believers. When He is come to dwell in the heart, He produces His fruit. The gifts of the Spirit are bestowed according to God's sovereign will and His wisdom. The selfsame Spirit divides to every man severally as He will (v. 11). It would appear that every Spirit-filled Christian has some capability for serving God.

There is a variety of gifts but the same Spirit. This eliminates rivalry, competition, and envy. Each one has a gift adapted to his assignment. He will prepare diligently for his work. But he can rest assured his labor is not in vain in the Lord.

There is unity in diversity. Paul uses the body to illustrate this harmony. A body is incomplete without all of its organs and members. Each one has its useful purpose. All are under the control of the brain. Every member has honor in doing what, by nature, it is designed to do. Every one helps every other one to fill its place in beautiful and satisfactory performance.

In the Church, the Holy Spirit is as the brain is to the body. He directs each member to his place of service according to his gift. He keeps all of them working in harmony. None are under discount, for all are important. Yet none are proud, for their gifts are from the Lord. All are employed to the glory of God.

September 15

The More Excellent Way

1 Cor. 12:31

All the gifts of the Spirit have value. But this word makes it clear that Paul did not consider them all of equal worth. The word "best" is also translated "greatest." Either way, it must mean there are good, better, best or great, greater, greatest gifts. The apostle gives insight to their relative importance in verse 28. Apostles, prophets, teachers are in that order. Those following may be considered desirable. Diversities of tongues may be last because it is less frequently needed. Most of those who are engaged in God's work are among those of their own language. Therefore, to them various languages would be relatively unimportant. Why cumber the Word of truth by use of a language that required an interpreter? No gift is the proof that one has received the fullness of the Spirit. That evidence is love out of a pure heart.

216

Therefore, Paul says, desire the best gifts. Nevertheless, the way of love is the more excellent way. This is in full accord with the teaching of Jesus who said, "Thou shalt love the Lord thy God with all thy heart, and with all thy soul, and with all thy mind. . . . And . . . thou shalt love thy neighbour as thyself. On these two commandments hang all the law and the prophets" (Matt. 22:37, 39-40). Paul said, "Love is the fulfilling of the law" (Rom. 13:10). John made it very strong: "We know that we have passed from death unto life, because we love the brethren"; and "he that loveth not his brother whom he hath seen, how can he love God whom he hath not seen?" (1 John 3:14; 4:20).

September 16
Love Is Indispensable

1 Cor. 13:1-3

The gift of languages, however desirable, is not enough. Neither inspiring eloquence nor command of all languages of men and angels will save preaching and testimony from hypocrisy. Without love they are insincere lip service.

The gift of prophecy may be the best gift, but it is no substitute for the love of God. The fruit of the Spirit is love. The understanding of all mysteries and the possession of all knowledge is disappointing if the heart is empty of love. "The gift without the giver is bare."

Achieving faith, able to move mountains, may be abortive and destructive without love. It equals zero without love. Devotion to truth is commendable. According to Jesus, to know the truth is to be free; but without the humility that love inspires, the free may become arrogant. In defense of truth and protest against error one may die a martyr. His charred body is no assurance that his soul is saved from hellfire. Only perfect love casts out fear that has torment.

Feeding the hungry and clothing the naked is commended by Christ and all the apostles; but such benevolence, without the motivation of love, is like hoarding money in bags that are full of holes. It leaves the benefactor bankrupt even if it saves the life of the beneficiary. Add all the gifts of the Spirit to all the virtues of Christian ethics; the total is still not sufficient without love. Absence of love is the fatal deficiency.

September 17

Love Is the Highest Good

1 Cor. 13:4a

Perfect love is without alloy, love supreme, pure, and absolute. It is love for God and all He loves, balanced by hatred of all that is evil. It includes all men, saint or sinner, friend or foe.

This divine love never runs out. No insult or injury can turn it to wrath, however deep the wound may be. The hands of love may be tied because a rebel will is unyielding, but patient love mourns the loss. It suffers long and is kind, while judgment is administered to the unrepentant sinner.

Pure and perfect love is rare. Its scarcity makes it more valuable. If gold were as common as clay, its worth would be as little. Long-suffering love is as infrequently found as gold.

The world's classic example is seen at Calvary. There the Eternal Father dipped His pen in the blood of His Son and wrote, "God is love," in language for all to read. There—among fake witnesses; bloodthirsty murderers; cowardly, self-saving officials; traitors; deniers; and deserters—Jesus prayed, "Father, forgive them; for they know not what they do" (Luke 23:34).

Under comparable circumstances Stephen, with countenance shining like the face of an angel, prayed, "Lord, lay not this sin to their charge" (Acts 7:60). He was as human as anyone saved by grace and filled with the Holy Spirit. If he could show such love, can't we do as well by God's grace?

Christ taught, "Love your enemies, bless them that curse you, do good to them that hate you, and pray for them which despitefully use you, and persecute you. . . . Be ye therefore perfect, even as your Father which is in heaven is perfect" (Matt. 5:44, 48).

September 18

Love Cures Envy

1 Cor. 13:4b

Envy entered the heart of man when Satan beguiled Eve. Her firstborn became the envious murderer of his brother. Envy is defined as "chagrin at the sight of another's excellence or good fortune, accompanied by some degree of hatred and a desire to possess equal advantage."

Envy is the most destructive force in the world. But for envy the discovery of atomic energy would be an unmixed blessing. It is envy that forces nations to live in fear.

Unrestrained envy may work destruction to its object, but it is certain destruction for the one who harbors it. A legend tells of a statue erected in honor of a noted wrestler. A contestant who had lost to him wrestled with the monument under cover of night until it fell on him and crushed him to death. He who indulges envy destroys himself. "Love envieth not." Pure love of God and man expels that form of self-love called envy.

Love rejoices in the good fortune of everyone. It does not covet the better clothing, house, automobile, or salary of another. Love does not begrudge his fellow his grace or gifts, his place of honor in church or community. He who loves will follow with enthusiasm as well as lead with humility. Love does not desire advancement at the cost of another's demotion. It does not discount a brother's success, not even a predecessor or a successor. "Love is of God."

September 19

The Charm of Love

1 Cor. 13:4c-5ab

The pure love of God in the heart transfigures the total person. It is refinement inspired and spontaneous.

Unassumed self-effacement is part of the irresistible charm of love. It shines like a light. There is no boasting, paraded righteousness, or condescending superiority. Love accepts praise

219

with humility and deftly turns a compliment upon its giver. It allows no ego inflation, intellectual pride, spiritual pharisaism, or rude discrimination against another.

Love is gentle and gracious. It permits no hot words of retaliation. It leaves no smoldering resentment to break out in biting sarcasm. The chastisement of love is healing, not withering.

Love does not seek its own glorification. It prefers the exaltation of another. Love does not insist on its own way. It may speak with conviction, but it yields in graciousness. Love can take a back seat without pouting. It demands neither justice nor recognition.

Love is "without offence." It does not carelessly give nor does it take offence. In love's garden there is no miff tree, but always there are found fresh, varied flowers, beautiful and fragrant. There are roses without thorns.

In Jesus Christ, we behold the glory of divine love incarnate. He draws men to himself in admiration and adoration by the irresistible attraction of love. The more completely He is stripped of the trappings with which men have clothed Him, the more magnetic He remains.

September 20

Love Is Fairness

1 Cor. 13:5c-6

Love is not blind but it is fair. It is quick to see wrong, but it does not withdraw mercy for the wrongdoer. Love inspires automatic reaction against rumor and gossip. It will have no part in "spreading evil surmises injurious to the good name of others." Love thinketh no evil.

The Christian in whose heart the love of God is shed abroad will base no conclusions upon his unfounded misgivings. He will argue against his mistrust until proof is established. He accepts the principle that all are innocent until proved guilty. When guilt is established, he grieves that he must admit the evidence is sufficient.

Jesus knew well the long record of rejection of God and willful transgression of His law by the people of Jerusalem. But His pronouncement of judgment was spoken in a heartbreaking lament. Love rejoiceth not in iniquity. It forbids repeating a damaging story even if regrettably true, except to protect an innocent person from being misled.

Can love render judgment upon the guilty? Yes, because justice administered in love can be redemptive. It leads to repentance. Love allows final condemnation only on the finally impenitent.

Love rejoices in the truth. A mind enlightened by the Spirit, whose fruit is love, accepts the truth with its implications even if its sharp, cutting edge brings self-condemnation. Such a Spirit-guided person will not defend himself by clever rationalization. He will admit he is wrong and amend his ways. The truth makes men free and whole.

September 21

The Mantle of Love

1 Cor. 13:7

Everyone wears a mantle. A spiritual atmosphere envelops the entire being if it is a cloak woven of silken threads of love. It is to the one who wears it a shield of defense against the arrows of hate. It is a powerful magnetism to draw all kindred spirits within its gentle folds.

Love "beareth all things." Attitudes, words, or deeds capable of double interpretation are taken in their better meaning. If there is no mistake possible, love says the motive was better than the appearance. If it was a vicious thrust, love is quick to forgive and heal the bleeding wound. Love is magnanimous.

Love "believeth all things." It is disposed to credulity. It prefers to be disillusioned rather than suspicious. Love does not reach conclusions based on prejudice. It would rather enjoy the confidence of the simple than the cunning discernment of the subtile.

Love "hopeth all things." It looks on the brighter side of life. It is not blind to dangers but hopes all things will get better. Love knows if defeat is possible, victory is not impossible. It would rather die in hope than to live in despair. The night may be dark but the morning cometh. The darkest cloud may have a silver lining.

Love "endureth all things." It never gives up. The long-delayed fulfillment of the promise is outlasted by love's endurance. Even treacherous betrayal cannot turn love to hate. Jesus said to Judas, the traitor, "Friend, wherefore art thou come?" (Matt. 26:50). Love never fails.

September 22

I Became a Man

1 Cor. 13:11

Infancy is characterized by simple dependence and unaffected love. Knowing this, Jesus said, "Except ye be converted, and become as little children, ye shall not enter into the kingdom of heaven" (Matt. 18:3).

The reactions of an immature mind are emotional, not rational. Conclusions are impulsive. Issues are drawn over inconsequential matters. Absence of sound arguments is camouflaged by loud, long talk. Small and often unintentional offenses are magnified in quarreling and abusive language. Small people often attribute the traits of their own dwarfed souls to other people. They use a vocabulary of intimidation. Paul was thinking of such practice when he said, "When I became a man, I put away childish things."

An innocent infant never loses his charm. A petulant child may be forgiven, in the faith that he will grow up. But childishness in adults, especially those who profess to follow Christ, is disappointing.

Small-minded people are never all on the same side of an argument; therefore, senseless controversies go on. Many times they are fostered by well-meaning people. They are easier to start than they are to finish. One group finds an inconsistency

222

and cries, "Compromiser." The answer "Radical" is never wanting. One may allow what another's conscience forbids. He is dubbed "carnal." The grieved defendant shouts, "Legalist." The work of mutilation goes on. Strength so much needed to combat sin and Satan and save the lost for whom Christ died, is worse than wasted.

Paul admonished, "Brethren, be not children in understanding: howbeit in malice be ye children, but in understanding be men" (14:20).

September 23

"Through a Glass, Darkly"

1 Cor. 13:12

Partial understanding is the inescapable lot of mortal man. Perhaps his greatest wisdom is the recognition that his knowledge is fractional. Cocksureness is unpardonable ignorance. The more learning one has, the greater is his understanding of the vastness of that beyond the grasp of his finite mind.

All anyone should need to keep him humble and charitable toward others is the knowledge of his own failures and limitations. God grant to us the ability to see ourselves as others see us and, far more important, to see ourselves as the all-wise Judge sees us.

One of the most amazing revelations of heaven may be the discovery of how wrong we were in our measurement of others. Some we did not expect may be there. Those we judged of little worth may be among the glorified. Man looks on the outward appearance. God knows true worth. Some we classified as inconsequential may be judged truly great. Some we overlooked here may have rich reward in heaven. God's righteous judgment is to be trusted.

From the viewpoint of one who knows as he is known, things we have considered of great importance may be seen of microscopic size. And things we reckoned as too small to notice may decide momentous issues.

223

Father, be pleased to let us sit at Thy feet and learn of Thee. Since at best we can know only in part, so fill us with Thy love that when that which is perfect is come, we may receive abundant mercy. For Jesus' sake, Amen.

September 24

Love Is the Greatest

1 Cor. 13:13

Faith, hope, and love are the noblest attributes of the human spirit. These virtues are comparable only to themselves. Doubt, despair, and desire can only be contrasted to these blessings of the Spirit. The legitimate material values are in a separate category from these things that abide. Even the best gifts of the Spirit are of temporary worth. Prophecies shall fail, tongues shall cease, knowledge shall vanish. Now abideth faith, hope, and love.

Paul told the Romans, "We are saved by hope" (8:24). From despondency and disillusionment we are lifted. The Christian's blessed hope is that someday we shall see the Savior and be with Him where He is.

By faith we enjoy the reality of things hoped for. Faith gives assurance when perplexity clouds our way. It sees with clear vision the way of holiness on which the redeemed walk.

"The greatest of these is love." All our hopes shall be fulfilled when Jesus shall appear and we shall be like Him for we shall see Him as He is. Faith also shall be changed to clear vision of the effulgent glory of the King eternal, immortal, invisible. But love shall abide forever, through everlasting years the same.

Anything not in harmony with love will be so discordant in heaven that banishment to outer darkness would be better than permanent residence there. "God is love," and only those who partake of the divine nature could feel at home where all is love.

Now abides faith, hope, and love; but the greatest of these is love.

"Comforted of God"

2 Cor. 1:3-4

Paul suffered many tribulations. Instead of languishing in self-pity, he rejoiced in the all-sufficiency of the grace of God. Even his thorn in the flesh by which he was buffeted, was proof that God's strength was made perfect in weakness. He looked upon his sufferings as supplemental to the sufferings of Christ. They identified him with the Suffering Servant. By them he grew in Christlikeness and shared in Christ's redeeming work.

His own tribulations qualified Paul to give a ministry of comfort to others. "For as the sufferings of Christ abound in us, so our consolation also aboundeth by Christ. And whether we be afflicted, it is for your consolation and salvation . . . And . . . as ye are partakers of the sufferings, so shall ye be also of the consolation" (vv. 5-7). Tribulation works patience, and patience experience, by which we are prepared for a ministry of comfort to those who suffer.

There is personal benefit in suffering for well-doing. Peter's benediction is: "The God of all grace, who hath called you unto his eternal glory by Christ Jesus, after that ye have suffered a while, make you perfect, stablish, strengthen, settle you. To him be glory and dominion for ever and ever. Amen" (1 Pet. 5:10-11).

And Paul includes this theme in that triumphant eighth chapter of Romans: "If . . . we suffer with him, . . . we may be also glorified together. For I reckon that the sufferings of this present time are not worthy to be compared with the glory which shall be revealed in us" (vv. 17-18).

The Priceless Treasure

2 Cor. 4:17

The vessel is fragile and of little worth. The treasure it contains is of untold value. A reading of the context reveals that Paul was using the vessel to represent his own person. He said, "We preach not ourselves, but Christ Jesus the Lord; and ourselves your servants for Jesus' sake. . . . always bearing about in the body the dying of the Lord Jesus, that the life also of Jesus might be made manifest in our body" (vv. 5, 10).

The vessel is always frail and fallible. The body is subject to disease and death. The mind is not free from mistakes, and even the spirit may be less than perfect. It has been marred in the Fall. It can, however, be remade to bear the image of God and contain the priceless treasure.

The treasure unmistakably is the light of the knowledge of the glory of God. That light shines in the face of Jesus Christ. Those who saw Him saw the glory of God shining in and through Him. That same light has shined in our hearts. It has transfigured our lives until these earthen vessels receiving the light shed forth its radiance for others to see.

Those whose lives shine as lights in the world are more conscious that the vessel is earthen than that they possess the treasure. If others behold it, they know the excellent power is of God, not of us. It is the resurrection life made manifest in us. The witness is authentic, but it is dependent on the Source of light and life.

September 27

"In Christ"

2 Cor. 5:17

"In Christ" is the most frequent and favored expression in Paul's terminology. It was the identification of a redeemed person with Christ. It was a confession of faith, implying union with Christ and fellowship with Him. In Paul's writings it is always *in* Christ, never *with* Christ. He uses that term or its equivalent 164 times in his writings. What air is to a bird and water is to a fish, Christ is to the Christian. He is at home in the Spirit of Christ. Paul said, "For to me to live is Christ" (Phil. 1:21). To have His mind is to manifest His attitude in every relationship of life.

226

To be a new creature in Christ means that in a spiritual understanding one is no longer of Adam's fallen race. Christ is now the Head of the family of God. The man in Christ has been born of the Spirit. "Old things are passed away; behold, all things are become new." He is no longer under the dominion of sin. He is a servant of righteousness. His life is no more fixed in the context of the world. He is otherworldly. His life center is in Christ.

The man in Christ has His attitude toward sin. He has no apology or defense for sin in practice or in principle. With Christ central, sanctification is the manifestation of Christ's character in the life of the believer. With eyes fixed on Jesus, we see the person we can be.

September 28

The Compelling Love of Christ

2 Cor. 5:14

To be "in Christ" is to see through His eyes. It is to see sin as exceeding sinful and Satan's malicious means for the destruction of men. It is to have a sense of values in complete contradiction to that of the worldly-minded. To Jesus, accumulated wealth was as nothing. He had not where to lay His head. Fame and prestigious position among men had no attraction for Him. Gratification of the desires of the flesh had no appeal. He said, "My meat is to do the will of him that sent me" (John 4:34).

The man in Christ sees all men as Christ saw them. He saw in the vilest of sinners and the most benighted pagan, men for whom the love of God was poured out. Every man was a soul worth more than all the world. Christ saw them as all dead, and He died for all. For their sakes He was obedient unto death, even the death on the Cross. He gave himself without limit. He died the death all sinful men should have died. He was made sin, "who knew no sin; that we might be made the righteousness of God in him. . . . God was in Christ, reconciling the world unto himself" (vv. 21, 19). Now being reconciled unto God, we are

227

made ministers of the reconciliation, as though God did beseech all men by us to be reconciled unto God.

Having received the love of God shed abroad in our hearts, we have no option. There is no room for self-centered living. Life in Christ is life poured out in a ministry of reconciliation.

September 29

"These Promises"

2 Cor. 7:1

A holy life is built upon the foundation of God's promises. He has given us exceeding great and precious promises. There is at least one to meet the need of every possible life situation. The veracity and faithfulness of God supports all the promises He has made. These promises are the ones which immediately precede the words of our text. "Therefore" turns attention to them. Here they are: "Ye are the temple of the living God; . . . I will dwell in them, and walk in them; and I will be their God, and they shall be my people. . . . I will receive you, and will be a Father unto you, and ye shall be my sons and daughters, saith the Lord Almighty."

These, as well as all God's promises, are conditional. They are made and fulfilled to those who are separate from unbelievers, unrighteousness, darkness, Belial, infidels, and idols. With a line clearly drawn, the question is asked, "Who is on the Lord's side?" A choice must be made and lived by. The one who lives a holy life has faith firmly anchored to the never failing promises of God.

There is a fountain in which the believer in the promises may wash and be clean. One cannot cleanse himself; but by voluntary exercise of faith, he can appropriate the means God provides for his cleansing. The blood of Jesus Christ, God's Son, cleanses from all sin. "The cleansing stream, I see, I see! I plunge and, oh, it cleanseth me!"

The fullness of a holy life is perfected in reverence for and worship of a holy God. "I have set the Lord always before me" (Ps. 16:8).

Riches Shared

2 Cor. 8:9

"Love that supplies its own motive" is one definition of grace. It is illustrated in the great gesture of God in that while we were yet sinners, Christ died for us. God held out the olive branch to rebellious man. While he was loveless and unlovely, God commended His love to him. It was no concession to sin. It was reconciliation on terms man could meet with no loss to himself and with well-being both now and forever assured. All man needs to do is to turn away from that which would work ruin and slavery in life and torment forever. "The wages of sin is death; but the gift of God is eternal life through Jesus Christ our Lord" (Rom. 6:23).

> *Oh, the mighty gulf that God did span*
> *At Calvary.*
> *Mercy there was great and grace was free;*
> *Pardon there was multiplied to me;*
> *There my burdened soul found liberty,*
> *At Calvary.*

The initiative was taken by God the Father, because He is holy love. The price was paid by the Son who did not grasp at equality with God. "Though he was rich, yet for your sakes he became poor, that ye through his poverty might be rich." He became the Son of Man that we might be the sons of God. He became the sin offering that we might offer to God a sacrifice acceptable, well pleasing, a reasonable service. He wore a crown of thorns that we might wear a crown of righteousness. He tasted death that we might live forever.

October 1

Abounding Grace

2 Cor. 9:8

Since God has given so lavishly to undeserving men, those who are recipients should abound toward others in gifts of love.

That kind of giving never impoverishes the giver. God's resources are not depleted by giving. Therefore, to the faithful steward of His bounty, there is an ever-abounding supply which more than equates what is given.

Stunted souls who give grudgingly may receive in proportion. But liberal souls who give cheerfully receive bountifully. The farmer who plants sparingly to save the seed gathers a meager harvest. The one who sees the harvest as 100-fold of what he plants commits his seed to the soil in faith and gathers the harvest with joy. In spiritual sowing and reaping, there is no risk; for "God is able to make all grace abound toward you; that ye, always having all sufficiency in all things, may abound to every good work." God will "multiply your seed sown, and increase the fruits of your righteousness" (v. 10). The one who demonstrates his righteousness in faithful stewardship and generous kindness will never want the means to do it. The more he gives, the more he will have to give.

His giving is in loving concern for those who receive of his bounty. It is also an expression of his gratitude to the Giver of every good and perfect gift.

"Thanks be unto God for his unspeakable gift" (v. 15).

October 2

The Glory of the Cross

Gal. 6:14

Paul wrote the Epistle to the Galatian church to withstand those self-appointed teachers who were insisting that Gentile Christians should be circumcised and keep the ceremonial law of Moses. He challenged the Galatians to testify whether they had received the Spirit by the works of the law, or by the hearing of faith. He declared that Christ had redeemed us from the curse of the law and that the blessing of Abraham had come on the Gentiles through Jesus Christ. "And if ye be Christ's, then are ye Abraham's seed" (3:29).

The apostle exhorts them to stand fast in the liberty wherewith Christ made them free. "For in Jesus Christ neither

230

circumcision availeth any thing, nor uncircumcision; but faith which worketh by love. . . . only use not liberty for an occasion to the flesh, but by love serve one another. For all the law is fulfilled in one word . . . Thou shalt love thy neighbour as thyself" (5:6, 13-14).

Paul concludes that those who were demanding that the Gentile Christians should be circumcised were insincere. They desired to glory in their flesh.

Paul's own testimony would indicate, I am crucified with Christ and I glory in the Cross by which I am dead to the world; and the word of pharisaical law is as though it did not exist to me. "For neither circumcision availeth any thing, nor uncircumcision, but a new creature. And as many as walk according to this rule, peace be on them, and mercy, and upon the Israel of God" (by faith in Christ) (6:15-16).

October 3

Chosen to Be Holy

Eph. 1:4

Holiness for man is not God's afterthought. It predates creation; it follows from the fact that God is holy and originates in the self-willed purity of God himself. Complete fellowship with God can only be known by one who is holy.

That God has chosen man to be holy is seen in that He created him in His likeness. He has commanded it in the law: "Ye shall be holy: for I the Lord your God am holy" (Lev. 19:2). It is further established that God wills man to be holy in that He sent Christ the Lamb of God to take away the sin of the world. And the Holy Spirit came to purify believers' hearts by faith.

God's purpose is nullified until man chooses to be holy. He must walk the path of obedience day by day, hour by hour, moment by moment.

The holiness which God willed for man has been provided in the atonement made by Jesus Christ. By His death He

231

opened the fountain that man may wash and be clean. By His ascension He made possible the coming of the Holy Spirit to abide in the cleansed temple of man's heart. Because believers are in Christ, they are partakers of the divine nature. They are built up in Him. He dwells in their hearts by faith. They pursue the goal of Christlikeness.

Holiness is manifested in a life without blame before Him in love. Those in Christ are living according to the eternal purpose of the God of holy love.

October 4

The Spirit's Seal and Pledge

Eph. 1:13b-14

This word of assurance is to those who have trusted in Christ for their salvation. They were living with Christ in view. Having already believed, they were sealed with that Holy Spirit of promise. The seal was the proof of genuineness. As an official seal testifies to the validity of a document, in like manner God stamps His own image on the spiritual nature of those who trust in Christ. They are renewed in knowledge after the image of Him that created them.

The seal of the Spirit is convincing evidence of exclusive possession by God the Father. It also is guarantee of security. Jesus said of His sheep, "I give unto them eternal life; and they shall never perish, neither shall any man pluck them out of my hand" (John 10:28). Only by willful rebellion can the seal be broken. There is safety in the Father's keeping.

The sealing of the Holy Spirit of promise is the fulfillment of the promise of the Father, reaffirmed by Jesus, and given in fullness at Pentecost and available to all believers thereafter.

The Holy Spirit is the earnest of our inheritance. The reference is to our future state of blessedness in the Father's house with many rooms. The present life in the Spirit is the pledge of that which shall be ours forever. It is a deposit in token of full payment. The life of the Christian is already in the kingdom of heaven. But what we now possess is only a small

232

fraction of the full endowment. It is heaven below, our Redeemer to know.

The Habitation of God

Eph. 2:22

The Church of Jesus Christ is the dwelling place of God. It
is built upon a sure foundation. It stands firmly on the revelation of God as found in the apostles and prophets. It is the truth
of God as contained in the message of holy men who were
inspired by the Spirit of God. The Chief Cornerstone is Jesus
Christ himself. "God . . . hath in these last days spoken unto
us by his Son" (Heb. 1:1-2). "Other foundation can no man lay
than that is laid, which is Jesus Christ" (1 Cor. 3:11).

The construction of the Church is of persons who, as living
"stones, are built up a spiritual house, an holy priesthood, to
offer up spiritual sacrifices, acceptable to God by Jesus Christ,"
and who "shew forth the praises of him who hath called [them]
out of darkness into his marvellous light" (1 Pet. 2:5, 9). The
redeemed are fellow citizens with the saints and are of the
household of faith. There is unity in variety. There are Jews and
Gentiles. The wall of separation has been broken down. All have
access by one Spirit to the Father. There is beauty in the sym-
metry of the Church. It is fitly framed together and groweth
unto an holy temple in the Lord. It will continue in process of
building until Christ comes to claim His own.

The Blood-washed people of God are the habitation of God
through the Spirit.

October 6

The Unsearchable Riches of Christ

Eph. 3:8

Humility is the primary virtue of one who has the mind of
Christ. That lowliness of mind qualified Paul to have an exalted

conception of Christ and the unsearchable riches in Him. He comprehended the fellowship of the mystery hid in God, the manifold wisdom of God, the eternal purpose in Christ, and unity of the family of God. These wonders brought him to his knees in awesome worship.

In this prayer Paul offered the Ephesians and the spiritually minded lovers of Jesus in all ages a glimpse of the depth of the riches both of the wisdom and knowledge of God. The prayer does more to clarify spiritual vision, increase faith, and deepen devotion than any exposition of it could do. It is to the Father of our Lord Jesus Christ that Paul prayed "that he would grant you, according to the riches of his glory, to be strengthened with might by his Spirit in the inner man; that Christ may dwell in your hearts by faith; that ye, being rooted and grounded in love, may be able to comprehend with all saints what is the breadth, and length, and depth, and height; and to know the love of Christ, which passeth knowledge, that ye might be filled with all the fulness of God.

"Now unto him that is able to do exceeding abundantly above all that we ask or think, according to the power that worketh in us, unto him be glory in the church by Christ Jesus throughout all ages, world without end. Amen" (vv. 16-21).

October 7
Toward the Ideal Church

Eph. 4:13

The ascended Christ had also descended to fill the Church with His Spirit to direct its operations and its growth. He is not only concerned with its expansion and numerical growth. His deeper desire is for it to grow in the knowledge and graces of the Spirit. When the ministries of the Church produce Christlike men and women, there will be no problem of addition; it will soon be multiplication, as it was in the days of the apostles.

Erection of buildings, raising money, enrollment statistics are good as secondary goals. Nevertheless, the primary purpose of all the services of the Church of Jesus Christ is "the perfecting of the saints, . . . the edifying of the body of Christ: till we all come in the unity of the faith, and the knowledge of the Son of God [in personal experience], unto a perfect man, unto the measure of the stature of the fulness of Christ."

To this end God "gave some, apostles; and some, prophets; and some, evangelists; and some, pastors and teachers" (v. 11). It would appear that pastors should be teachers as well as preachers, shepherds, and administrators. There is a teaching phase of the ministry, that the Church may be built up in the holy faith. Many others may share in this work of instruction, but the pastor is a teacher too.

The ideal is a Church composed of people who are mature even unto the fullness of Christ. They will be established in love and unity. The Church will be the Body of which Christ is the Head.

October 8

A Glorious Church

Eph. 5:25b-27

Paul saw the Church as the Body of Christ becoming the Bride of Christ. That invisible Church is contained within the visible church. It is not coextensive with the ecclesiasticism as men behold it. There are many nominal church members who do not qualify as composing the true spiritual Body of Christ. No one denomination constitutes that organism. But in almost any company of church people there are those who by faith in Christ have been "born again, not of corruptible seed, but of incorruptible, by the word of God, which liveth and abideth for ever" (1 Pet. 1:23). They now are members of Christ's Body.

Jesus "loved the [unsanctified] church, and gave himself for it"; that He might sanctify it with His own blood, He

235

suffered without the gate. "That He might sanctify her, having cleansed her," is a helpful translation. The Bible always places remission of sins before sanctification. It is after the washing as with water and the renewing of the Holy Spirit in regeneration that the purification follows. Since these verbs "sanctify" and "cleanse" are in the aorist tense, they may be understood to imply two crisis experiences. The sacraments may be symbolic of those experiences: baptism suggesting the washing has taken place; and the New Testament in Christ's shed blood, as received in the Lord's Supper, signifying the Blood that washes whiter than snow.

All this Christ did for His Church in His atoning death that He might present it to himself as His Bride. He has prepared her for himself, a glorious Church with no stain of sin and no marks of age upon her.

October 9

Love Abounding

Phil. 1:9

The Epistle to the Philippians has been called a love letter. Paul's love for them is expressed eloquently and repeatedly in many expressions of his deep affection. He said, "I have you in my heart," and, "I long after you" (vv. 7, 8). He had proof that the Philippians loved him. They had sent their love offerings to him in Thessalonica, in Corinth, and now in Rome. Their love was not on the human level; it was agape, the love of God. Paul was concerned that their love for one another should continue and increase. Therefore he includes in his letter a prayer that their love might abound more and more like a river at flood time.

The love that God sheds abroad in the hearts of those who receive the Holy Spirit in fullness is perfect love. It is unrivaled love for God, and it is love for others without taint of selfishness.

Nevertheless, it is love that can be improved in its expression. Love finds ways for its own increase. Love can so permeate our being that the words we speak have overtones of tenderness and compassion. Love is constantly contriving ways to show itself in deeds of kindness and generosity.

Love is not blind. It has 20/20 vision. With friends, it loves in spite of faults and failures. With enemies, it overcomes evil with good.

There is insight in the lines of Edwin Markham.

> *He drew a circle that shut me out,*
> *Heretic, rebel, a thing to flout;*
> *But love and I had the wit to win,*
> *We drew a circle that took him in.*

October 10

The Mind Which Was in Christ Jesus

Phil. 2:5

Anyone of thoughtful, devout mind stands in awe at the mention of this text. The finite mind cannot reach the sublime heights or measure the fathomless depths of truth contained in this passage. Yet is is offered by Paul as the solution to a very practical problem in the church at Philippi. And if accepted, this admonition would resolve many tense situations in the churches of our day.

Paul was not writing to his beloved church at Philippi because it was torn by divisions. But he realized there was potential schism among those for whose continued unity in holy fellowship he was jealous. It was for that purpose he offered this timely counsel, "Let this mind be in you, which was also in Christ Jesus." It is clear that there were three characteristics of Jesus' mind that he wanted them to imitate. First, it was a mind in complete obedience unto death, even the death of the Cross. This is a principle which no earnest Christian can take time to debate. Obedience is a joy to those who supremely love God.

The second disposition that Jesus exemplified was selfless

living for the sake of others. He did not grasp equality with God as the first Adam did. He emptied himself for others' sake. His was the mind of a servant.

The third trait of the mind of Christ, which Paul cited, was the willingness to offer himself a sacrifice to reconcile all penitent, believing sinners to God. To such a purpose every Christian should offer himself a living sacrifice.

October 11

No Impossibilities

Phil. 4:13

This is more than "positive thinking" or "possibility thinking." It includes both but it is above the level of humanism. It is a declaration of faith in Christ. He is the dynamic of the Christian's life. Paul testified to the Galatians, "Christ liveth in me" (2:20); and to Timothy he humbly professed, "I thank Christ Jesus our Lord, who hath enabled me" (1 Tim. 1:12). Weymouth translates this verse, "I have strength for anything through Him who gives me power."

This would be the language of the Stoics, who taught that man could of himself overcome in all human circumstances by his own will, but for the fact that Paul ascribed his strength to the power of Christ working mightily in him. There are those who protest that any confession of dependence on a source outside themselves is weakness. To the Corinthians Paul said, "I rather glory in my infirmities, that the power of Christ may rest upon me. . . . for when I am weak, then am I strong" (2 Cor. 12:9-10). It is when the man of faith realizes his inadequacy, that the power of God's mighty Spirit works in and through him. Dependence on human resources and personal capabilities is weakness. The more we learn to lean on Christ, the more power He supplies. Given a man living in complete yieldedness to the will of God, everything is in the realm of possibility.

It is not power to turn on by command. It is His strength within us. Because He is our life, we are more than conquerors.

238

October 12

Established in the Faith

Col. 2:6-7

Paul addressed his letter to the Colossians "to the saints and faithful brethren in Christ." Epaphras had declared to him their love in the Spirit. Paul had expressed his concern that they might be "strengthened with all might according to his glorious power, unto all patience and longsuffering with joyfulness" (v. 11).

In the words of this text, he assumes that their conversion was real and the transformation of their lives was complete. Therefore, he exhorts, as ye have received Christ in full surrender and in faith, continue to live in Him. As the branch lives by union with the vine, so you, being joined to Christ by faith, abide in Him.

The apostle uses a double metaphor, rooted like a tree and built up like a house. The tense of the first verb is aorist. That of the second is present. You have chosen and received Christ by faith and have become a new creature. You are rooted in Him. Some trees spread their roots on the surface of the ground. Others strike deep taproots and from them send out others into the soil. Such a tree stands firm in the storm of wind that topples those that have only shallow roots. Paul is saying, Your roots are deep in the soil of God's truth.

The building rises on its foundation in a continual progress toward completion. Weymouth translates verse 7 thus: "having the roots of your being firmly planted in Him and continually building yourselves up in Him and always being increasingly confirmed in the faith as you were taught it, and abounding in it with thanksgiving."

October 13

Risen with Christ

Col. 3:1

Paul had reminded the Christians at Colosse that they had been dead in their sins. They were quickened with Christ in

239

forgiveness. They were buried with Him in baptism. They now walked with Him in newness of life. He now calls upon them to "seek those things which are above" and set their "affections on things above . . . where Christ sitteth on the right hand of God." They are new persons. They have more than a new set of rules to live by. It is life with a new motive and a new purpose, not simply good resolutions. It is life different in kind, not in degree only. It is of different quality. It is supernatural. They have the stamp of eternity upon them. They are citizens of heaven here and now.

Christ has become a great spiritual magnet to lift them out of their worldly context. Their desires and aims are no longer for the sensuous and the material. They seek the things spiritual and eternal. The love of earthly things has been neutralized, cancelled out. Their affections are set on things above. Christ is the new life center. They are drawn toward Him where He is at God's right hand. Their lives are submerged with Him in the will and love of God. They have put off the old man with his deeds. They are renewed in knowledge, righteousness, and holiness. They have put on Christ. He is in them and they are like Him now. When He shall appear, they will appear with Him in glory.

October 14
Exemplary Christians

1 Thess. 1:5-7

The beginning of the church of the Thessalonians is recorded in Acts 17:1-10. Paul had been hurried out of the city under cover of night because of violence aroused by Jews who were stirred with envy. The first Epistle to that church was sent from Corinth within a few months of Paul's departure. It is an intimate personal communication expressing the apostle's loving concern for his brethren in God the Father and in the Lord Jesus Christ. He opens with the apostolic salutation of grace and peace and an expression of thanksgiving to God for them and assurance of his prayers on their behalf.

Paul is so certain of their genuine conversion that he commends them as examples to all believers. He calls to remembrance their work of faith which was evidenced by their turning from the idols of paganism to serve the living and true God. He was encouraged by their labor of love which motivated them to witness to the power of the Word of the Lord in all their home mission field. He was gratified that their patient hope was directed toward the coming from heaven of the Son of God, whom God had raised from the dead.

The gospel had been proclaimed to them in the power of the Holy Ghost and in much assurance. Their faith had been tested in affliction, and their joy in the Holy Ghost attested to their transformation. They had sealed their election to salvation by believing the Word of God and by their obedience to it.

October 15

Something Lacking in Their Faith

1 Thess. 3:10

Paul had no doubts about the regeneration of the believers at Thessalonica. They gave full proof that they were new creatures in Christ Jesus. He did have deep concern that they should be steadfast in the Christian faith and that they should continue toward completeness. He assured them that even in his absence his love for them had not abated. He testified, "We were gentle among you, even as a nurse [mother] cherisheth her children: so being affectionately desirous of you, we were willing to have imparted unto you . . . our own souls" (2:7-8).

The apostle had earnestly wanted to return to them but was hindered by Satan. Therefore, he had sent Timothy to establish and comfort them lest his labor be in vain. Now Timothy had returned with a good report which brought comfort to Paul and was cause for his rejoicing. He said, "We live, if ye stand fast in the Lord. For what thanks can we render to God again for you, for all the joy wherewith we joy for your sakes . . . ?" (vv. 8-9).

Paul, however, is concerned for them and is praying night and day that he might see them and perfect that which was lacking in their faith. His prayer for them was that they might increase and abound in love for one another and for all men even as he loved them. That was in fact a prayer that they might be made perfect in love. The end result would be establishment in holiness. It was perfect love and purity of heart that was lacking in their faith.

October 16

The Will of God

1 Thess. 4:3

We are now into the practical portion of this Epistle. The focus of Paul's exhortations is on the will of God for the sanctification of all Christian believers. The apostle has expressed his strong desire that the Thessalonians should go forward in their devotement to God. In going on they would be saved from going back to their old pagan life. There is no stopping place provided in the will of God. Progress in faith and love is not an option; it is a must. The growing Christian discovers his need for a pure heart that is full of love divine. Sooner for some and later for others, God not only convicts of inward sin but also reveals that a cleansing fountain has been opened for all. The blood of Jesus Christ cleanses from all sin. This is entire sanctification which is the entrance into a life of holiness.

Holy living calls for discipline of natural desires. Sexual indulgence, gluttony, and intemperance are contrary to God's commandments. God has not called us to uncleanness but unto holiness.

Deceitful practice in business is forbidden among brethren and with those that are without the Christian community.

Brotherly love is taught of God, and in it the Christian is to grow more and more.

Meddling in the affairs of others is condemned, while diligence in work in keeping with God's will is urgently recommended.

Holiness is full devotement to God, who has given us His Holy Spirit, whose office is to make and keep men holy.

October 17

"Sanctify You Wholly"

1 Thess. 5:23-24

Paul has left no doubt as to the reality of the experience of initial salvation experienced by the Christians at Thessalonica. He has received a recent report of their steadfastness in the faith. He now makes known to them the ethical implications of a life of holiness. In verses 12-22, he sets before them the spiritual concepts by which they should abide. Finally he climaxes the message from his heart of love with a prayer for them to be wholly sanctified.

The apostle places within the reach of their faith an experience that would cleanse their entire being—body, soul, and spirit—from all sin. They would be made holy or pure through and through. It was not to be a continuing process but an instantaneous act of God.

The verb "sanctify" is in the Greek aorist tense, which is never used for continuous action, but rather something completed now.

This prayer is for purity and perfect love. It did not assure perfection in performance, but complete submission to the will of God and intentions that were all according to His holy dispositions. This would result in a blameless life before God. It would not be faultless before men. They would do as Paul testified, exercise themselves to have always a conscience void of offense toward God and toward men.

In the gracious experience of grace received by faith, Christians are preserved unto the coming of Christ.

Paul adds the promise, "Faithful is he that calleth you, who also will do it."

243

October 18

Love out of a Pure Heart

1 Tim. 1:5

This Epistle is addressed to Timothy, whom Paul called his own son in the faith. He would be expected to make this letter personal, not controversial. He would by intention emphasize the essentials for Christian doctrine, experience, and ethics.

In this text, the apostle spells out the maximum demand upon one who is a Christian and the minimum expectation. This is the lowest common denominator; true Christianity need be no more and can be no less.

To be a Christian one must have sincere faith in the revelation of God as taught and exemplified in the life, death, and resurrection of Jesus Christ. When men depart from the simplicity that is in Christ, they almost certainly read into their creed their own opinions and interpretations. Such may be acceptable and important to oneself, but if made the criterion by which to judge others, they may only exclude them. It is characteristic of the finite mind to make one's own opinions essential to orthodoxy, and all who disagree are therefore heterodox.

To those who have an unfeigned faith is given a pure heart, a single mind, and a life elevated and holy. The end result is expressed in word and deed.

The only source from which such love can be obtained is God, who is love. It is received by faith. It is love of one's neighbor. This, said Paul, is the fulfilling of the law. Such a Christian has a conscience enlightened by God's Word and quickened by His Spirit. It is sensitive, yet approving.

October 19

Serene Faith

2 Tim. 1:12

That which is anticipated by faith is in possession of the believer now. When one believes for salvation, he is saved. One

244

who has faith for grace and strength to meet his daily needs has that grace and strength. He who has faith for eternal life has it now.

Unqualified commitment to God is the basis of faith for God's safe keeping. Paul is saying in this text that he has deposited his life and his all in God's care. Therefore, whatever of threat may come in life and whenever and however death may come, he has no cause for anxiety. He lives in the confidence that he is completely in the hands of God. This is the security that the committed Christian enjoys.

Paul said, "I know whom I have believed." The preposition *in* is often inserted. The apostle's faith was fortified by long acquaintance. He had met Jesus more than 30 years before on the Damascus road. The One in whom he trusted had never failed. In Corinth, beset by malicious foes, the Lord said to him, "Be not afraid . . . for I am with thee" (Acts 18:9-10). In Jerusalem the Lord stood by him and said, "Be of good cheer, Paul" (Acts 23:11). Again in the fierce storm at sea when all hope of being saved was gone, there came the reassuring word, "Fear not, Paul . . . God hath given thee all them that sail with thee" (Acts 27:24).

To all who trust Christ with their all, He will prove himself trustworthy. Heaven and earth may pass away, but Jesus never fails.

October 20

The Grace of God Brings Salvation

Titus 2:11-14

The grace of God has been manifested to all men. Christ is the "Light, which lighteth every man that cometh into the world" (John 1:9). To be saved, men must walk in that light voluntarily and by faith receive the salvation available to all. God in Christ teaches the believer how to live negatively—he rejects godlessness and worldly desires. Positively, he, by the help of the Holy Spirit, practices self-control and integrity in all human relationships. He has God who is holy as the center of his worship, and His revealed will as the rule of his life. All this is what it means to have full and free salvation now. We live out our redemption in a world in which evil is prevalent.

This great salvation has been provided by Jesus Christ who gave himself for us in the sacrifice offered on the cross of Calvary. In that great deed of love divine, He redeemed us from all iniquity, all willful sinful practice, and all impurity of heart. Justification and sanctification are included provisionally in Christ's offering himself once for all. Those who will trust and obey become a special possession of the Redeemer. They are not their own, they are bought with a price. Therefore, they glorify God in their bodies and spirits which are His.

Paul's faith in the coming of Christ a second time was firm. He offers that blessed hope as a compelling motive for holy living and zeal for good works.

October 21

A Slave Emancipated

Philem. 17-18

Slavery is not consistent with Christian principles now and never has been. The Christian does not defy the laws of the country of which he is a citizen; he lives above them.

Onesimus was owned by Philemon as a slave. He ran away; and with money he had probably stolen from his master, he made his way to Rome. He remembered Paul as a friend and benefactor to his master and sought him out in desperation. The apostle had received him and obtained his confession. Onesimus became a new man in Christ.

Playing on the meaning of his name, Paul said, "Onesimus is profitable to me or to you." But he knew by law he was the property of Philemon. Upon the apostle's advice Onesimus returned to his master. He carried this beautiful letter with its delicate touches of loving entreaty.

Paul does not invoke apostolic authority. He appeals to Philemon as a friend who owed his soul to him. He suggests that

246

Onesimus had departed for a while that he might be received forever not as a slave but as a brother beloved. Master and slave were one in Christ.

The apostle offers to be the mediator. He wrote, "If he has wronged you or owed you anything, charge it to me." He expressed his confidence that Philemon would do more. This was a veiled suggestion that he would emancipate Onesimus. Apparently he did; for, according to Early Church history, the runaway slave became bishop of the church at Ephesus.

October 22

"God Is Light"

1 John 1:5

The apostle John has given us some of the clearest insights into the pure essence of the nature of God. In chapter 4, verse 24 of his Gospel he records the words of Jesus who said, "God is a Spirit." That was to testify to the omnipresence of God. He is to be worshiped in spirit and in truth. Therefore, where two or three are gathered in Christ's name, He is in the midst. His presence in one place does not forbid the same glorious reality anywhere.

John also declares God is love (1 John 4:8, 16). Because He is love, He is motivated to communicate the knowledge of himself to man. He so loved that He gave His only Son to seek and to save the lost. Christ is God's supreme gift to man to woo and win him back to His fellowship.

From our text for today, we learn that God is light. Jesus said, "As long as I am in the world, I am the light of the world . . . he that followeth me shall not walk in darkness" (John 9:5; 8:12). Jesus came to restore the fellowship with God which man knew before the Fall. "If we walk in the light, as he is in the light, we have fellowship one with another . . . truly our fellowship is with the Father, and with his Son Jesus Christ" (vv. 7, 3). That fellowship is extended to all who dwell in love, for God is love.

247

October 23

Forgiveness of Sins

1 John 1:9

One of the facts of life is that man is a sinner. He who denies it deceives himself. To change the name does not alter the fact. What is assumed in the entire Bible is summarized by Paul, who wrote, "The scripture hath concluded all under sin" (Gal. 3:22); and, "All have sinned, and come short of the glory of God" (Rom. 3:23). John adds his penetrating conclusion, "If we say that we have not sinned, we make him [God] a liar, and his word is not in us" (v. 10).

As clearly as the Word teaches that man is sinful, so clearly does it offer forgiveness of sins. David prayed, "Have mercy upon me, O God, according to thy lovingkindness: according unto the multitude of thy tender mercies blot out my transgressions" (Ps. 51:1).

Isaiah's message from the Lord was, "I have blotted out, as a thick cloud, thy transgressions, and, as a cloud, thy sins" (44: 22).

Jesus commissioned Paul to preach "forgiveness of sins."

Forgiveness, according to John, is conditioned upon confession or acknowledgment of sins committed. This is to be accompanied by repentance or turning from sin. Then faith in Christ the Savior brings forgiveness. *God is faithful* to keep His promise to forgive or to blot out our sins, that is, to clear the record as though the sins had never been committed. God is *just* to forgive our sins because Christ died to provide atonement for sin. Now God can be just and the Justifier of all who believe in Jesus.

October 24

The Blood Cleanses

1 John 1:7

In God's gracious act of forgiveness the guilt of sin is gone. But the sin that dwells within remains. The guilt of sin is for

248

voluntary transgressions of God's known law. For the continued practice of sin the conscience may be seared as with a hot iron until one can sin and seem to enjoy it. Or guilt may lie so heavy on the conscience that it drives the sinner to emotional and mental distraction. Thank God, there is another alternative, namely, to seek and find forgiveness and peace with God.

The sin that remains is the propensity to sin because of what a man is. If in ignorance of God's provision for cleansing one struggles against it, the result is frustration and intermittent defeat and victory. But God is light, and the believing, obedient child of God sees the light. If he will walk in that path of light, it will lead him to make a total consecration to God and His holy will. He discovers that within the reach of his faith there is cleansing from all sin.

That cleansing is possible through the Blood that Jesus shed on the Cross. The life is in the Blood. On the Cross Christ made the supreme sacrifice. By it He made possible forgiveness of sins and cleansing from all sin. It is complete but it is conditional. All light on the path must be obeyed. This cleansing is present but it is continuous. The Blood cleanses now and continues to cleanse as light is obeyed.

October 25

"We Have an Advocate"

1 John 2:1-2

John, the aged apostle, rightfully thinks of himself as a father and those to whom he is writing as children. He is deeply concerned that his children sin not.

The right concept of one who has believed in Christ and seeks to follow Him is that he does not commit sin. In the background of this text are forgiveness of sins and cleansing from all sin by faith in Christ. John has made it clear that to sin is not impossible; but not to sin, is possible.

For the Christian who unknowingly comes short of the perfect will of God, Jesus Christ the righteous is his Advocate. He is at God's right hand, making intercession for him. He is pleading the merits of His sacrifice on the behalf of all who in limited knowledge come short of the glory of God. Here is John Wesley's reasoning: "Everyone may mistake as long as he lives. A mistake in opinion may occasion a mistake in practice. Every such mistake is a transgression of the perfect law. Every such mistake were it not for the blood of the atonement would expose to eternal damnation. It follows that the most perfect have continual need of the merits of Christ even for actual transgressions and may say for themselves as for their brethren, forgive us our trespasses."

Christ interposed His precious blood on behalf of the Christian who trusts in Him. He is the atoning Sacrifice for the sins of the whole world. He is the Mercy Seat.

October 26

"Love Not the World"

1 John 2:15

The love of the world and the love of the Father are mutually expulsive. This is a logical deduction from the word of Jesus, "No man can serve two masters" (Matt. 6:24). When the love of God is shed abroad in our hearts by the Holy Spirit, there is at that moment expulsion of the love of the world. This is "the expulsive power of a new affection."

This is no contradiction to the glorious proclamation that God so loved the world that He gave His only begotten Son that whosoever believes in Him might have everlasting life. This is love for all people of the world. This love is in the heart of every Christian. Such love reaches out in compassion, sharing, and sacrifice to bring salvation to all men.

John defines the world, which is anti-God, in the next verse. In the world gratification of the desires of the flesh is dominant. The love of God expels perverted desires and refines those that are a part of a normal person.

The lust of the eyes is the covetous disposition to possess the things of the material world beyond all present and future

250

need. Love of God and greed are utterly incompatible.

The boastful pride of life is the passion for power, prestige, and exaltation over one's fellowman. Love is expressed in the desire to identify with the need of all men. Love of the world is supreme folly. It passeth away. He that does God's will abides forever.

October 27

Supreme Love

1 John 3:16

Adam Clarke observes that 1 John 3:16 is the counterpart of the great text that is identified by the same numerals in the Gospel by John. Certainly both declare that God's love for man is supreme. Here, however, there is a clearer identification of God the Father with the sufferings of Christ the Son. "God was in Christ, reconciling the world unto himself" (2 Cor. 5:19). It was God incarnate who died on the Cross. God the Father suffered in the death of His beloved Son. Even in that brief separation in which Jesus cried, "My God, my God, why hast thou forsaken me?" (Mark 15:35), the Father was draining the bitter cup to the last drop. He was not a detached judge on His throne. He too was involved in the sacrifice.

John does not imply that the Christian can add anything to the sacrifice made once for all to make an atonement for sinners. "For by one offering [Christ] hath perfected for ever them that are sanctified" (Heb. 10:14). He does say that the selfless love manifested in the death of Christ should be in Christians. Jesus said, "This is my commandment, That ye love one another, as I have loved you. Greater love hath no man than this, that a man lay down his life for his friends" (John 15:12-13). This is the strong bond that unites Christians to one another and to Christ.

John lengthens the cords of love to include any brother in need. If the Christian closes his heart of compassion from need, how dwelleth the love of God in him?

251

October 28

Perfect Love

1 John 4:17

God manifested His love toward us, "because that God sent his only begotten Son into the world, that we might live through him" (v. 9). We did not love God, but He loved us and sent His Son to be the atonement for our sins. In Jesus, God, who is love, was made flesh. In Him, His life and His death, we have seen a perfect revelation of love.

Love is not only seen in Jesus, it is communicated to us through Him. We love God because He first loved us. Our love to God is in response to His love which we have received through Christ. Now this love is to be seen in us because we love one another. Thus, God dwells in us and love is perfected in us. The One who dwelleth in love dwelleth in us. We bear His image; and as He is, so are we in this world. In the true Christian, love is demonstrated. This commandment we have from Him, "That he who loveth God love his brother also. . . . he that loveth not his brother whom he hath seen, how can he love God whom he hath not seen?" (vv. 21, 20).

Christian perfection is perfect love in motive and intention. That love casts out fear that hath torment. There is no fear in love—no fear of what the future holds, no fear of death, and no fear of the judgment. "He that feareth is not made perfect in love. . . . perfect love casteth out fear" (v. 18).

October 29

"Fellowhelpers"

3 John 8

John addressed this brief letter to Gaius, who was well known to the apostle. His generous spirit and his good works had been reported to John. This letter opens with words of affection and approval. Evidently Gaius had received some itinerant evangelists with hospitality and had given them encouragement. This called forth a word of commendation which may be understood to be representative of the spirit in which Christians should support one another.

They are fellows, that is, peers, joined together in a common cause to make the truth of the gospel known to all men. It is a fellowship in Christ that levels those who are included. In spirit there are no superiors and none are inferior. "He that is joined unto the Lord is one spirit" (1 Cor. 6:17). There is no cause for jealousy among the servants of God. There is no condescension. And none need fall down to any, except the Lord. The followers respect leaders; and leaders do not lord it over the followers. They are all "members one of another."

John's word is "fellowhelpers to the truth." They have received and obeyed the truth. That truth has made them free. They are called to proclaim the truth, first by living according to it. They stand up to the corrective plumbline of truth. They bear witness to the truth as it is in Jesus. They speak the truth in love. Jesus said, "For this cause came I into the world, that I should bear witness unto the truth" (John 18:37).

October 30
The White Stone

Rev. 2:17

To hear was not only to listen attentively but to respond in obedience. The Spirit had a message for the church at Pergamos. He has a word for all churches. To those who obey His instruction with love, rich promises are given. There is the possibility of living the life of an overcomer.

The hidden manna which was kept in the ark of the testimony was representative of Christ, the Bread of Life. It never deteriorated. Christ is the same yesterday, today, and forever. The Christian may feed on Him by faith with thanksgiving.

The gift of the white stone has several possible interpretations. It was used by jurors to signify acquittal. It could mean that a sinner had received forgiveness and remission of sins. It could also be like a ticket of admission to royal assemblies and a banquet. All who know Christ as Savior have received a passport to heaven and an invitation to the marriage supper of the Lamb. White is the appropriate dress of heaven. The saints are clothed in robes of fine linen, pure and white.

Upon the white stone there is "a new name written, which no man knoweth saving he that receiveth it."

An aged black man who had served the Lord for many years knew death was near. He testified to his daughter, "Years ago God gave me a little book down in my heart. No one could read it but me. But I know what it said." That was his new name. He had the witness of the Spirit.

October 31

The Open Door

Rev. 3:8

The figure of the open door occurs several times in the New Testament. Usually, if not invariably, it represented an opportunity to preach the gospel of Christ, the power of God unto salvation, in an area untouched by the missionary movement. That is doubtless the significance of our text for today. The church at Philadelphia was in an advantageous location for extending the influence of the gospel. This special assignment was a challenging responsibility. The door was open and no man could shut it. The forces of evil were present, but they could not prevail. Jesus had said, "I will build my church; and the gates of hell shall not prevail against it" (Matt. 16:18). Included in the promise to the church at Philadelphia was the assurance that the enemies present would bow and worship.

There is admission that this church was limited in strength. But there was another door open that none could shut. It was the door that opened the resources of God to the faith of His people. No church has adequate numbers or reserves to match its responsibility in world evangelism. But the resources of heaven and the power of the Spirit are adequate if our faith can unite us to them.

The word of God to Zerubbabel is valid now! "Not by

might, nor by power, but by my spirit, saith the Lord of hosts" (Zech. 4:6). Jesus promised, "Ye shall receive power, the Holy Spirit coming upon you, and ye shall be witnesses unto me . . . unto the uttermost part of the earth." The promise is to all that are afar off.

The Permanent Versus the Perishing

Psalm 1

Psalm 1 may be considered an introduction to the entire collection. Its central theme is that God's blessings come to the righteous, while His judgments fall on the ungodly. It would seem that the author had been reflecting upon the history of God's revelation of himself and His will for His people.

The fact that there is a negative aspect to holiness does not escape his notice. The one who does not abhor and resist evil is soon on the path of progressive sin. He is listening attentively to the counsel of the ungodly. He is acting in accord with the practice of sinners. He is passively accepting the blighting influence of the scorners.

Genuine piety must be nourished by the milk and meat of God's Word. "His delight is in the law of the Lord; and in his law doth he meditate day and night." There must be knowing that comes by obedience; experience that comes with loving; wisdom to put into practice what has been learned. Such habitual consideration of the known law of the Lord will result in present and permanent blessedness.

This righteous man will be like a tree planted by an intelligent person where soil is fertile and the water supply is certain. Its life is evident by the leaves; it is perpetually fruitful. The ungodly are in striking contrast: They are like chaff which has no value, driven away by the wind.

The conclusion in the last verse is focused on the contrast between the permanent and the perishing, between the righteous and the ungodly.

November 2

Holiness, Positive and Negative

Psalm 15

This classic poem is a summary of the qualities of a holy life. The positives and the negatives of holiness are listed. Both are an invariable part of a life which is completely yielded to God. As it should be, the positives come first.

Conformity to God's will takes knowledge of His Word. It calls for motivation stimulated by the Holy Spirit. It is reinforced by fellowship with those of like precious faith. It is a delight to the one who is aware of his divinely appointed destiny.

Holy conduct is the spontaneous expression of holy character. That character is conditioned upon a continuous relationship to God, maintained by habitual, voluntary abiding in God's presence. It is a place of permanent residence; dwelling in God's holy hill includes the comfortable feeling of being at home with the family of God.

From such inner adequacy issues a blameless life of honesty and uprighteousness. Nothing reveals the heart condition more certainly than the words which proceed from the lips. Speaking the truth is the evidence of absolute sincerity.

If the positive virtues of holiness are in full manifestation, then the negative vices are excluded. There can be no starting or passing of stories injurious to the good name of others. All sin will be condemned and not condoned. A promise given will be fulfilled even if keeping it is costly. Exorbitant interest or profits will not be charged. Holy hands will never be contaminated with bribes. Holy people stand firm in righteousness. They are rooted and fixed in God.

November 3

Trust in God

Ps. 16:1

This golden poem, ascribed to David, is an expression of loyalty to God. It is one of the Messianic psalms. Adam Clarke identifies its entire content with the Christ of God. This does not make it any less meaningful to Christians. That all its truth is related to Him, only makes it more real to us. He was a brother most human. It is a declaration of the faith that we are His and He is ours. By Him we have been redeemed.

From such a vantage view we look at the past with gratitude. We say, "The Lord is the portion of mine inheritance . . . The lines are fallen unto me in pleasant places; yea, I have a goodly heritage" (vv. 5-6).

We have a confident view of the present. "I have set the Lord always before me: because he is at my right hand, I shall not be moved" (v. 8). Here I enjoy security. He is with me wherever I go. All I possess are gifts of His love. All I do is in the power of His Spirit.

The future look is glorious because we have hope that is firmly anchored within the veil, where Jesus the Forerunner is entered for us. Because the Holy One saw no corruption, my flesh shall rest in hope. My heart is glad, and my glory rejoices. If He is risen, those who die in the faith shall also rise. They have beheld the path of life. With Him there is fullness of joy. At His right hand there are pleasures forevermore.

November 4

God Vindicates the Righteous

Ps. 17:15

This psalm is a prayer of David. Many believe it came out of that period when his life was in danger because of the jealousy and hatred of Saul.

David makes his appeal to God for protection. He places his life completely in the hands of God. "Let my sentence come forth from thy presence" (v. 2). His trust is implicit. He calls upon God and feels assured of His marvelous loving-kindness. His believing plea is that God will keep him as the apple of His eye.

The enemies of the fugitive are described as greedy, bloodthirsty lions lurking in hidden places. His final entreaty is "Arise, O Lord . . . deliver my soul from the wicked" (v. 13).

Then David declares his faith: "As for me, I will behold thy face in righteousness: I shall be satisfied, when I awake, with thy likeness."

The inheritance of the righteous is unmixed satisfaction. There will be no haunting regrets. There will be sweet and sacred memories instead of unrelenting remorse. There will be heard songs of triumph. There will be companionship with saints and angels. The righteous will enjoy a permanent dwelling with no threat from enemies and no tempter to fear.

Having been made partakers of the divine nature, the righteous will behold the face of the holy God unveiled. They shall awake in His perfect likeness. This is not awakening from the sleep of a night but the awakening in the resurrection morning.

November 5

God's Work and His Word

Ps. 19:1, 7, 12

C. S. Lewis judged Psalm 19 to be the greatest poem in the Psalter and one of the greatest lyrics in the Word. It is divided into three parts. In the first six verses, the poet beholds with wonder the revelation of God in the universe. He sees the glory of the heavens as a revelation of the majesty and power of God. Their voice is not heard. Theirs is a silent but eloquent testimony.

The second section of the poem is devoted to the revelation of God in His Word. The Psalmist employs a varied vocabulary with slightly different shades of meaning, but all speaking of the Holy Scriptures as the message of God for man to believe and obey.

God's Word, the Bible, is not an expressed opinion which man is free to contradict with his opinions. It is a message with which man has no controversy. The divine command is perfect. Obedience to it transforms the soul. The affirmation of the Lord is certain. It makes the teachable one wise unto salvation. The established rules of God are righteous. They make the heart glad. With God's final decisions there is no error. Even

258

the transgressor will acknowledge their justice. The willing and obedient will be rewarded with treasures more precious than fine gold.

No matter how persuasive the revelation of God may be in His works and His words, it is of no effect until man opens his mind to receive it.

The last three verses of this psalm frame in words man's appropriate response.

November 6

"The Lord Is My Shepherd"

Psalm 23

I shall not want for acceptance. The Shepherd is mine and I am His. He knows my name. I know His voice; I am never alone. There is always protection from the wolf that comes to destroy. There is fellowship among the sheep of His pasture. I belong to the Shepherd who gives His life for the sheep. He carries the lambs in His bosom. When the way is rugged and steep, He gently leads. I shall not wander beyond the boundaries of His loving care. He is forgiving of my waywardness. When I fall, He lifts me up.

I shall not want for guidance. He leads me by a path which is always safe. The darkness is made light by His presence. He takes away reluctance and hesitation and makes me delight in obedience. The way may lead through a tunnel, but there is light beyond.

I shall not want for assurance. I fear not poverty; He will supply all my need. I fear no evil; He will not allow me to be tempted above that which I am able to bear. I fear no enemies; He prepares a table before me in their presence. I fear no overpowering foe; His anointing will make me adequate and victorious. I fear no limitations; my cup runneth over. I fear no defeat; His rod and His staff strengthen me. I will not fear death; He will be with me. I fear not the venture into eternity; He will not fail me then. Goodness and mercy have followed me all the days of my life; therefore, I can trust the Shepherd to bring me to the fold.

November 7
Worthy to Worship

Ps. 24:3-5

Consider the greatness of God. He is the supreme Possessor of the whole universe. "The earth is the Lord's, and the fulness thereof; the world, and they that dwell therein" (v. 1). He is the Creator and the Preserver of all. "He hath founded it upon the seas, and established it upon the floods" (v. 2). His right to possession is supported by the fact that He is the Creator. His right to rule as absolute Sovereign cannot be challenged. His Lordship over all that dwell therein is further confirmed because according to the New Testament gospel, He is the Redeemer. All are His by right of purchase as well as by right of creation.

Who is worthy to worship the God of matchless majesty, universal sovereignty, and spotless holiness? Who can come near to Him? Who can stand in His awesome presence? Holiness alone can qualify anyone to approach God and be comfortable in His acceptance.

The reply of the Psalmist to his own question is descriptive of the one worthy to worship such a high and holy God. "He that hath clean hands, and a pure heart." The one who has confessed his sins and received the pardon that God bestows. Outward sins must go and inward impurity must be purged. "Purify your hearts, ye double minded" (Jas. 4:8).

It is not simply the one who knows the crisis experiences of forgiveness and cleansing who is worthy to worship God. He must also live a life above reproach. He must live according to the straight line of truthfulness.

November 8
One Supreme Desire

Ps. 27:4

Can all the longings of the human spirit become only one desire? Probably that is not a possibility. David could say, however, that all conflicting desires had vanished. All permissible cravings had been so refined that they blended into one supreme desire, and in the realization of that yearning there was blessed contentment.

Actually, there were three deep needs of David's soul which were all supplied. To dwell in the house of the Lord all the days of his life was to find permanent residence in the glory of God's holy presence. There the beauty of the Lord is beheld. Nothing can draw the eyes from such transcendent beauty. Any other scene is like a blank wall of obstruction in comparison. The mind can meditate in God's presence until anything material is like dust and ashes compared to priceless diamonds.

God is my Light and my salvation. He is my security, my Pavilion. His call to seek His face finds ready response in my will. His face is not hidden from me. He will teach me the truth that makes me free and pure. He will lead me on the path of righteousness unto the perfect day. He will deliver me from all my enemies, both within and those that rise up against me.

The psalm ends with an exhortation, "Wait on the Lord." Continue with that one supreme desire. Be persevering in courage. "He shall strengthen thine heart."

November 9

No Good Thing Wanting

Ps. 34:10

Here is an inverted metaphor. Unlike the young lions who lack and suffer hunger, those who seek the Lord shall not want any good thing. The lioness, strongest, most stealthy, most successful hunter of food to satisfy the hunger of her whelps, may fail in her effort to supply their need. In contrast, David declares, they that seek the Lord shall not want any good thing. This does not promise there will be no desire, but that there will be no good thing lacking. God is the One who knows what will be for the good of those who seek Him. They are submissive to Him who possesses unlimited resources, infinite wisdom, and eternal goodness.

To the one who has sinned against Him and seeks forgiveness, He will have mercy according to His loving-kindness. To those who are aware of inner conflict with the will of the flesh, the cry for holiness will be met with full cleansing. To all who seek God's protection from the foes that come with fierce attack from the evil in the world, the angel of the Lord encamps round about them that fear Him, and delivers them. The righteous whose afflictions are many will be delivered out of them all. To those who seek the presence of the Lord, it is never denied. He is always nearby. If the seeker is not always conscious of His nearness, he can be always confident that He is there.

November 10
A Delightful Walk

Ps. 37:23

Who is a good man? He is one who knows God's commandments and obeys them. He is characterized by uprightness and honesty in all his dealings with his fellowmen. He is aware that he is not faultless and is therefore charitable to those whose faults he knows. Such a man is guided by the Lord on the path of life. He is not self-righteous; the source of his goodness is in God.

The good man is not standing still. Taking steps means he is moving. They are not backward but always forward. He is pursuing a straight course. The road sometimes leads over steep hills. The Lord who put the hills there gives the strength for climbing. The footing can be rough but God provides shoes to protect the traveler's feet. There is no assurance that the good man will not stumble. Nevertheless, he does not give up. He never quits; he will not be a dropout. The hand of the Lord lifts him and upholds him.

The good, strong, courageous man sees beyond the roadblock. There is light shining ahead. The adventure on the good way may not always be inspiring, challenging, exciting. But the determination to persevere will be renewed until the goal is reached. For the good man, there is pure delight in the way God leads, and such a man brings delight to the heart of God.

November 11

God's Answer to Man's Cry

Ps. 40:1-3

Serious-minded, honest men confess a deep need in their souls. Many cannot define it and some do not admit it. There are those, however, who voice it in a cry of desperation. In His great mercy, God may come to the rescue of one who has neglected to call upon Him. God will hear the call of one who prays habitually. David's cry for God's deliverance was from a background of patient waiting upon God. Because of his persistence in prayer, he had the attention and readiness of the Lord to answer. Patient waiting is the greatest assurance that an answer is on the way.

David bears testimony that in man's desperate predicament, God is the Deliverer. Man is in a horrible pit of despair. He is sunken in the miry clay. He cannot save himself. The help of men is inadequate; sinful man needs higher help. God is mighty to save and strong to deliver.

God does more than lift a man from the quagmire. He sets the feet of the redeemed on a rock. It is not a static life. His *goings* are established. He puts distance between where he is and where he was. His aim is higher ground. To make His redeemed a joyful and an attractive person to others, God puts a new song in his mouth, even praise unto our God. It is a victor's song of praise and thanksgiving. Others, seeing the manifestation of the grace and power of God, shall put their trust in the Lord.

November 12

Walk About Zion

Ps. 48:12-14

The Temple was beautiful for situation on Mount Moriah. It was the joy of all that land. God was known there. He was the object of worship and the inspiration for praise.

The poet invites all to walk about Zion to survey the impressive features of the City of God.

This psalm may be considered a preview of the Church that Christ loved and gave himself for, that he might present it to himself a glorious Church. The towers could not be overlooked. There they stood, rising far above all the surroundings. They were for landmarks to guide travelers in their search for the City of the Great King. They were lighthouses sending out their beacon rays. There were at least two, one for the prophet to proclaim warning and one for the teacher to instruct. So it is with the Church.

The bulwarks of the Church are her holy doctrines. The strength of the Church is maintained more in loyalty to her basic doctrines than by any other means. These must be vitalized by the presence of the Holy Spirit. They must be translated into ethical practice in the transformed lives of those who compose the Body of Christ.

The palaces are to be considered as the dwelling place of God, the Holy One of Israel, here applied to Christ Jesus, who is Lord of all. His presence in the person of the Holy Spirit is the attraction, the distinction, and the abiding glory of the Church.

November 13

Sin Confessed

Ps. 51:3

Nathan, the prophet, had led David into a pronouncement of judgment upon the representative character in a parable describing what the king himself had done. The prophet said, "Thou art the man" (2 Sam. 12:7). The king could not repudiate his own sentence of death for the transgressor. He was guilty, condemned, and worthy of the death sentence.

This psalm of confession, contrition, and repentance is therefore the anguished cry of a soul whose only hope was not that justice should be done him but in the mercy of the righteous God who pardons iniquity. It is the confession of a man trapped, convicted, ready to turn to God in true repentance.

Under such conditions, the sinner at last had come to that

state of mind in which he was utterly honest. David said, "I acknowledge my transgressions." His pronouncement of the death sentence upon himself is proof that he knew God's commandments, "Thou shalt not kill. Thou shalt not commit adultery" (Exod. 20:13-14). He knew he had sinned against a woman less responsible than himself. He had sinned against Uriah. He had sinned against all the subjects of his kingdom. But in its final essence, he knew his sin was against God. This was the most reproachful thought of all.

David not only confessed his sinful deed, he went further to admit that the act was only the outward evidence of his depraved heart. He said, "I was shapen in iniquity; and in sin did my mother conceive me" (v. 5). This was a confession all truly convicted sinners could make.

November 14

Full Salvation

Ps. 51:6-12

This prayer psalm not only treats of the doctrine of sin; it just as clearly shows that God provides the cure for the disease. And as sin is twofold in its nature, therefore salvation must be a double cure.

There are four phases of holiness in David's prayer for purity. Each of them is reinforced by a second petition.

First he prays, "Purge me with hyssop"; wash me with the strongest detergent. Let me be washed as garments are washed, and all the ingrained dirt is beaten out by smiting on the rock. Let there be no residue of impurity as particles of dust in the snow. Make me whiter than snow.

Second, "Create in me a clean heart, O God; and renew a right spirit within me." Reconditioning of the polluted nature was not satisfactory. There must be a new creation. David prayed, in effect, "Give me, O God, a heart like Thine." Renew in me the life of God. "Stamp Thine own image deep on my heart."

Third, "Cast me not away from thy presence." Only in

265

Thy conscious presence can I live apart from my sinful environ- ment. "Take not thy holy spirit from me." Only by His indwell- ing can I be strong enough to resist the enemy which comes as a roaring lion to devour me.

Fourth, "Restore unto me the joy of thy salvation." That joy will be my strength. "Uphold me with thy free spirit." Then with that freedom I will always shun the wrong and do the right.

November 15

A Reclaimed Life

Ps. 51:13-17

God never offers a premium for sin. He forgets man's sins, but the sinner lives with his regrets. He also carries with him the liability that he will fall into a former pattern of conduct. Nevertheless, God does, by the alchemy of His grace, restore those of a sinful past to lives of usefulness. They have been forgiven much and they love proportionately. Their gratitude to God for His merciful restoration may be deep and enduring. It may be expressed in testimony and devoted service.

David pledged, in response to God's pardon, "I will teach transgressors thy ways; and sinners shall be converted unto thee." J. J. S. Perowne comments, "Terrible had been the fruit of his sin, not only in wasting his own soul, but in injury done to others. Terrible was his punishment in witnessing this; and therefore, the more anxious is he, though he cannot undo his own sin, to heal the breach, and repair the evil of sin in other souls."

The humble king cried out, "Deliver me from blood- guiltiness, O God, thou God of my salvation: and my tongue shall sing aloud of thy righteousness." I will not keep my praise to myself. I will let it be heard. "O Lord, open thou my lips; and my mouth shall shew forth thy praise." He would offer to God a broken and a contrite heart which would not be de- spised. He would forever be the grateful, humble, obedient servant of God.

November 16

The Creator and the Creature

Ps. 90:12

The 90th psalm is among the most treasured and quoted of this entire collection of Hebrew poems. Some scholars believe that evidence is convincing that Moses produced this masterpiece of literature. Others consider that all but impossible. Whoever he was, the author must have had the mind and the faith of Moses if not the name.

The theme of the psalm is the utter dependence of man, the creature, upon God, the Creator. God is the Giver; man is the receiver.

God is eternal, changeless; man is transitory. God had no beginning and shall have no end. The life of man is like the passing of a few hours in the night while he is unconscious in sleep. It is as the grass that is green in the morning and withered and brown in the evening. God is holy. Man is sinful; he must see his sins in the blazing light of God's holy face.

God is all wise. Man gropes his way in the darkness of his own self-imposed blindness. Therefore he prays, "Teach us to number our days, that we may apply our hearts unto wisdom." The heart cry is, "Satisfy us early with Thy mercy that even the days of youth may not be squandered. The days of our lives are few. Let us rejoice and be glad all our days" (see v. 14).

God is gracious. Man echoes the Psalmist's prayer, "Let thy work appear unto thy servants, and thy glory unto their children" (v. 16). The life of man can be crowned with God's glory. The beauty of the Lord God may rest upon him. His work can have permanent value because it is done for God.

November 17

Almighty God Is Near

Ps. 91:1

In no portion of the Holy Scriptures is the nearness of God proclaimed so certainly and repeatedly as in Psalm 91. He is offered as a dwelling, a refuge, a fortress, a shield, a buckler, a hiding place, as a mother bird covering her young under her feathered wings. He is the One who warns of the hidden snare and delivers from it. He is there in the terror of the night to give assurance. He is the shield against the arrow that flies by day. He is the antitoxin to ward off the pestilence that comes unawares. He is the guard to sound the warning of the destruction that wasteth at noonday. He dispatches His angels as ministering spirits to guide our way in safety. The fiercest of beasts and the most poisonous serpent shall not invade our dwelling. Honor and promotion are promised. The answer to our prayers and satisfaction as long as life shall last, are assured.

The fulfillment of all these promises which inspire faith and complete trust in God is sure, because He is near. Even the blind can see His face and the deaf can hear His voice. Those numb with pain can feel His touch. He is light in darkness; He is strength in weakness. He is a companion in loneliness; He is comfort in grief. He is protection in peril; He is wisdom in perplexity. He is confidence in discouragement; He is hope in despair. He is life in death.

November 18

Thanksgiving Is Good

Ps. 92:12

Psalms 90—92 belong together. There is a line of thought that ties them each to the other. The first is a prayer for deliverance. The second is a declaration of trust. The third is a song of thanksgiving.

Herein is a practical lesson for all God's people. They should commit themselves to God in prayer, then rest in total confidence that what is for their good and God's glory will certainly come to pass. And whether the answer is immediate or ultimate, they should sing a hymn of praise that the answer has come or is on the way. In such joyous, victorious living they do show forth God's loving-kindness in the morning and His faithfulness every night. As the trusting heart waits and watches the progress of divine providence, he is made to wonder at the greatness of His works and be glad for the goodness and wisdom of his Heavenly Father. He knows God's way will prove to be the best way.

To encourage one to righteousness, the Psalmist employs the most inspiring metaphors imaginable. He shall flourish as the palm tree; he shall grow like the cedar in Lebanon. The harvest of a date palm has been known to total 600 pounds. While the palm tree represented fruitfulness, the cedar in Lebanon spoke of vitality and perpetuity.

The poet saw in the double metaphor of the fruitful palm and the long-lasting fragrant cedar a likeness to the righteous bringing fruit in old age.

November 19

A Song of Praise

Psalm 100

Thanksgiving is not only an expression of gratitude for blessings received; it is also an admission of dependence upon God and His wisdom and grace. Psalm 100 is one of the most adequate thanksgiving songs in all literature. It is titled "A Psalm of Praise."

A more definitive title would be "A Psalm for the Thank Offering." Vocal praise to God is appropriate. It can scarcely be restrained by those who are aware of the gifts of God, so many and so measureless. But the offering of the sacrifice of praise as the fruit of the lips is superficial if it is not accompanied by suitable offerings for the advancement of God's kingdom. The worshiper's sincerity is attested by the consecration of his possessions to God. The genuineness of his dedication is indicated by his sharing for the sake of others and for the glory of God. The ultimate testimony is to present oneself a living sacrifice upon the Christian's altar which sanctifieth the gift.

The inspired poet sees that singing songs of thanksgiving and praise is a normal pattern of life for every individual. He is to sing and make melody in his heart to God. He must let it be heard of men also.

All God's chosen people shall also lift a mighty chorus of jubilant song because God has created and redeemed them. The Psalmist cried, "Make a joyful noise unto the Lord, all ye lands." God's eternal purpose includes full salvation, free salvation for all men. There is nothing exclusive in the provisions made by the God of all grace.

November 20
"Forget Not All His Benefits"

Ps. 103:1-2

In this beautiful and much-loved psalm Israel's sweet singer pours out his soul in an ecstasy of thanksgiving. "Forget not all his benefits." Many do forget shamefully.

The Psalmist, who was almost certainly David, calls for all that is within him to give praise to the Lord. If he was to praise God with all that was within him, then God must have answered his prayer to create in him a clean heart.

In verses 3-5 we have a summary of benefits which could be expanded without limit. Very correctly forgiveness tops the column. How wonderful that all our iniquities can be forgiven, removed as far as the east is from the west.

"Healeth all our diseases" is next. God gives wholeness to the soul. Nevertheless the healing of the body is included. Augustine said, "To an omnipotent Physician no sickness is incurable. God made the body, God made thy soul, He knows how to recreate that which he created." "Who redeemeth thy life from destruction"; He will save the soul from hell. He will salvage the life already far spent in sin.

"Who crowneth thee with lovingkindness and tender mercies." With beautiful, fragrant flowers of loving-kindness and tender mercies, God weaves a crown for His chosen ones to wear every day. "He satisfieth thy mouth with good things." He regenerates desires until they are clean and good, then satisfies with the most pleasant fruit. As a result, youth is renewed as the eagle's which molts and lives in the beauty of feathers all new, fresh, and befitting.

270

November 21

The Gladness of God

Ps. 104:31

In the 104th psalm the gladness of God is expressed.

This is in poetic form the story of creation as recorded in Genesis 1. From the first day when God said, "Let there be light," until His works were finished, He rejoiced in what He had made. He saw that it was good. All His works praise Him.

In this review of creation the poet goes beyond the Genesis account. The psalm shows the beginning of the eternal order, and the continual support and supervision of the all-wise, all-powerful, and ever-present Creator. "He holds the whole world in His hands."

God created all the life on this planet, and He provides for the perpetuation of that life. The plant reproduces through the seed; the animals, the birds, the fishes of the sea, by their innate powers of reproduction. No kind of life is left without provision for its day-by-day existence. In the world of nature there is heard a continuous symphony of praise to God.

God climaxed His creation by making man in His own likeness. He was crowned with glory and honor and set over all the works of creation. God gave His only Son to reclaim and re-create sinful man who is the only creature that does not render praise to God his Creator and his Savior. Let all God's people say with the Psalmist that as long as each of us live, "I will be glad in the Lord" (v. 34). This will cause the heart of God to be glad.

November 22

The Antidote to Sin

Ps. 119:11

This is the longest of the 150 psalms and the longest chapter in the entire Bible. Possibly that is the excuse for failure to mine out its rich treasures. No portion of the Holy Book of equal length affords more wealth to discover than this most carefully structured poem.

271

It has 22 stanzas, 1 for each letter of the Hebrew alphabet. Each verse has two members, all written in the form of acrostics, opening with the same letter. Only verse 132 fails to include the "law" of God or one of the synonyms—"testimonies," "precepts," "statutes," "commandments," "ordinances," "judgments," "word." Where in all the Holy Scriptures is the value of the Word of God so elaborated?

Verse 11, the third in stanza two, gives the most effective antidote for sin that has ever been prescribed. "Thy word have I hid in mine heart, that I might not sin against thee." The wonder is that the Word is not merely a rule of outward conduct; it is a power of a life within. Every other verse in this section offers an evaluation of the Word as it relates to day-by-day holy living.

Verse 9 offers the Word as a detergent for sin. "Wherewithal shall a young man cleanse his way? by taking heed thereto according to thy word." In the Ten Commandments, religious principles provide the incentive to seek God's will as a safeguard from wandering from the narrow way. In the 12th verse the statutes, social regulations given by the blessed Lord, quench the thirst for spiritual understanding of the will of God in our human relations.

November 23

The Way of Truth

Ps. 119:29-30

Truth is defined as "conformity to reality." It is verified fact. God has implanted in the mind of man the desire to know the truth. His choice to act according to truth is the verification of truth to him. The Psalmist prayed, "Remove from me the way of lying: and grant me thy law graciously." That his prayer might be answered, he declared, "I have chosen thy way of truth: thy judgments have I laid before me." It was as if he said, My will is to reject error and falsehood; therefore it is conditioned to obey the truth of Thy law.

Jesus said, "For this cause came I into the world, that I should bear witness unto the truth." Again He said, "Thy word is truth," and yet again, "I am . . . the truth" (John 18:37; 17:17; 14:6). To choose Christ is to choose the way of truth. That way is made plain by the Word of God. What the Bible says is true not because it is in the Bible; rather, it is in the Bible because it is true. I do not judge the Bible and its truth; it judges me. I choose the way of truth even if it convicts and condemns me.

Obedience to the truth brings cleansing and purity through faith in the sacrifice made for me on Calvary. It also brings emancipation and freedom through the truth. "Ye shall know the truth, and the truth shall make you free" (John 8:32). This is the way of fulfillment and victory.

All who choose this way walk on a shining path. They are true to themselves and cannot be false to any man.

November 24

Light on the Way

Ps. 119:105

The people of ancient Israel were led from Egypt to Canaan by a pillar of cloud by day and of fire by night. The people of God today have more dependable guidance through knowledge of God's Word and the personal leadership of the Holy Spirit.

The words of our text for today are often quoted. They are a source of comfort and assurance to those who are pilgrims on the way of holiness. God's Word gives those who trust and obey a clear and certain sense of direction. It is a light on the long road of life. It keeps the final destination in focus. Such far vision is a reinforcement to determined purpose in the routine of daily life.

But the Word of God is a lamp to our feet as we go on step by step. We have the precepts of the Word for guidance, and its promises to give support to faith. There will be widsom for every decision and a light at the end of every tunnel.

The Psalmist knew he needed to perform his vow to keep

God's righteous judgments. His offerings of praise and gratitude received His approval. He took his life in his hand, that is, he staked his life on the dependability of God's law. There is no risk in dependence upon God's veracity. God was his heritage and the source of his joy. He had disciplined his will in performance of God's statutes. This is a pattern for all who will have light on their daily path.

November 25

Deep, Settled Peace

Ps. 119:165

Peace is freedom from anxiety, a serene state of mind. When the Psalmist said, "Great peace have they which love thy law," he was surrounded by his foes. They had the power and the desire to destroy him. His peace was undisturbed because his relationship to God was fully assured. When David was a captive among the Philistines, he said, "In God I have put my trust; I will not fear what flesh can do unto me" (56:4). Here he declares his love for God's law. He rejoices at His Word as one that finds himself in possession of great spoil which a fleeing enemy has left. He declares his sincerity. He abhors lying. Testimony with reservations is lying. But he loves God's law. Every day is filled with praise for His judgments. His hope for salvation is supported by obedience to God's commandments. He loves God's testimonies. He makes no vain boast, for all his ways are as an open book before God.

This poet loves and therefore obeys. All who love, obey, and trust are at peace.

"Nothing shall offend them" may be translated, "There is not for them a stumbling block." They walk on a smooth, straight path of righteousness. And the fruit of righteousness is peace.

It is also blessedly true that one who is in such a state of mind will be no cause for others to stumble. His faith will be supportive to all who observe his righteous conduct and behold his peaceful face.

November 26

The Lord Is Thy Keeper

Ps. 121:8

The theme of this beloved psalm is that one who trusts in God is safe in His keeping. In the original language, the word translated "keep" occurs seven times in the last six verses. It is translated "preserve" to avoid repetition. God's presence is assurance of security from all evil. It is preservation of those who persevere.

What the Psalmist knew of God's keeping grace can be the experience of all who trust and obey. The writer of this devotional guide, in answering the call of duty for 22 years, rested in the promised security of the last verse of this psalm with confidence. He traveled by every conveyance from jeep to jet over mountains, deserts, and stormy seas. The total distance would not be less than 1.5 million miles. Lands of many languages and variable cultures were visited. Strange foods were eaten. Beds made of feathers, straw, ropes, and boards were sometimes the best available. Some countries were in the throes of revolution. Many were dominated by religions hostile to evangelical Christianity.

In the beginning, Ps. 121:8 was given as a reassuring comfort. The report is: Life was never in danger from disease or accident. No schedule was more than marginally missed. Not one piece of luggage was lost. No temptation was ever encountered without a way to escape. No loneliness was unbearable, and God watched between loved ones at home and the one 10,000 miles away. To God be the glory!

November 27

Joyful Worship

Ps. 122:1

The inspiration for this psalm was the practice of the Hebrew people to go up to Jerusalem to celebrate the great festivals of their calendar. Their loyalty to the God of their fathers, the Holy One of Israel, made them willing to make long journeys over land and sea. The anticipation of standing within the gates of the Holy City and worshipping in the sacred courts of the house of God made the journey a joy. They held in their memory the glories of the days of David and Solomon. They cherished the hope that such glory would return to Israel.

What they now experienced was anticipation of the fulfillment of the promised glory of the future, when David's great Son, the Lord Jesus Christ himself, should establish His kingdom forever. Thus anticipation and realization combined to make their worship the most joyful experience of life on earth. With one voice they could say, "I was glad when they said unto me, Let us go into the house of the Lord."

True worship flows from the mind and spirit that are harmonized with the holy nature of God. To all such there are no barriers to the reality of God's presence. There is a spontaneous exclamation of admiration, praise, and thanksgiving. The sanctuary of the church is the house of God and the gate of heaven. Worship alone with God has its rich reward, but worship together with God's wonderful people is a foretaste of heaven. Note the Psalmist said, "Let *us* go into the house of the Lord." He did not want to go alone. To meet with God in worship and with His people in fellowship is unmixed joy.

November 28

Sowing and Reaping

Ps. 126:5-6

There is general agreement that this psalm was born in the mind and heart of an unnamed poet soon after the first return to Jerusalem from the Captivity. The edict giving permission to go back to their own land, by Cyrus the Persian king, had all but overwhelmed them. It seemed too good to be true. They sat by the rivers of Babylon to weep as they remembered Zion. When their captors required of them to sing one of the songs of Zion, they said, "How shall we sing the Lord's song in a strange land?" (137:4).

But now they were back in their beloved Zion. Their mouths were filled with laughter and their tongues with singing. They were saying, "The Lord hath done great things for us; whereof we are glad" (v. 3). Nevertheless, they were reminded only a few had come home. It was a trickle of a brook across a desert land. Their prayer was that God would bring back more until it would be like surging rivers.

Their situation is comparable to the experience of newborn Christians. They are often made glad because their bondage to sin is turned to glorious freedom. But soon their thoughts turn to those they love who are still in bondage to sin and Satan. With their rejoicing there is a deep longing for others to find the Savior. This rejoicing remnant understood that to reap they must sow; and they knew if they sowed, they would reap.

November 29

Brethren Dwell in Unity

Psalm 133

Any of a number of historical events may have been the inspiration for writing this poem. No matter what the occasion, it has the beauty and fragrance of a rose. Its message is dateless and timeless.

The holy anointing oil is the first figure used to illustrate how good and how pleasant it is for brethren to dwell together in unity. Aaron is used as a representative of all priests in all generations. One is reminded that all Christians are "a royal priesthood." Therefore, this ointment may be poured upon all who are of the household of faith.

The holy ointment was a composition of olive oil mixed with aromatic spices. The fragrance filled the house. It symbolized the Holy Spirit, who makes the life He possesses beautiful and attractive. That Spirit-anointed one was joined in the unity of holy fellowship with all who were sharing the same Spirit. The sweet-smelling savor was the evidence that all in the communion were united by the bond of love. This unity should prevail in every congregation of Spirit-filled Christians.

277

There is no exclusiveness in the Spirit's availability. The Holy Spirit is for all believers. Martin Luther, commenting on this psalm, said, "By the beard and the extreme parts of the garment, he signifieth that as far as the church reacheth, so far spreadeth the unity which floweth from Christ her Head."

Men may differ widely in their interpretation of Scripture and yet live in love and unity. The love of Christians for one another has no boundaries.

November 30

A Model Prayer for a Holy Man

Ps. 139:23-24

Nowhere in all the Psalter or in all the Bible are the attributes of God more clearly declared than in this psalm. It has been called the crown of all the psalms. Here God is seen as all-wise, everywhere present, and almighty. He is man's Maker, his Teacher, and his Keeper. Yet man is not absorbed in Deity. He has the right to self-determination. He shapes his own destiny. God is his Judge to be respected, and He is his Friend to be loved.

The first petition of this prayer is "Search me." The darkness could not hide anything from the all-seeing eye. The man who prayed was ready now for God to make all known to him. To know oneself as God knows him is essential to holy living. To be honest with ourselves is a primary characteristic of purity. *Let me know as I am known. This is my sincere desire.*

"Try me." *There is no escape from Thy presence. I do not seek to get away from Thee. I want Thee ever before me, that I may have Thee as my Example. I submit myself to Thee as my Mentor. Check me if I go one step astray. Implant right and holy thoughts in my mind. Then reinforce my will and my ability to do the good which I would. Let my performance be righteous and my motives pure. Be Thou my wisdom and my might.* "Lead me in the way everlasting." *Lord, help me to follow the path of righteousness.*

December 1

"God with Us"

Isa. 7:14

In his own day Isaiah faced a king who trembled with fear. Already Judah had been invaded and plundered by each of two kings. Now they had formed an alliance to resist a powerful foe —the king of Assyria. They had invited Ahaz, king of Judah, to join with them. He refused, and they were proposing to force him from his throne and place another, who would co-operate with them, in his stead. Ahaz considered an alliance with the Assyrians. Isaiah warned him that such trust in man would only be betrayed. He urged Ahaz to trust in God. He stressed the importance of relying upon God's presence. He could depend upon "God with us" and be saved from disaster.

But the prophecy of Isaiah had a far greater fulfillment. With the passing of the centuries the virgin-born Son of God was called "Emmanuel, which being interpreted is, God with us" (Matt. 1:23). That of which prophets inquired and angels desired to look into came to pass. "The Word was made flesh, and dwelt among us, (and we beheld his glory, the glory as of the only begotten of the Father,) full of grace and truth" (John 1:14). This is Immanuel, God with us.

Christ companied with the disciples who walked with Him by Galilee. Where they went, He was with them. He is the Eternal Contemporary. He is our Immanuel—God with Us— on every long and lonely journey, in every dreary day and every dark night. He is the Pilgrim Christ—God with us.

December 2

His Name Is Wonderful

Isa. 9:6

Holy men of the Old Testament had some idea of the Messiah to come. Isaiah was the prophet who spoke more often and more clearly of the Savior.

There are wise students of this unequalled Book of Isaiah

who have suggested that the word "Wonderful" qualifies all other identifications that follow. For this brief meditation let the Wonderful stand alone as one of the names given to the Savior by the Seer who proclaimed His advent as he gazed into his telescope seven centuries before the dawning of that blessed day when they that walked in darkness saw a great light.

Into the name Wonderful may be read these definitions: miraculous, marvelous, awesome, adorable, unique. All of these characteristics can be ascribed to Him who was called Jesus the Nazarene. His birth was miraculous: He was conceived of the Holy Ghost and born of a virgin. His works were marvelous: He opened blind eyes and unstopped deaf ears. He cleansed the leper and made the lame to walk. He cast out demons and restored the dead to life. The winds and the waves obeyed His voice.

The wisdom of Jesus was awesome. Paul declared that Christ was the wisdom of God. He also wrote that in Him "are hid all the treasures of wisdom" (Col. 2:3).

The character of Christ is adorable. He is worshipped by millions. Before Him angels prostrate fall and demons fear and fly.

This One whom Isaiah called Wonderful is unique. He died and He arose from the dead. And because He lives, we shall live also. He is wonderful!

December 3

"Counsellor"

Isa. 9:6

In another description of the One destined to be omniscient Counsellor, He soliloquizes, "The Lord God hath given me the tongue of the learned, that I should know how to speak a word in season to him that is weary . . . he wakeneth mine ear to hear as the learned" (50:4).

Jesus said, "My judgment is just; because I seek not mine own will, but the will of the Father which hath sent me." He listened to the voice of the Father and could say, "The words

280

that I speak unto you I speak not of myself: but the Father that dwelleth in me" (John 5:30; 14:10). Therefore, when He taught, it was not as the scribes, in meaningless theories and rote sayings; it was as one having authority. He was the all-wise Counsellor.

To obey His command to love your enemies is the cure for all lust, revenge, hatred, murder, and war. Heed His word, "Lay up for yourselves treasures in heaven" (Matt. 6:20). Then there will be no greed, no stealing, no lying, no blinded vision of values that are eternal. Learn from the omniscient Counsellor that no man can serve two masters. Then avoid the pitfalls of divided loyalties and split personalities. Love God supremely and your neighbor as yourself, then all other passions of life will be refined and made to fit into a pattern of harmonious symphonies of praise to God. Obey His wise command, "Seek ye first the kingdom of God, and his righteousness; and all these things shall be added" to bring the gain of contentment.

December 4

"The Mighty God"

Isa. 9:6

In Isaiah's vision of the Son to be given, not only was He anointed with the Spirit of God, but the nature of essential deity resided in Him. He saw the Suffering Servant in clear perspective, but he also saw Him as the mighty God.

There are many Old Testament scholars who identify the Angel of the Lord as the preincarnate Son of God. In such a role Isaiah saw the One of whom he prophesied. In John 1:3 we learn that "all things were made by him; and without him was not anything made that was made." The theology of John is anticipated by Isaiah. This same mighty God, the Holy One of Israel, is the One to whom no other gods can be equal.

Isaiah saw Him as the conquering Warrior. He is described as "glorious in his apparel, travelling in the greatness of his strength[.] I that speak in righteousness, mighty to save" (63:1).

Isaiah saw the Messiah as the Almighty Deliverer, the

Redeemer. The prophets recalled God's deliverance of Israel from bondage in Egypt. Isaiah in particular looked to the day when the remnant should return from Babylonian captivity. But he looked beyond to the fulfillment of God's promise of a universal salvation from the captivity of sin. He said, "Behold, God is my salvation" (12:2). He expanded his vision when he said, "Look unto me, and be ye saved, all the ends of the earth: for I am God, and there is none else" (45:22). My God, how great Thou art!

December 5

The Eternal Father

Isa. 9:6

This name again identifies the child of Isaiah's prophecy with God the Father. Jesus confirmed the unity when He said, "I and my Father are one. . . . he that hath seen me hath seen the Father" (John 10:30; 14:9). Here is one of Isaiah's great promises to his people, "The Lord hath comforted his people, and will have mercy upon his afflicted. . . . Can a woman forget her [nursing] child, that she should not have compassion on the son of her womb? yea, they may forget, yet will I not forget thee. Behold, I have graven thee upon the palms of my hands" (49:13, 15-16).

Being one with God the Father, the Eternal Son is omniscient, omnipotent, and omnipresent. Even as we know that the Son is like the Father, so we know the Father is like the Son. He is "the brightness of his [Father's] glory, and the express image of his person" (Heb. 1:3). What we believe God to be we see complete in Christ. What we see in Christ the Son we know to be in God the Father.

The compassion that the Son had for man is the same as God manifested when "he gave his only begotten Son, that whosoever believeth in him should not perish, but have everlasting life" (John 3:16). All the best in the ideal, human father is found in perfection in the Father of Eternity. "Like as a father pitieth his children, so the Lord pitieth them that fear him" (Ps. 103:13).

282

"The Prince of Peace"

Isa. 9:6

Isaiah saw the One whose birth he foretold as a beneficent Ruler. He proclaimed Him the Prince of Peace, the One in whom God's promises to Abraham and His covenant with David should be fulfilled. He said, "Of the increase of his government and peace there shall be no end, upon the throne of David, and upon his kingdom, to order it, and to establish it with judgment and with justice from henceforth even for ever" (v. 7). It was to be a kingdom that would never end. It would be not temporal but eternal. It would not be a rule dependent on military might; it would be established with judgment and justice. It would be a reign in righteousness and peace, producing prosperity and having perfection as its goal.

Anyone who lives in the world of today or has any knowledge of history knows that such a utopia does not exist now and never has. Therefore in a literal fulfillment the prophecy can only refer to a future kingdom. It will come to pass when "the kingdoms of this world are become the kingdoms of our Lord, and of his Christ; and he shall reign for ever and ever" (Rev. 11:15).

Jesus said, "My kingdom is not of this world" (John 18:37). There is a realm in which Jesus now rules and administers peace. To those who will receive Him as Lord of all, He imparts peace. He is the Reconciler, who harmonizes the nature, the mind, and the will of man with the holy God. "The work of righteousness shall be peace; and the effect of righteousness quietness and assurance for ever" (Isa. 32:17).

The Ideal King

Ps. 2:8

The Psalmist was endowed with prophetic vision. He doubtless had in view a contemporary king. As was usually the case in any age, the one he saw was beleaguered by raging enemies, foes of God as well as of His human representative. In the wisdom of the prophet, the success of this king was in his alliance with God rather than in his own resources or in a confederacy with other nations.

But the Psalmist saw farther than the events of the immediate future. The temporal kingdom of the present and near future blended into a description of the Messiah and His eternal kingdom. He was the ideal to whom the king now ruling should look as his inspiring Example.

Thus the prophetic vision of the Psalmist was expanded from the temporal and local to include the eternal and universal kingdom of God. This was in full harmony with the word of the prophet Isaiah, who cried, "Arise, shine; for thy light is come, and the glory of the Lord is risen upon thee" (60:1).

It is Jehovah who says, "Thou art my Son; this day have I begotten thee. Ask of me, and I shall give thee the heathen for thine inheritance, and the uttermost parts of the earth for thy possession." Five times in the New Testament this prophecy is applied to Christ. The qualifications for citizenship in His kingdom are submission to the Son and service to the ideal King with reverence and rejoicing. Blessed are all they that trust in Him.

December 8

No Other Name

Acts 4:12

Peter and John were summoned to appear before a court which had prejudged their case. Evidence made no difference to them. Their minds were closed. The judges were the rulers, elders, scribes, and the high priest. Their only restraint was fear of public opinion. They acknowledged that a notable miracle had been done which they could not deny.

They asked, "By what power, or by what name, have ye done this?" Peter gave an unequivocal answer. "Be it known unto you all, and to all the people of Israel, that by the *name of Jesus Christ of Nazareth,* whom ye crucified, whom God raised from the dead, even by him doth this man stand here before you whole" (vv. 7, 10; emphasis added).

The *name* stood for all the power that was so miraculously manifested when the Son of God was doing mighty works in Capernaum. By the Spirit the apostles were partakers of His nature, and they had authority to do His work in His name. Through faith in that almighty name, the crippled had been given perfect soundness. It was in that name that the apostles were saved. There is salvation for whosoever will in that blessed name. There is none other whereby we must be saved.

Jesus is the sovereign name. He is the Stone rejected of the builders, which has become the Head of the Corner. He is Savior now. He will be the righteous Judge.

The name of Jesus Christ is solitary. It belongs in no list of names. It stands alone.

December 9

Why Did Jesus Come?

John 18:37

It was not to receive the homage paid Him on Palm Sunday. Neither was it to be a powerful monarch to conquer the world with the might of the sword.

Repeatedly He said He came to do His Father's will. This consciousness was compelling Him from the time He was 12 years old until Gethsemane and the Cross. That imperative kept Him on the path of obedience day after day.

The knowledge that He was doing His Father's will made a life of self-denial and sacrifice a joyful experience. This was the joy that was set before Him.

To Pilate, Jesus said, "For this cause came I into the world, that I should bear witness unto the truth." In His condescension, by His words and deeds, and by His death on the Cross, He testified that "God is love."

Jesus came in the role of a servant. He washed the disciples' feet and wiped them with the towel with which He had girded himself. He said, "I have given you an example, that ye should do as I have done to you" (John 13:15). He came to be the Redeemer. Mary and Joseph were told, "He shall save his people from their sins" (Matt. 1:21). The angel announced to the shepherds, "Behold, I bring you good tidings of great joy . . . For unto you is born . . . a Saviour" (Luke 2:10-11). Jesus said, "The Son of man came . . . to give his life a ransom for many" (Matt. 20:28).

December 10

"The Light of the World"

John 8:12

"God is light" (1 John 1:5). Therefore, it is appropriate that when God broke through the darkness, His coming should be heralded by an angel surrounded by the glory of the Lord. It is also significant that a star of light should guide wise men to the place of the Savior's birth.

It is not surprising that Jesus announced, "I am the light of the world." John said of the Word, "In him was life; and the life was the light of men. And the light shineth in darkness" (1:4-5).

Christ is a floodlight on the face of God. The light of the glory of God shines in the face of Jesus Christ. He said, "He that hath seen me hath seen the Father" (14:9). In Jesus we see God, who is invisible, upon whom man cannot look and live. Christ is a beacon light whose rays pierce the darkness of the night of sin. They guide all who will follow the gleam to salvation and heaven.

One may stand on the shore of a lake and see the moon rise in radiant splendor. It seems to illuminate the whole earth. But there is a bright path on the water that comes to the feet of the observer. In like manner Christ is the Light of the World. The Holy Spirit causes the message of the gospel to be personal.

Light dispels darkness and it heals diseases. Christ is the inner Light in the soul of man to bring health and wholeness.

286

December 11

Jesus Is Lord

Phil. 2:11

"Jesus Christ is Lord." This is the essence of the doctrine of Christ. It is arranged in climax. *Jesus* is the man of history. His birth is the pivotal point around which recorded history revolves. As the shepherds and the wise men came to recognize His birth, so commoners and kings pay tribute to Him today. His name is high over all in art, music, literature, and architecture. "No mortal can with Him compare among the sons of men."

The Jesus of history is the contemporary *Christ*. He is the same yesterday, today, and forever. To His disciples He said, *"go . . .* and, *lo,* I am with you alway" (Matt. 28:19-20). Another like Him, even the Comforter, has come to abide with those who love and obey Him forever. He is Emmanuel, God with us.

Jesus Christ is *Lord* of eternity. He had no beginning. He shall have no end. He is Alpha and Omega. He entered and made history. He is Lord of all. His coming will climax history. He, as King of Kings, shall reign forever and forever.

In the sanctuary of a church in St. Paul, Minn., was a marble statue of Thorwaldsen's *The Appealing Christ*. With outstretched hands He was saying, "Come unto me." A fire destroyed the church. Miraculously, the statue escaped injury. It stood among the ruins in original beauty. Passersby stopped to look upon that statue.

Christ stands today in majesty and glory. He will remain to all eternity. He is indestructible.

December 12

The Preeminence of Christ

Col. 1:15-20

In this characterization of Jesus Christ, Paul sees from vantage viewpoint with inspired vision. He was familiar with

Moses and the prophets. He had the full account of the life of Jesus from His birth to His ascension. He had seen Jesus, as one born out of due season. He had moved from hostile opposition to become the most ardent apostle of the One he had persecuted. No man could be better qualified to bear convincing witness to the preeminence of Christ.

Paul saw Jesus as "the image of the invisible God, the firstborn of every creature." He held first place in creation. "By him were all things created, that are in heaven, and that are in earth . . . he is before all things, and by him all things [hold together]."

Christ, according to Paul, was preeminent in redemption, "having made peace through the blood of his cross, by him to reconcile all things unto himself." Jesus of Paul's vision was the firstborn from the dead. "Now is Christ risen . . . and become the firstfruits of them that slept" (1 Cor. 15:20). "Christ being raised from the dead dieth no more" (Rom. 6:9).

Christ "is the head of the body, the church . . . that in all things he might have the preeminence. For it pleased the Father that in him should all fulness dwell." The glory of the mystery of the gospel is "Christ in you, the hope of glory" (v. 27). He would present you holy and unblameable in His sight.

December 13

Christ Seeks the Lost

Luke 19:10

There are two aspects of man's lostness. Man has wandered away from God. "All we like sheep have gone astray; we have turned every one to his own way" (Isa. 53:6). Like the lost sheep, man is helpless in his lostness.

The other side of the coin is that God lost man. Sin brought separation. In the tragedy of the Fall, God suffered the loss of His supreme creation. He made man for fellowship in voluntary obedience and reciprocal love. God was grieved at the loss He sustained. His great heart of love has yearned for the restoration of that relationship to man which was enjoyed in Eden.

It was to Zacchaeus Jesus said, "The Son of man is come to

seek and to save that which was lost." It is past tense. The loss was sustained in the act of man's rebellion. Finally God sent His Son to seek and to save that which was lost. Sinful man is incapable of saving himself. There is nothing in him to cause him to repent and convert and be healed. It is the prevenient grace of God that by the Holy Spirit awakens desire to return to God.

As the shepherd seeks the wandering sheep, the Son of Man seeks the lost soul. The prodigal comes to himself because the seeking Savior shows him his lostness. It is God who reaches down to sinful men. He takes the initiative. The up-reach of faith is in response to the down-reach of love.

December 14

The Seamless Coat of Christ

John 19:23-24

Christ is not divided. He cannot be taken only as Example without being taken as Savior; nor can He be received as Redeemer, yet not be received as Teacher. The story of His seamless tunic may be understood to illustrate the unity of His person. He was the God-Man. He was one Person with two natures, Son of God and Son of Man.

He said, "I and my Father are one. . . . If ye had known me, ye should have known my Father also: and from henceforth ye know him, and have seen him" (John 10:30; 14:7). There was never a rift between the Father and the Son.

In His condescension by God's appointment and His own choice, Jesus was perfectly identified with man, except in His sinlessness. In the circumstances of His birth He became one with humanity. He was ever on the level of the need of those He came to redeem.

At His baptism when John protested, Jesus said, "Suffer it to be so now: for thus it becometh us to fulfil all righteousness" (Matt. 3:15). He was tempted in all points as we are. His temptations are typical of our own. Jesus shared man's sorrow.

He wept at Lazarus's grave. On the Cross God "made him to be sin for us, who knew no sin; that we might be made the righteousness of God in him" (2 Cor. 5:21). In death He went all the way with man. "He by the grace of God [did] taste death for every man" (Heb. 2:9). "If we have been planted together in the likeness of his death, we shall be also in the likeness of his resurrection" (Rom. 6:5).

December 15

Love Survives Rejection

John 1:11

In his prophetic description of the Suffering Servant, Isaiah said, "He is despised and rejected of men" (53:3). He was born in a stable. There was no room in the inn. To escape the murderous wrath of Herod the king, the angel of the Lord warned Joseph to flee to Egypt. In His infancy He was a fugitive in a strange land. In His hometown of Nazareth, after He had identified himself as the Messiah of the prophet's vision, He reminded his fellow townspeople that a prophet was not accepted in his own country. All who heard Him were filled with wrath. They rose up and thrust Him out of the city and led Him to the brow of a precipice to cast Him down headlong. "But he passing through the midst of them went his way" (Luke 4:30).

Those who saw Jesus cast the demons out of a tormented man besought Him to depart out of their coasts. He wept over Jerusalem, saying, "How often would I have gathered thy children together, even as a hen gathereth her chickens under her wings, and ye would not!" (Matt. 23:37). The people to whom He came as their Savior called for a murderer to be released and that Jesus should be crucified. They cried, "Away with him."

In spite of rejection, His love was the same. He prayed, "Father, forgive them." "He came unto his own, and his own received him not." His loving appeal to sinful men has never changed. He is still kindly saying, "Behold, I stand at the door, and knock" (Rev. 3:20).

December 16

Jesus, Our Emmanuel

Matt. 1:21, 23

There is prediction in Moses and the prophets. There is fulfillment in the Gospels. Matthew wrote his story about Jesus to the Jews especially. He therefore sought to show how the Old Testament Scriptures in which they thought they had eternal life actually foretold the coming of Jesus as the Messiah-Savior.

Here in his report of the birth of Jesus as Son of Mary, he relates it to the prophetic word of Isaiah in whom his fellow countrymen had such great faith. In doing so, he points up the heavenly descent and the earthly origin of the One whose mission he records.

Jesus was the name given to the Son of Mary. Its meaning, "Jehovah is salvation," is implied in the announcement made to Joseph and Mary, "He shall save his people from their sins." Without Him all men are sinners separated from God. Through Jesus they are freed from sin and reconciled to God. The gospel makes no allowance for sin. It offers salvation. It does not excuse sin, it destroys it.

Emmanuel, meaning "God with us," was the name given by Isaiah some seven centuries before the birth of Jesus. The prophet proclaimed Him as adequate to the need of his people then. Matthew applies the same name to the One who came to bring salvation and be the constant Companion of all their journey. Jesus said, "I will not leave you orphans. I will come to you" (see John 14:18). His other self, the Holy Spirit, would abide with them forever.

December 17

Born of a Virgin

Matt. 1:18, 21

God had sent His messenger to Mary to inform her that she was chosen to be the "blessed . . . among women." His message was, "Behold, thou shalt conceive . . . and bring forth a son, and shalt call his name JESUS." In her bewilderment Mary asked, "How shall this be?" The answer was delicate and satisfying to the virgin, even if the aura of mystery was not removed. By the superhuman power of the Highest, the Holy Ghost would come upon her, so the One to be born of her would "be called the Son of God" (Luke 1:28-35).

To relieve the perplexity of Joseph, God sent His messenger to inform him of the divine origin of the Son Mary was to bear. He added, "Thou shalt call his name JESUS: for he shall save his people from their sins."

The position that the Virgin Birth is not an essential in the doctrine of Christ involves several fallacies. First, the account of the supernatural birth of Jesus is a part of the Sacred Record. If it is not true, we have a fallible Bible. Second, we are left without any knowledge of the divine origin of Jesus, which is to discount His uniqueness. We would then be obliged to be in the same boat as the murderers of Christ, the Pharisees, who had to admit, "As for this fellow, we know not from whence he is" (John 9:29). Third, to deny miracle in His birth prepares the way to invalidate His redeeming work done on the Cross and finally to deny the resurrection of Christ. That is a fatal blow to the gospel.

December 18

The Word Made Flesh

John 1:14

John identified the Word as coexistent and coequal and coeternal with God. We sing, "Veiled in flesh the Godhead see." We have a full revelation of the invisible God. He "dwelt among us, (and we beheld his glory, the glory as of the only begotten of the Father,) full of grace and truth." "In him dwelleth all the fulness of the Godhead bodily" (Col. 2:9). In the law and prophets we learned the attributes of God in the abstract. In the Jesus of the Gospels we have all those characteristics of Deity in a tangible, visible, approachable Person. John said it strikingly, "That which was from the beginning, which we have heard, which we have seen with our eyes, which we have looked upon, and our hands have handled, of the Word of life" (1 John 1:1). From the Word in flesh we have all our concepts of God verified.

Jesus was a manifestation of all that His disciples ought to be. He was a living parable of a perfect life. In the days of His passion, from the acclaim of Palm Sunday through Gethsemane and to the dark hours on the Cross, His faith in the Father was firm. "God is love." Jesus was love made flesh. That love was manifested in perfect obedience. He said, "As the Father hath loved me, so have I loved you: continue ye in my love. If ye keep my commandments, ye shall abide in my love; even as I have kept my Father's commandments, and abide in his love" (John 15:9-10).

December 19

The Star of Bethlehem

Matt. 2:10

The greatest event of history had transpired. Those to whom the oracles of God had been committed were blind and dull of hearing. When they should have been aware, they were asleep.

Strangely enough, God had made known to men of devotion and wisdom in a distant land that the King of the Jews was born. Little is known about them. They have been called kings, and names have been given them, but that is legendary. Even from where they came is not certain. They were listening and God spoke to them. They were the firstfruits of the Gentiles. God used a star of unusual appearance to awaken their desire to make a long journey that they might worship the King of recent birth.

In faith they pursued the path by which the star led until that path came to the region of Jerusalem. Assuming the King would be born where kings resided and ruled, they went to Jerusalem. They made inquiry of Herod. He called for those who were most knowledgeable and was told that Micah had pointed to Bethlehem as the birthplace of the Messiah.

293

When they heard the report, they departed; and then the star appeared again. When they trusted their own impulsive judgment, they lost their way. Now being informed by the Spirit-inspired word to turn to Bethlehem, the star appeared and led them to the place where the infant Jesus was found.

Those who follow the Spirit, the Day Star, in their hearts according to God's Word, are wisely led.

December 20
The House of Bread

Luke 2:15

Bethlehem means "the house of bread." It was so named centuries before the birth of Christ because from the nearby fields was harvested the grain of which bread was made to feed the inhabitants. No name could have been more appropriate for the native city of the Christ who is the Bread of Life.

The very mention of Bethlehem as the house of bread brings to mind the miracle of feeding 5,000. There follows one of the most meaningful discourses Jesus ever gave to His disciples. In it He said, "I am that bread of life. . . . This is the bread which cometh down from heaven, that a man may eat thereof, and not die. I am the living bread which came down from heaven: if any man eat of this bread, he shall live for ever: and the bread that I will give is my flesh, which I will give for the life of the world" (John 6:48, 50-51).

Christ is the spiritual Bread which supplies sustenance and strength for every day. Those who feed on Him in their hearts by faith with thanksgiving hunger for nothing else. Their emptiness is filled. Their craving is satisfied. "Bread of heaven, feed me till I want no more."

This is the bread that was symbolized by the pot of manna that never spoiled. Christ as the Bread of Life is memorialized in the bread of the Lord's Supper which is a means of grace to all who worthily partake. Those who eat this bread shall not die but will live forever.

December 21

Our Best for God's Best

Matt. 2:11

The Magi recognized in the Christ child One to be worshipped. They bowed before Him. Surely they did not know all that has been revealed concerning His kingship, His priesthood, and His death. But they brought gifts as appropriate as if they had known. They knew that when they came into the presence of a king, they should present a gift. Gold was the most acceptable because it was the most priceless. Frankincense was offered by the priests in the Temple worship. It was therefore suggestive of the role that Jesus would perform as the High Priest for all believers. Myrrh was the spice used for embalming the dead. Since this Messiah-Servant would die as His final redemptive deed, this gift was prophetic.

Without attempting to read too much into the meaning of the gifts that these wise men brought as tokens of their homage, we can be sure they were what they had to give and the best they had. They were evidently men of wealth. Therefore, their gifts were not cheap. Had they been of the poverty level, flowers from the field might have been as acceptable. They knew that the One they had come to worship was Heaven's Best, God's best Gift to men. Therefore, they brought their best.

These gifts were representative of the readiness of those wise men to give themselves in worship, obedience, service, and love to the One before whom they bowed in adoration.

God gave His Best. All who truly worship Christ give themselves.

December 22

Little Town of Bethlehem

Mic. 5:2

This prophecy by Micah spanned eternity. He saw that Bethlehem would be the birthplace of One who was in the bosom of God from eternity. He also saw that He should be Ruler of a kingdom that would have no end. The Messiah King was to be supreme Lord of a spiritual dominion in the hearts of men. Isaac Watts saw the increase of that Kingdom until

> *Jesus shall reign where'er the sun*
> *Does his successive journeys run;*
> *His kingdom spread from shore to shore,*
> *Till moons shall wax and wane no more.*

The revelation of Micah's prophecy could come to him only as he was moved by the Holy Spirit. He knew that Bethlehem was the birthplace of David. Only God could know that from a town "too little to be among the clans of Judah" would come One whose redeeming grace and power would change the history of nations by transforming the lives of men.

But for the fact that Micah's prophecy was fulfilled in the birth of Jesus there, Bethlehem would have remained in obscurity forever. It is He who has made it renowned until millions make their pilgrimage to that remote village every year. There is an abiding glory because Jesus was born there.

Phillips Brooks expressed it beautifully in his beloved carol:

> *O little town of Bethlehem,*
> *How still we see thee lie!*
> *Above thy deep and dreamless sleep*
> *The silent stars go by.*
> *Yet in thy dark streets shineth*
> *The everlasting Light;*
> *The hopes and fears of all the years*
> *Are met in thee tonight.*

December 23

"Peace on Earth"

Luke 2:14

God is glorified in heaven. All is harmonious there. There is no will in rebellion with God's will, and no nature that is not in harmony with the divine nature. Jesus the Savior came that God might be glorified on earth as He is in heaven. He came with God's offer of peace. He was the catalyst. Without being contaminated by compromise with sin, Jesus took on himself the sins of the world that He might be the reconciliation of man to God. In so doing He became the Savior. All who are forgiven know the peace of God. They are not at peace with the world but with God. They are harmonized with God even as the celestial beings in heaven.

The heavenly host sang of peace among men with whom He is pleased. Therefore, the peace of heaven is to be known among those who know the Reconciler. Tension is not found in homes where Jesus is known. Envy, strife, and division in churches, according to Paul, if proof of carnality. All war is abhorrent to God, but so-called holy wars must cause Him unspeakable grief.

The hope of peace on earth is in Jesus, the Prince of Peace. When families, fellow churchmen, leaders of nations bow in surrender to Christ the Lord and accept His will, there will be peace among men with whom God is pleased. Then God will be glorified in earth as in heaven. "Of the increase of his government and peace there shall be no end" (Isa. 9:7). "Even so, come, Lord Jesus" (Rev. 22:20).

December 24

Joy to the World

Luke 2:10

The salient note in the announcement of the angel was joy. The good tidings would have been disappointing without that accent. The promise was not ecstatic exuberance for a passing moment. It was fulfilled in a well-spring of joy which would flow continually through all the adversities as well as the victories of a lifetime. It was all who would receive the Savior who was born in the City of David. He came to banish their fear and in its place implant faith. He would pardon their guilt and give them peace with God and goodwill to all men.

The joy of the Advent season is primarily the joy of giving, inspired by the fact that God so loved that He gave His only

Son—the unspeakable Gift. Challenged by His readiness to give up the glory He had with the Father, all Christians find their greatest joy, not in receiving, but in giving. The angel made it clear that the good tidings of great joy should be to all people. It is a joy that passes away if it is not shared.

In the traditional practice of giving at the Christmas season is found the greater joy. "It is more blessed to give than to receive" (Acts 20:35). In giving we open our hearts to receive with gratitude. This teaches us that all we receive by grace is to be given in the same measure.

Jesus said, "These things have I spoken unto you . . . that your joy might be full" (John 15:11).

December 25
The Wonder of It All

Luke 2:12

Isaiah said, "His name shall be called Wonderful" (9:6). What an appropriate name for One whose birth was in circumstances of such surprise and wonder! Nothing was as it might have been expected to be.

Caesar Augustus was serving the purpose and plan of God without knowing it when he decreed that all the world should be taxed. It brought Joseph and Mary from Nazareth to Bethlehem that the birth of the Messiah should be according to Micah's prophecy. The result was that the Governor who should rule Israel was born in a manger with lowing cattle as attendants. And a peasant girl was His mother.

The announcement of His lowly birth was made to wondering shepherds by the angel of the Lord. It was not by the usual excited father or friend. It was to uninformed, unsuspecting shepherds rather than to the priests and elders of the Temple. They needed a sign by which to identify the Baby. He was wrapped in strips of cloth and was lying in a manger. When they made known the saying which was told them, all that heard it wondered. Strangers from a far country came to worship Him who was born "King of the Jews." Those who should have rejoiced at His birth seemed ignorant of it. And to save His life, flight to another country was necessary.

All this was preliminary to the life of One who had not where to lay His head. If He saved others, He could not save himself.

December 26

"We Would See Jesus"

John 12:20-21

Jesus rises above all racial, national, and social boundaries. He is the universal Man. To all men He is "the way, the truth, and the life" (14:6). A university professor was asked recently, "What is the most common disease from which people of today suffer?" He answered in one word, "Emptiness." Jesus Christ is the answer.

Most of the earth's billions suffer from the malady. They neither have the diagnosis nor the knowledge of the remedy. The Greeks wanted to see Jesus. He was obscured by the crowds that were shouting, "Hosanna: Blessed is the King of Israel that cometh in the name of the Lord" (v. 13). Instead of making Jesus the Great Physician for the souls and bodies of men known, they were the obstruction to those who would see and know Him.

This generation of the human family would like to have a good look at Jesus. Unfortunately, those who surround Him, those who go to our churches, those who are called Christians, all too often hide Him instead of lifting Him up. If only we as Christians could improve the visibility of Jesus, many would see Him and find in Him the answer to the deep need of their lives and their souls' insatiable longings.

What a world of faith and love we would have if all who name the name of Jesus were really new creatures in Christ, transformed by His indwelling Spirit, living transparent lives through which the Light of the World could shine!

December 27

The Consummation

John 14:3; Acts 1:10-11

The message of the advent of Christ is incomplete without the promise of His coming again. The prophecy of the Messiah's role as the Son of David to reign upon His throne and to order and establish it forever, had no semblance of fulfillment in the coming of the Suffering Servant. Therefore, in the far view of the prophets, the first and the second coming of the Messiah were seen. In His first coming, He established a spiritual kingdom that would continue until it reaches consummation in His second coming. "The kingdoms of this world are become the kingdoms of our Lord, and of his Christ; and he shall reign for ever and ever" (Rev. 11:15). In His first coming he brought "peace among men with whom he is pleased" (Luke 2:14, RSV). In His second coming there will be universal peace, for we "look for new heavens and a new earth, wherein dwelleth righteousness" (2 Pet. 3:13).

In His first coming He provided salvation for whosoever will. In His second coming He will lift the curse from all creation. He will come again to rule on David's throne, as the holy men of God, who spoke as they were moved by the Holy Spirit, said He would. He will come again in His visible, personal presence just as those who followed Him until He ascended, saw Him go into heaven. This was a steadfast word spoken by angels. He will come again according to the unanimously expressed expectation of the apostles.

He will come again according to His own explicit promise, "I will come again."

December 28

Unprofitable Servants

Luke 17:10

This parable is not intended to represent God or to show His attitude toward those who serve Him. God is not a slave

300

owner. He is not a hard taskmaster. To gain a true picture of the Lord's role in relation to His servants, we turn to Luke 12:37. "Blessed are those servants, whom the lord when he cometh shall find watching: verily I say unto you, that he shall gird himself, and make them to sit down to meat, and will come forth and serve them."

The point of this parable is to show what the attitude of the servant should be. Indeed, as God looks upon those who are His, they are sons, not servants. Jesus' word to His disciples was "Henceforth I call you not servants . . . but . . . friends" (John 15:15).

It is for love and gratitude to God that one thinks of himself as a servant. Paul was a self-styled love slave for Christ. The Christian recognizes that he is owned and controlled exclusively by his Lord. "Ye are not your own[.] For ye are bought with a price" (1 Cor. 6:19-20). We have a debt of gratitude and love which can never be paid. However much we may do for Christ, we can never do enough. When added burden is laid on us, we can not complain or whimper in self-pity. When compensation is neither proportionate nor adequate, there is no protest.

Love of God and delight in doing His will carries the Christian far beyond duty. He esteems himself an unprofitable servant.

December 29

A Christian and Time

Eph. 5:16

A dedicated Christian recognizes the Lordship of Christ. His life is wholly consecrated to doing the will of God. Life is made up of years. The years consist of days, days of hours, hours of minutes. Therefore, living to the glory of God calls for thoughtful consideration of how one spends his moments and his days.

An alternate translation of our text for today is "Buy up the time." That implies that time is precious. It is too valuable to be squandered. When once spent, it is gone beyond recall. As time passes, opportunities are presented. They too come but once. They never return. God has "made every thing beautiful in his time" (Eccl. 3:11). In God's scheme nothing is out of place. Therefore, in planning a life, let God's will be the first consideration. The same rule applies to the daily schedule. Wisdom rules out chaotic living, which is time wasted in duplicated effort. A Christian, however, cannot be a slave to his schedule. Some of his great opportunities to serve God and man may come as interruptions of his systematic order. He may sometimes sacrifice a moment, an hour, even a day to seize the opportunity to do a kind deed and thus do God's will.

Still another translation of our text is "Make the most of your time," or give consideration to priorities. That means that some things enjoyable, even profitable, must be eliminated. Some things important may be postponed. "To every thing there is a season, and a time to every purpose under the heaven" (Eccl. 3:1).

December 30

The Unchangeable Record

John 19:22

These words spoken by Pilate have the accent of finality. The translators have found no way to vary the interpretation. The governor had already stretched his conscience to the limit. He would not be cajoled into changing the superscription. It was a sop to his conscience, which was the more troubled by the warning of his wife. It was an attempt to justify his cowardly deed in the light of known law. It was a barb in the closed minds of the envious Jews. Pilate's superficial effort to rid himself of responsibility only mocked him. He could have changed what he had written, and indeed his unjust sentence, if he would. He was a free agent before God. But his mind was set. His will was determined. He would not be changed.

As free moral agents approach the end of another year, they look at the record they have written. They are in a decidedly different situation than was Pilate. It is not possible to revise what has been written on the page of personal history. It was written with indelible ink. It cannot be erased.

302

Deeds done, good or bad, remain. Words spoken, harsh or kind, are beyond recall. Influence, helpful or hurtful, has gone forth not to return. The regrettable omissions cannot be corrected. The saddest words on tongue or pen are "It might have been." Since the record is unchangeable, it behooves everyone to think soberly, act wisely, and keep in mind the Day of Judgment. The Holy Spirit is the Helper.

December 31

One More Year

Luke 13:8-9

The symbolic subject of this parable is a fig tree. The real subject was the Jewish nation. Here, as elsewhere, the words of Jesus were unmistakable in their application. Everything was favorable to fruit bearing for the fig tree. If it did not bear, it was good for nothing. It was planted in the most conducive place. It had been pruned, cultivated, and fertilized. But it was barren. It was a disappointment. This is the history of Israel in brief.

The pronouncement of judgment on the fig tree was not unreasonable. "Cut it down; why cumbereth it the ground?" The dresser of the vineyard interceded. "Give it one more chance," he pleaded. "I will dig about it, fertilize it, and water it. If it doesn't bear fruit then, you can cut it down."

There is a personal message in this parable. God has done His best to make our lives fruitful. He has loved us. He has redeemed us. He has placed us in circumstances conducive to fruitfulness. The fruit He seeks "is in all goodness and righteousness and truth" (Eph. 5:9). Absence of it is cause for God's disappointment. What would come if He should judge us as we are?

In mercy and in answer to the prayers of intercession, we have an extension of time.

There are two pertinent questions to answer: Are we bearing fruit according to God's will? and, Are we intercessors for those who now are disappointing God?

303